Geography

a visual encyclopedia

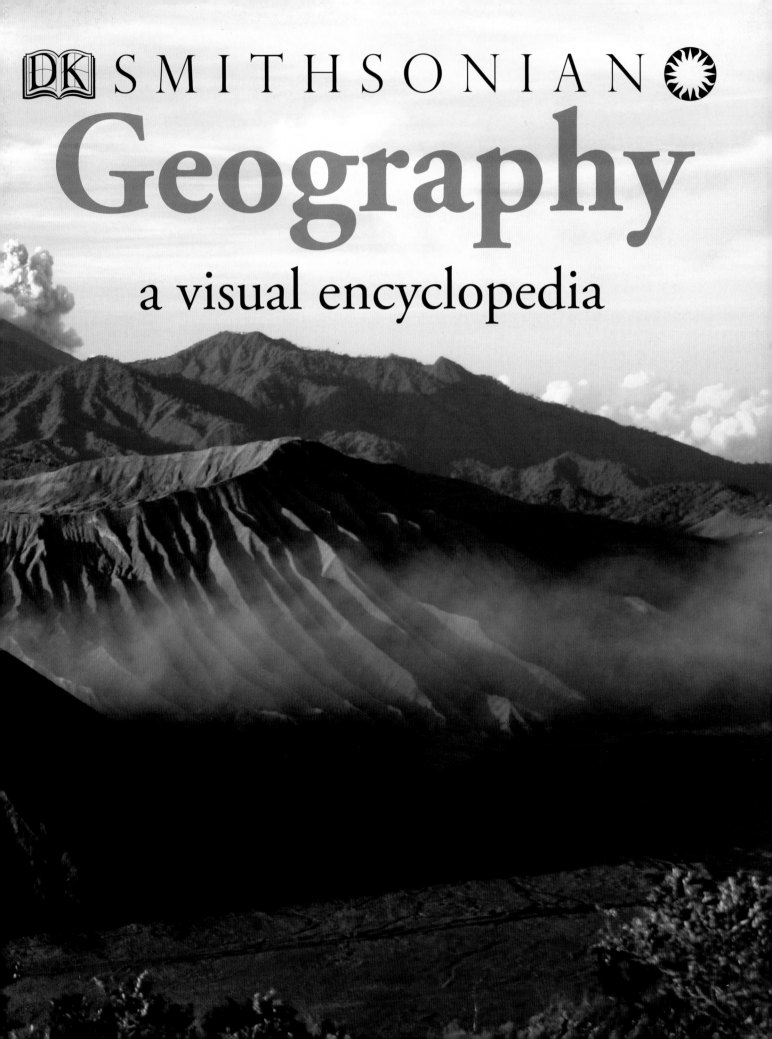

DK SMITHSONIAN

Geography

a visual encyclopedia

LONDON, NEW YORK, MUNICH,
MELBOURNE, DELHI

Written by John Woodward
Consultant Dr. Kim Bryan

Senior Editor Jenny Sich
Senior Designer Stefan Podhorodecki
Managing Editor Linda Esposito
Managing Art Editor Diane Peyton Jones
Cartographer Simon Mumford
US Editor John Searcy
Jacket Design Development Manager Sophia M.T.T.
Jacket Editor Manisha Majithia
Jacket Designer Natalie Godwin
Producer, Pre-production Nikoleta Parasaki
Senior Producer Gemma Sharpe
Publisher Andrew Macintyre
Art Director Philip Ormerod
Associate Publisher Liz Wheeler
Publishing Director Jonathan Metcalf

Tall Tree Ltd.
Editors Joe Fullman, Camilla Hallinan,
David John, Catherine Saunders
Designers Ben Ruocco, Malcolm Parchment,
Marisa Renzullo, Ed Simkins

Smithsonian

This trademark is owned by the Smithsonian Institution and is
registered in the United States Patent and Trademark Office.

Smithsonian Consultants Bruce Smith, Dr. Jeffrey E. Post,
Dr. M.G. (Jerry) Harasewych, Dr. Don E. Wilson, Andrew K.
Johnston, Julie A. Herrick, Jennifer Zoon, Peter Liebhold,
Melinda Zeder, Jim Harle, Thomas F. Jorstad, J. Daniel Rogers

First American Edition, 2013
Published in the United States by
DK Publishing
375 Hudson Street
New York, New York 10014

13 14 15 16 17 10 9 8 7 6 5 4 3 2 1
001–184806–July/2013

Discover more at
www.dk.com

Contents

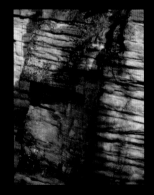

Introduction

Earth is an astonishing place. Somehow, a mass of gas and shattered rock swirling around a hot star evolved into a living planet, unique in the Solar System.

By sheer luck, Earth formed at exactly the right distance from the Sun for water to lie on its surface without freezing or boiling away into space, forming broad oceans that cover more than two-thirds of the globe. Water seeping down into the searingly hot rocks below makes them melt and erupt from volcanoes—a process that, over billions of years, has created immense continents.

Circulating air currents in the atmosphere carry moisture over the land. There, it soaks into the ground and fuels the growth of plants—just one aspect of the incredible web of life that makes Earth so special. As part of that life, we in turn have changed the face of our planet in countless ways.

Using a rich combination of vivid images and clear text, this book is the perfect guide to how planet Earth works, and what humanity has made of it. It covers every aspect of its geography, from its formation and structure to its turbulent weather, restless geology, living landscapes, and the countries and peoples of the world. This is our planet, in all its glorious complexity.

PLANET EARTH

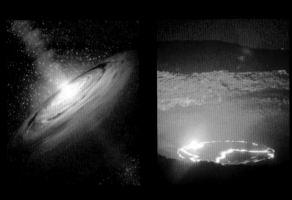

Created from a cloud of dust more than 4.5 billion years ago, Earth is still evolving. Heat deep within the planet drives a relentless process of rocky upheaval and renewal.

The Solar System

When the Sun formed from a cloud of dust and gas, some of the material spread out into a spinning disk. From this came eight orbiting planets and vast numbers of asteroids, comets, and smaller bits of space rock that sometimes crash to Earth as meteorites.

THE SUN

A star like many others in the sky, the Sun is a giant ball of hot gas that formed about 4.6 billion years ago. Nuclear reactions in its core release nuclear energy that heats its surface to around 10,800°F (6,000°C)—six times as hot as volcanic lava.

◄ HOT GAS
Colossal plumes of hot gas erupt from the Sun's surface and spill out into its atmosphere. Each one is far bigger than planet Earth.

Mercury

Mars

Saturn

Jupiter

Earth

Venus

ORBITING WORLDS

All the major planets orbit the Sun in almost the same plane, but at different distances. The planetary system is 7.5 billion miles (12 billion km) across, but since many comets and asteroids have much bigger orbits, the entire Solar System is at least 9.3 trillion miles (15 trillion km) wide.

ASTEROIDS AND COMETS

Asteroids are lumps of rock, iron, and nickel, and are much smaller than planets. Many orbit the Sun in the Asteroid Belt between the orbits of Mars and Jupiter. Comets are chunks of ice and dust that grow tails of glowing dust and gas when their orbits take them close to the Sun and they are blasted by its radiation.

◄ STREAK IN THE SKY
Sometimes comets come close enough to Earth to be seen in the night sky, as when Comet McNaught streaked past our planet in 2007.

FACT!

The Sun is made of the lightest elements in the Universe —hydrogen and helium—but despite this the Sun is at least 333,000 times as heavy as planet Earth.

Uranus

◄ THE PLANETS
The four rocky planets—Mercury, Venus, Earth, and Mars—consist of solid rock, some with shallow atmospheres. The gas giants Jupiter and Saturn have small rocky cores surrounded by thick layers of gas. Uranus and Neptune are similar, but they are mostly frozen because they are so far from the hot Sun.

Neptune

METEORITES

The meteorites that land on Earth range from small pebbles to truck-sized or even larger chunks of space rock. Some are mixtures of rock and iron that formed before the Solar System. Others are parts of shattered planets. This one came from the Moon.

DWARF PLANETS

Astronomers have named five rocky objects as dwarf planets: Ceres, Pluto, Haumea, Makemake, and Eris. Although they are smaller than the eight major planets, they are larger than the thousands of other tiny worlds in the Solar System. Pluto has a moon called Charon, which is almost half the size of Pluto—the two orbit each other like twins, as seen in this distant view from Earth.

The planets

Earth is one of four relatively small rocky planets orbiting the medium-sized star that we call the Sun. Mercury and Mars are smaller than Earth, while Venus is about the same size. The other four planets are far bigger, but even the biggest, Jupiter, is one thousand times smaller than the Sun.

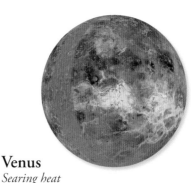

Venus
Searing heat

Diameter 7,521 miles (12,104 km)
Mass compared to Earth 0.82
Average distance from Sun 47 million miles (108.2 million km)
Number of moons 0

Although it looks beautiful in the night sky, Venus is shrouded with thick clouds of sulfuric acid. Its dense atmosphere of mainly carbon dioxide gas traps so much heat, the lava-covered surface of the planet reaches a blistering 867°F (464°C)—a temperature hot enough to melt lead.

Mercury
Cratered world

Diameter 3,029 miles (4,875 km)
Mass compared to Earth 0.06
Average distance from Sun 36 million miles (57.9 million km)
Number of moons 0

The smallest planet, Mercury is similar to our Moon with its cratered, barren surface and broad plains of volcanic lava. Mercury is the closest planet to the Sun but, although it has scorching hot days, its nights are freezing. This is because it has virtually no insulating atmosphere to retain heat.

Mars
Rock and ice

Diameter 4,213 miles (6,780 km)
Mass compared to Earth 0.11
Average distance from Sun 142 million miles (227.9 million km)
Number of moons 2

Only half the size of Earth, Mars does not have enough gravity to cling on to much atmosphere. Water once flowed on the planet, leaving dry riverbeds and floodplains, but the water that remains is now all frozen at the planet's north and south poles, or beneath its dry, dusty, rock-strewn surface.

▼ DISTANT WORLD
Tire tracks made by the rover vehicle Spirit *scar the rocky surface of Mars, 48 million miles (78 million km) from Earth. The whole planet is tinted red by iron oxide—the same material as rust.*

Earth
Living planet

Diameter 7,926 miles (12,756 km)
Mass compared to Earth 1
Average distance from Sun 93 million miles (149.6 million km)
Number of moons 1

As far as we know, Earth is the only planet in the Solar System with any form of life. This is mainly because the other planets, even the rocky ones that are similar to Earth, do not have large amounts of liquid water—they are either too hot or too cold. Earth is the only planet with oceans of water, which cover 72 percent of its surface.

Jupiter
Banded giant

Diameter 88,846 miles (142,984 km)
Mass compared to Earth 318
Average distance from Sun 484 million miles (778.3 million km)
Number of moons 63

Jupiter is a colossal ball of mainly hydrogen and helium gas, with more than twice the mass of all the other planets put together. Huge storms rage across the surface, including the Great Red Spot, which is twice the size of Earth. One of Jupiter's 63 rocky moons, Europa, is covered by ice that may conceal liquid water.

▼ MANY MOONS
This image, taken by the space probe Voyager 1, *shows two of Jupiter's 63 moons: Io (left) and Europa (right). Io is passing over Jupiter's Great Red Spot.*

PLANET EARTH

Saturn
Icy rings

Diameter 74,914 miles (120,536 km)
Mass compared to Earth 95
Average distance from Sun 891 million miles (1.4 billion km)
Number of moons 60

The second largest planet, Saturn, is famous for its rings of fragmented ice. The planet itself is mostly hydrogen and helium gas, like Jupiter, but much of the gas is in liquid form. This is because the planet is so far from the Sun that it's extremely cold—at such low temperatures hydrogen and other gases become liquid.

▼ RING SIZE
Saturn's distinctive rings are made up of billions of particles of ice ranging in size from dust-like specks to boulders several yards across.

Uranus
Frozen planet

Diameter 31,763 miles (51,118 km)
Mass compared to Earth 14.5
Average distance from Sun 1.8 billion miles (2.9 billion km)
Number of moons 27

Bitterly cold methane clouds cover the massive ball of gas and ice that forms Uranus. The planet is tilted sideways on its axis—probably because of a huge collision early in its history—so its north and south poles are almost aligned with the Sun. This means that its many rocky moons seem to orbit the planet from top to bottom, rather than from side to side.

Neptune
Windy world

Diameter 30,760 miles (49,532 km)
Mass compared to Earth 17.1
Average distance from Sun 2.8 billion miles (4.5 billion km)
Number of moons 13

Neptune is so far from Earth that no one knew for certain that it existed until the 19th century. Like Uranus, it is largely made of a mixture of frozen gases, including the methane that gives it its deep blue color. It has a stormy atmosphere with recorded wind speeds of up to 1,300 mph (2,100 km/h), the fastest in the Solar System.

How Earth formed

Earth was created from rock fragments, dust, and gas orbiting the early Sun. As this material smashed together, it heated up, until the whole mass melted. The heavier metals sank towards the center of the young planet to become its core, leaving the rest to form its thick rocky mantle, crust, and atmosphere.

▼ SPINNING DISK
The whole Solar System was formed from a cloud of dust and rock called the solar nebula.

ACCRETION

Earth and all the planets were made in the same way, from the giant spinning disk of rock and dust left over from the formation of the Sun. The rocks collided and became welded together in larger lumps— a process called accretion. The lumps joined together to form several small planets. As each one grew, it developed the gravity to attract more and more material, until there was no more within its range.

FACT!

Earth's mass is still growing as chunks of space rock called meteorites hit its surface. Luckily, Jupiter's immense gravity attracts most of the bigger objects and stops them from hitting us.

IMPACT ENERGY

Energy cannot be created or destroyed, but it can be converted into different forms. When two objects slam together at high speed, the energy of their speed is turned into heat. This is why big meteorites create impact craters surrounded by pieces of rock that have been melted. The Barringer Crater in Arizona was created by a meteorite 165 ft (50 m) wide—the impact energy was converted into enough heat to melt the rock.

MELTDOWN

As space rocks crashed into the early Earth, the impacts generated so much heat that the whole planet was kept hot and molten. Gravity dragged most of the heaviest ingredients of the molten rocks towards the center, creating a metallic core surrounded by layers of lighter, less metallic rock.

NUCLEAR FURNACE

As the rate of accretion slowed, Earth started to cool and solidify again, this time in layers surrounded by the cool, brittle crust. However, radioactivity within the interior of the planet keeps it hot, and this drives the geological processes that generate earthquakes and volcanoes.

◄ RED-HOT LAVA
Radioactive rocks deep inside Earth produce nuclear energy that is transformed into heat. This can melt solid rock and turn it into volcanic lava, like this on Hawaii.

LETTING OFF STEAM

As the crust was forming, gas erupting from huge volcanoes formed Earth's early atmosphere. The volcanic gas included vast amounts of water vapor that created enormous clouds. Over millions of years, torrential rain poured down to fill the first ocean, which probably covered the entire planet.

The Moon

The Moon is Earth's only natural satellite. It is one of the biggest moons in the Solar System compared to the planet that it orbits, and its gravity has a significant effect on Earth. However, it does not have enough gravity to cling to an atmosphere, and this makes it a very different world from ours.

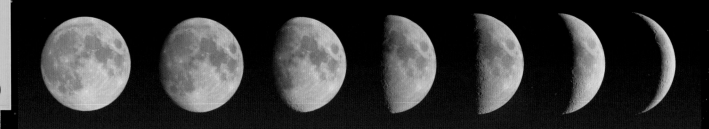

▲ WANING MOON

Over the two weeks following a full moon, the area lit by the Sun gets smaller every night, dwindling to a bright crescent and eventually an almost invisible "new moon."

ORBIT AND PHASES

The Moon takes just over 27 days to orbit Earth. It spins on its axis at the same rate, so the same side always faces us. During its orbit, the angle between the Earth, Moon, and Sun changes, altering how much of its surface seems to be illuminated when viewed from Earth. Once a month, the whole face is lit up, but the bright area gradually shrinks (wanes) to nothing, and then grows bigger (waxes) again.

AIRLESS WORLD

The Moon has only one-sixth of Earth's gravity, which is not enough to hold on to an atmosphere. This means that there is no air, no weather, and nothing to protect the surface from solar radiation by day or to retain heat at night. Each Moon day lasts for 13 Earth days, so almost two weeks of scorching heat are followed by the same period of extreme deep freeze. Any water is either instantly boiled away or frozen in deep, permanently dark craters. This is why there is no life on the Moon.

FAST FACTS

- **Average distance from Earth** 237,034 miles (381,470 km)
- **Size (diameter)** 2,160 miles (3,476 km)
- **Mass compared to Earth** 0.0123
- **Average surface temperature** −9.4°F (−23°C)
- **Maximum surface temperature** 225°F (107°C)
- **Minimum surface temperature** −243°F (−153°C)
- **Day length** 13 Earth days
- **Orbit period** 27.3 Earth days

FORMATION OF THE MOON

The Moon was probably created by the biggest crash in Earth's history, when our newly formed planet collided with a smaller planet, roughly the size of Mars. Molten material from the impact formed the Moon. The smaller planet seems to have been completely destroyed, because analysis of Moon rock shows that it is made of the same material as Earth's deep rocky mantle. Earth would have been partly melted again by the impact, but it would then have solidified in layers, as before.

Mars-sized object

Hot, newly formed Earth

Debris forms an orbitng ring around Earth

Moon forms from accreted debris

Earth cools down again

▲ COLLISION
Around 4.5 billion years ago, Earth was hit by another planet.

▲ DEBRIS
Broken rock formed a debris cloud.

▲ SOLID PARTNERS
The debris clumped together and then melted to form the Moon.

IMPACT CRATERS

The Moon's surface is marked by craters, caused by big meteorite impacts in the distant past. Some of the biggest craters have been flooded with volcanic rock to form dark maria (seas). Many smaller, younger craters also cover the surface of the Moon.

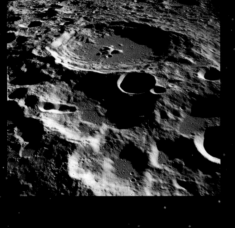

LUNAR EXPLORERS

In July 1969, America's Apollo space program sent the first human explorers to set foot on the Moon. This image shows the second man on the Moon, Buzz Aldrin, photographed by the first, Neil Armstrong. Just 12 people have explored the Moon as part of six Apollo missions, the last of which was in 1972. The final three missions explored the surface using a Lunar Roving Vehicle, seen in the main image (left).

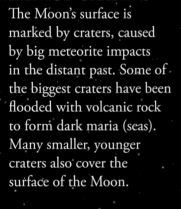

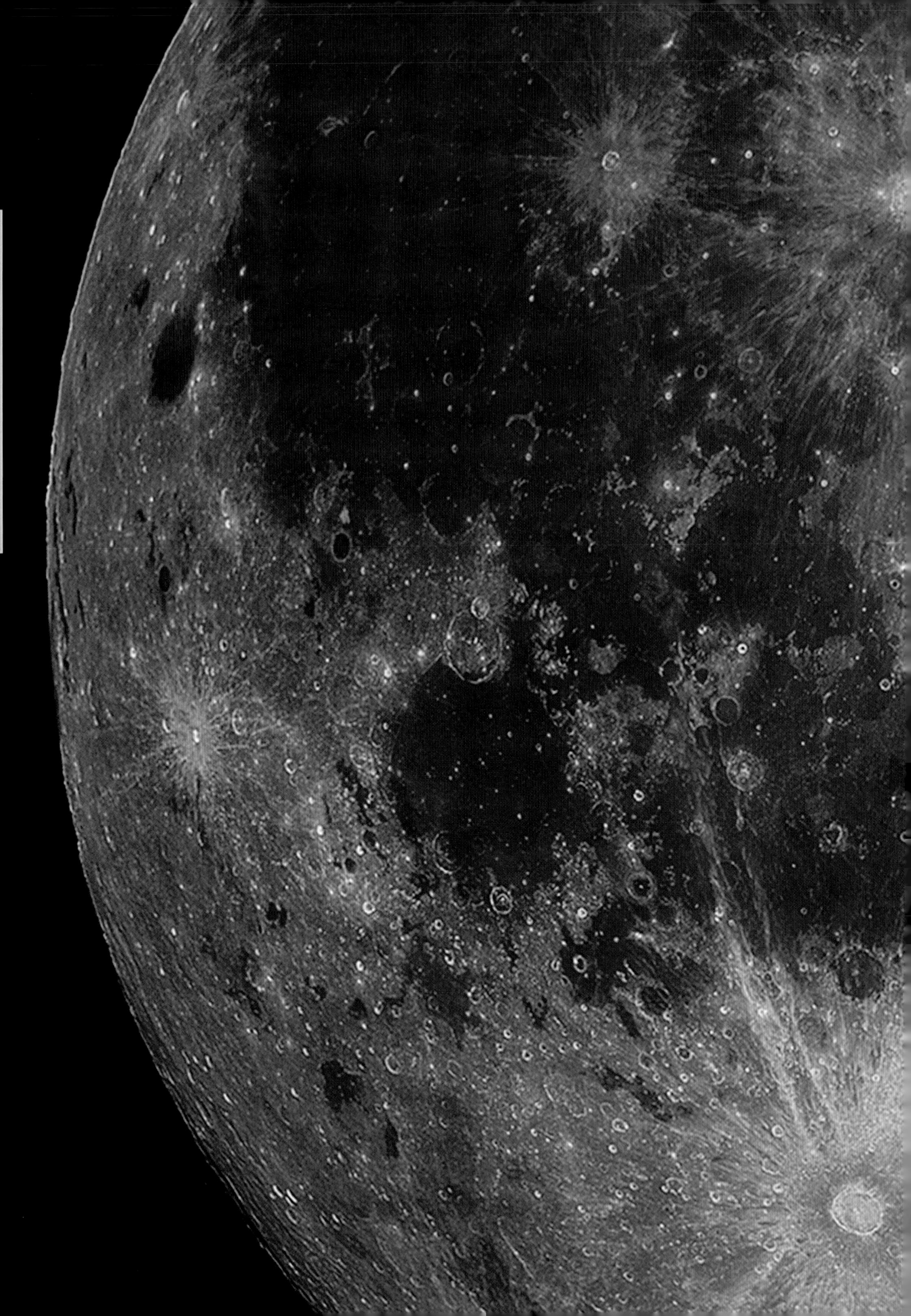

SCARRED SURFACE

A close view of the Moon reveals that it is scarred by hundreds of overlapping craters. Most of these were made by meteorites that hit the surface more than 3.7 billion years ago, at a time when Earth was being bombarded in the same way. Similar impact craters on Earth have been worn away, but those on the Moon have survived because the Moon has no weather.

Inside our planet

As Earth cooled, most of it turned to solid rock. It formed layers, with the heaviest material at the center (the core), surrounded by a deep, rocky mantle and a thin, brittle crust. Nuclear reactions inside the planet make the rocks much hotter than their normal melting point, but intense pressure keeps the rock solid, except for the outer core, which is liquid.

THE CORE

Most of the planet's weight is concentrated in the core, which is mostly iron mixed with nickel. The inner core is solid, but surrounded by a liquid outer core. Together, they form a metallic ball almost 4,350 miles (7,000 km) across—roughly the size of Mars. Some meteorites are made of these same metals, and may be fragments of shattered planet cores.

▶ IRON METEORITE
This meteorite looks rusty because, like Earth's core, it contains large amounts of iron. It probably came from the core of a planet destroyed long ago.

THE MANTLE

The core is surrounded by a mass of solid rock called the mantle. It is rich in iron and very heavy, but not as heavy as the metallic core. The mantle rock is extremely hot, and this makes it moldable, like modeling clay. The intense heat deep within the planet keeps the mantle moving very slowly, in currents that cause earthquakes and volcanic eruptions.

The liquid outer core is mostly molten iron, plus some sulfur.

The lower mantle is less mobile than the upper mantle due to intense pressure.

Mantle

Outer core

Inner core

Crust

The inner core is a ball of solid metal, and extremely heavy.

The upper mantle is kept moving by heat currents rising from near Earth's core.

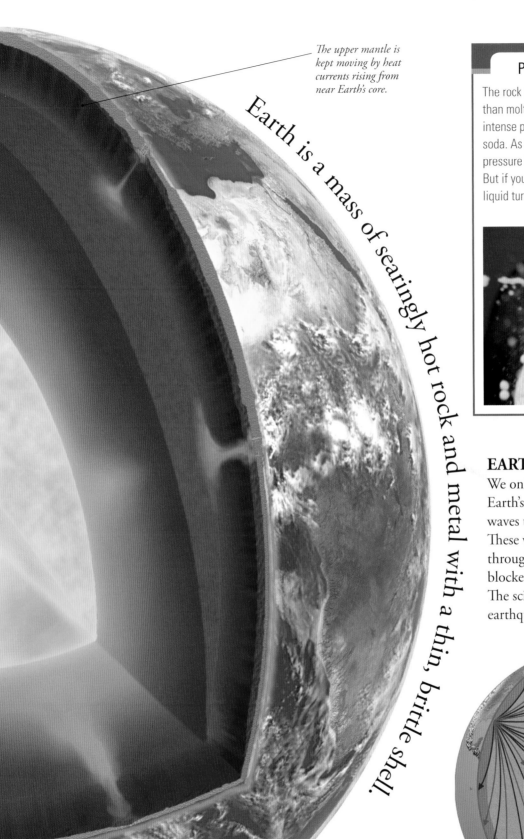

Earth is a mass of searingly hot rock and metal with a thin, brittle shell.

PRESSURE AND HEAT

The rock deep within the planet is far hotter than molten lava, but it is kept solid by intense pressure. It's similar to a bottle of soda. As long as the cap stays on, high pressure inside the bottle keeps it liquid. But if you release the pressure, some of the liquid turns to gas that fizzes out of the top.

EARTHQUAKE CLUES

We only know what lies beneath Earth's crust by studying the seismic waves that radiate from earthquakes. These waves pass at various speeds through the planet, but can be blocked by its different layers. The science of interpreting these earthquake clues is called seismology.

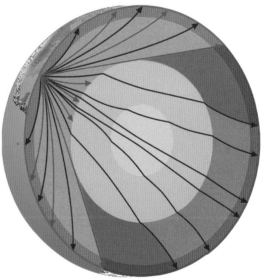

▲ SEISMIC WAVES
Some waves (blue) can pass through the core, but others (red) cannot and must go around it.

FAST FACTS

Diameter of the inner core 1,516 miles (2,440 km)
Depth of the outer core 1,408 miles (2,266 km)
Depth of the mantle 1,800 miles (2,900 km)
Depth of the crust 3–43 miles (5–70 km)

Magnetic Earth

Earth's liquid metallic outer core is constantly in motion. The moving molten metal acts as an electromagnetic dynamo, generating a magnetic field around the planet. This is the same magnetism that makes a compass needle point north or south. More importantly, the magnetic field also deflects harmful rays from the Sun.

GEODYNAMO

The molten metallic outer core is kept in motion by heat currents and Earth's spin. This generates electrical currents in the iron-rich metal. In turn, these induce a magnetic field extending into space as the magnetosphere. It is similar to the field of a bar magnet roughly aligned with Earth's spin axis.

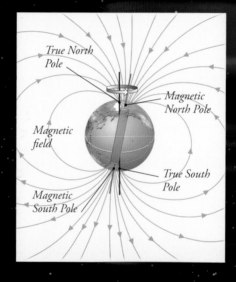

True North Pole

Magnetic North Pole

Magnetic field

True South Pole

Magnetic South Pole

▶ OFFSET FIELD
The magnetic field is tilted at an angle to Earth's spin axis, so magnetic north is not true north.

Earth

Deflected magnetic field

WANDERING POLES

The strength of the magnetic field changes and so does its alignment with Earth's spin axis. This means that the magnetic North Pole keeps moving, at up to 25 miles (40 km) per year. Currently, it's very close to the true North Pole, but a century ago it was a long way south of it, in Arctic Canada. The magnetic South Pole also wanders, and the two magnetic poles are not always opposite each other.

Magnetic North Pole in 1900

Magnetic North Pole today

True North Pole

MAGNETIC SHIELD

The magnetosphere acts as a barrier to the solar wind. This stream of charged particles would otherwise strip away the atmosphere's ozone layer, which protects us from harmful ultraviolet radiation. The solar wind distorts the magnetosphere so it is compressed on the side facing the Sun, but extended on the other side.

MAGNETIC REVERSALS

Earth's magnetic field is so unstable that its poles may completely reverse. These reversals have taken place many times in Earth's past. They are recorded by magnetized particles in lava flows that aligned themselves with the magnetic field when the rock was molten. The last time this happened was 780,000 years ago, around 580,000 years before modern humans evolved.

Solar wind

Magnetosphere

Sun

FINDING THE WAY

A magnetized compass needle aligns itself with the planet's magnetic field, so it points to magnetic north. Since this is not the same as true north, anyone using a compass has to make a correction to allow for the difference. Using satellites instead, GPS navigation is not affected in the same way.

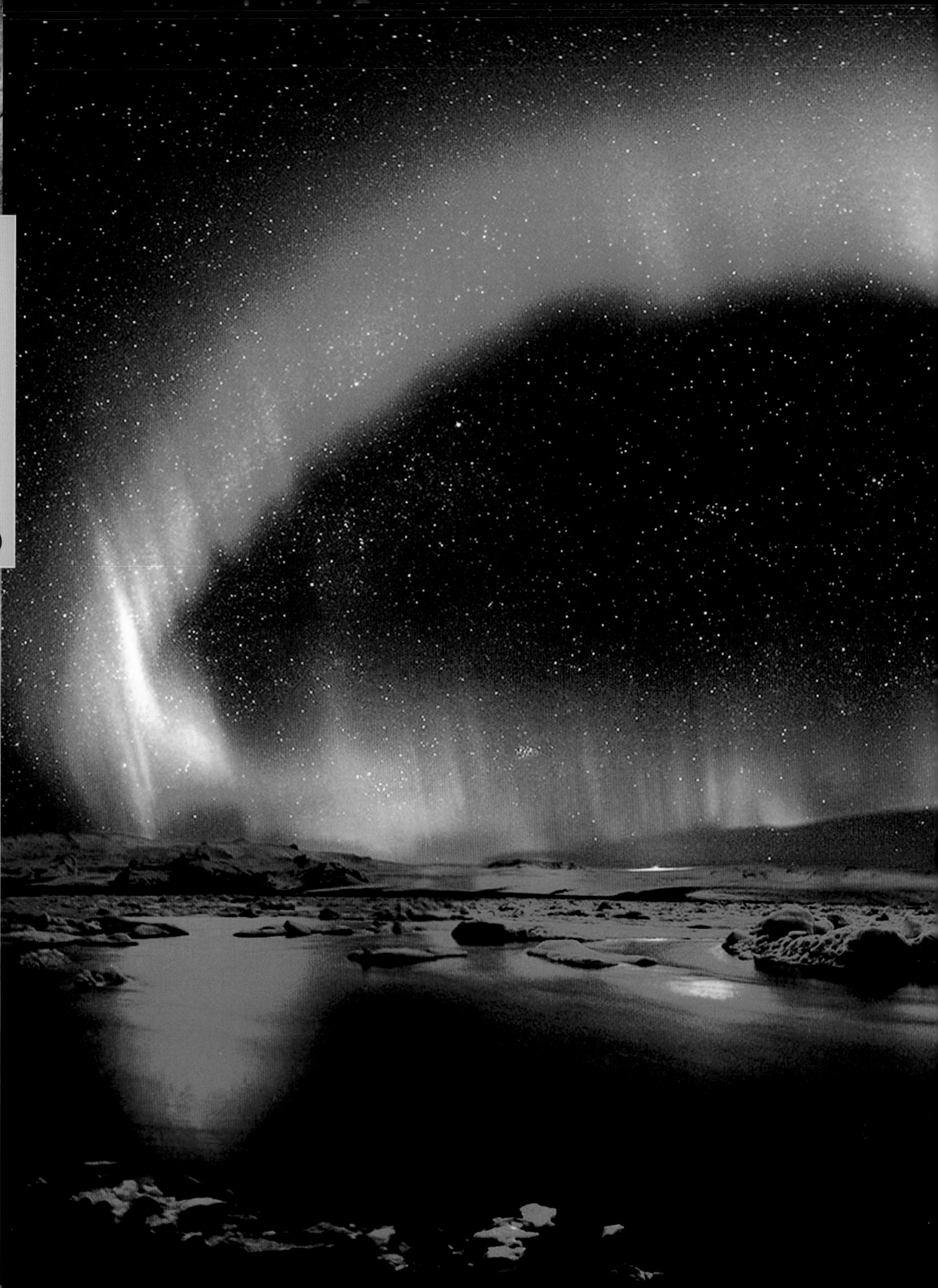

NORTHERN LIGHTS
Earth's magnetic field shields us from the stream of charged particles radiating into space from the Sun. However, some particles get through near the poles, where they energize atoms high in the atmosphere. This creates the spectacular Aurora Borealis in the north (seen here above Bear Lake in Alaska) and the Aurora Australis in the south.

Earth's crust

The hot, mobile rock of Earth's thick mantle is enclosed by an outer skin of cool, brittle rock known as the crust. This is divided into oceanic and continental crust. The thin oceanic crust covers more than two-thirds of Earth's surface and is mainly made of a dark, heavy rock called basalt, while the thicker continental crust is made of lighter rock such as granite. The hard bedrock of both types of crust is often covered by softer rock.

OCEANIC CRUST

The crust beneath the ocean floors is about 5 miles (8 km) thick. It is made of basalt lava flows, which erupt from oceanic volcanoes. The basalt lava is basically the same as the rock of the mantle below, but not as heavy. This is because some of the heaviest ingredients of the mantle rock are left behind when it forms molten lava.

◄ BASALT LAVA FLOW
This lava erupted from a Hawaiian volcano is cooling and solidifying into black basalt—the same rock that forms the bedrock of the ocean floors.

CONTINENTAL CRUST

In mountainous regions, the crust that forms the continents can be 43 miles (70 km) deep. It is made of many types of rock, but at its heart lies very hard rock such as granite. This rock is lighter than the basalt that forms the ocean crust because it lacks some of its heavier ingredients.

▼ GRANITE OUTCROP
The cores of continents contain granite, which is paler than basalt because it contains fewer dark, metallic ingredients such as iron.

THE BRITTLE SHELL

Both types of crust are bonded to the upper layer of the mantle to form a vast cool shell around the planet called the lithosphere. This lies above a hotter, more fluid layer that is always moving. The movement makes the lithosphere crack, so it is split by rifts and faults, and peppered with volcanoes.

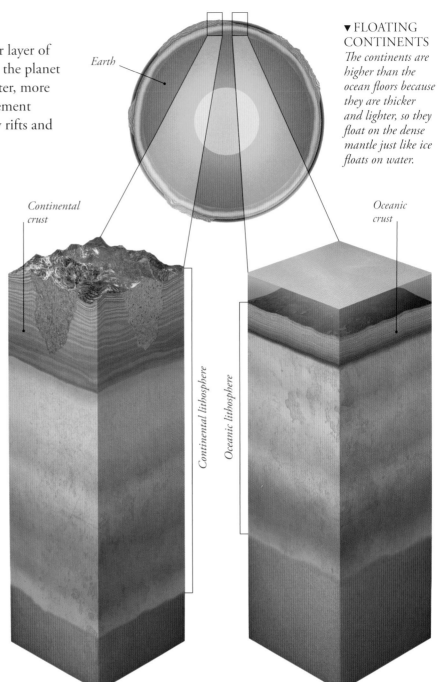

Earth

Continental crust

Oceanic crust

Continental lithosphere

Oceanic lithosphere

▼ FLOATING CONTINENTS
The continents are higher than the ocean floors because they are thicker and lighter, so they float on the dense mantle just like ice floats on water.

SOFT SKIN

The hard basalts and granites that form the basis of the crust are often covered with softer sedimentary rock made of cemented rock fragments and the compacted remains of living things. On land, these decay to form soils.

DRILLING DOWN

Scientists can investigate the deeper layers of the crust by drilling down into the rock to bring up samples. The Kola Superdeep Borehole project on the Kola Peninsula of Russia penetrated more than 7.5 miles (12 km) below the surface. Special drilling ships, such as this one in the Gulf of Mexico, have drilled boreholes more than 1.2 miles (2 km) deep into the ocean floor.

▲ DEEPWATER DRILLSHIP
The drilling rig mounted on this research ship allows scientists to probe deep below the ocean floor.

27

Impact craters

Our planet is continually showered by meteorites. Most of these are very small, but sometimes Earth is struck by a meteorite big enough to create an impact crater, just like the ones you can see on the Moon. It is likely that at least one such impact caused a mass extinction of life long ago. Simple craters are deep, but complex craters are wider, often with rings of ridges and a central dome.

Barringer Crater
United States

Location Painted Desert, Arizona
Date of impact 50,000 years ago
Width 0.75 miles (1.2 km)
Type Simple

Also known as Meteor Crater, this is one of the best-preserved impact sites on the planet. It was probably made by a nickel-iron meteorite roughly 150 ft (50 m) across. Remains of the meteorite are still scattered around the rim of the crater, in the form of tiny metal balls that formed when it vaporized on impact.

▼ CLEAR IMPACT
Barringer Crater was caused by a recent impact, which is why it is still well defined.

Spider Crater
Australia

Location Kimberley Plateau, Western Australia
Date of impact 600–900 million years ago
Width 8 miles (13 km)
Type Complex

Hidden away in a remote region of northwest Australia, this very ancient structure was only identified in the 1970s. The crater has a massively eroded central dome created by the recoil of Earth's crust after the impact. This is now carved into spiderlike, radiating ridges of very hard quartzite rock.

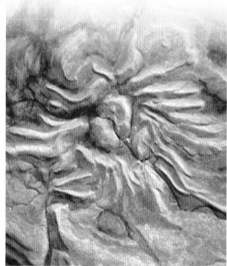

Lonar Crater
India

Location Maharashtra, near Mumbai
Date of impact 50,000 years ago
Width 1.1 miles (1.8 km)
Type Simple

Lonar Crater is similar to Barringer Crater, but slightly bigger. It was formed at about the same time in very hard basalt rock, and is beautifully preserved. The monsoon climate has turned it into a lake 560 ft (170 m) deep. It is almost perfectly circular and surrounded by dense woodland and several Hindu temples.

Ouarkziz Crater
Algeria

Location Northwest Algeria
Date of impact 70 million years ago
Width 2 miles (3.5 km)
Type Simple

Originally called Tindouf when it was discovered in 1997, the Ouarkziz impact crater appears as an almost perfectly circular scar in the barren layers of sedimentary rock of the northern Sahara Desert. Occasional rainstorms feed a stream that has cut across the crater, but it looks far more recent than its true age of 70 million years.

▶ VISIBLE FROM SPACE
The Ouarkziz Crater was photographed in 2012 by a crew member on the International Space Station.

Manicougan Crater
Canada

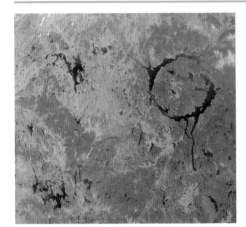

Location Québec, northwest of Montreal
Date of impact 212 million years ago
Width 60 miles (100 km)
Type Complex

After Spider Crater, this huge crater in Canada is one of the oldest that has been found. It was formed by a massive impact that made Earth's crust rebound into the peak of Mont Babel at the center of the crater. It is surrounded by the vast, ring-shaped trough of Lake Manicouagan.

Chicxulub Crater
Mexico

Location Northern coast of Yucatán
Date of impact 66 million years ago
Width Up to 150 miles (240 km)
Type Complex

Discovered by accident by an oil prospector in the late 1970s, this truly colossal crater and its rings mark the catastophic asteroid impact that almost certainly triggered the extinction of the dinosaurs 66 million years ago. It is now buried beneath later rocks, and is only detectable using high-tech surveying equipment.

Wolfe Creek Crater
Australia

Location Great Sandy Desert, Western Australia
Date of impact 300,000 years ago
Width 2,870 ft (875 m)
Type Simple

Most meteorite craters on Earth have been virtually destroyed by erosion, but recent desert sites like this one survive almost intact. It has features typical of many small craters, including a central hollow that sometimes holds water, and a circular rim covered with debris blown out by the force of the impact.

Kaali Craters
Estonia

Location Saaremaa Island, Estonia
Date of impact 4,000–10,000 years ago
Width 40–130 ft (12–40 m)
Type Complex

One of the most recent meteorite impact sites, Kaali is a group of nine craters. It was formed when a meteorite broke up into fragments several miles above the surface, each of which formed its own small crater.

Moving plates

Earth's crust is always on the move, driven by heat currents that rise from deep within the planet. The movement is extremely slow, but hugely powerful. It has ripped the brittle lithosphere into great rocky plates that are pulling apart in some places and grinding together in others. These movements trigger earthquakes and volcanoes, especially in the frontier zones where the plates meet.

MOBILE MANTLE

The heat generated deep within the planet rises through the mantle to the surface, just like heat rising through soup simmering on a kitchen stove. It drives convection currents that circulate through the solid but very hot mantle rock, and keep it moving very slowly. The currents make the mantle rock rise to beneath the crust, spread sideways, then sink again as it cools.

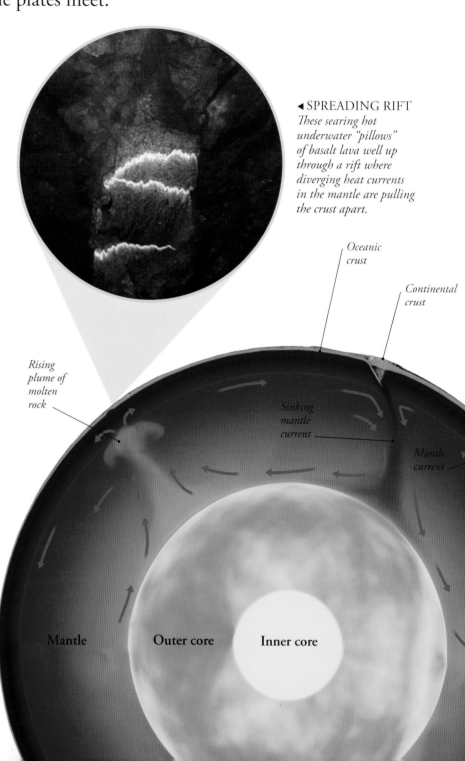

◀ SPREADING RIFT
These searing hot underwater "pillows" of basalt lava well up through a rift where diverging heat currents in the mantle are pulling the crust apart.

Oceanic crust

Continental crust

Rising plume of molten rock

Sinking mantle current

Mantle current

Mantle   Outer core   Inner core

HEAT SOURCE

Deep in Earth's mantle, uranium and other radioactive elements release nuclear energy in the form of heat. The process is the same as the reaction that takes place in this nuclear reactor. Some elements, such as uranium-238, have been generating heat in this way since the planet was formed.

▲ NUCLEAR ENERGY
Uranium fuel rods in a nuclear reactor radiate the same type of energy as the uranium inside the planet.

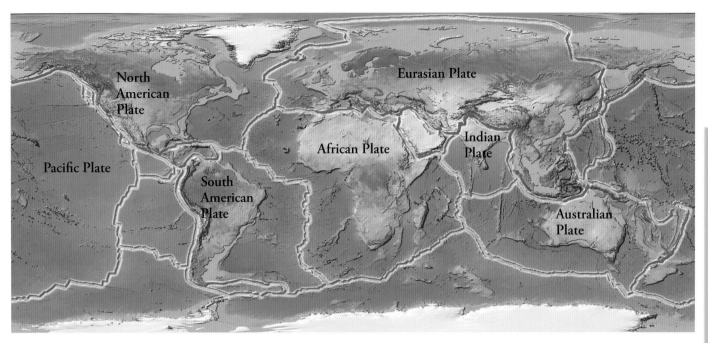

North American Plate

Eurasian Plate

Pacific Plate

African Plate

Indian Plate

South American Plate

Australian Plate

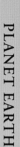

FRACTURED SHELL

The relentless movement of the mantle has broken the brittle lithosphere into sections that resemble fragments of a giant eggshell. The pieces are known as tectonic plates. Some are huge (the largest are labeled on the map above), but there are also many much smaller ones. Some plates form the ocean floors, while others underlie both continents and oceans.

▲ COLLIDING CRUST
The way the crust crumples up where plates push together is clear in this satellite view of the Alps.

PUSH AND PULL

When the convection currents rise through the mantle they push the plates apart, and when they sink back down again they pull the plates together. This means that the plates are always moving very slowly, at about the same rate as your fingernails grow. New crust is created where the plates pull apart, and old crust is crumpled up or destroyed where they push together.

CONTINENTAL DRIFT

The plates underlying the continents are constantly shifting relative to each other. Over vast spans of time, they are split up and pushed together in different arrangements. This is called continental drift. The continents that make up our present world are fragments of a giant supercontinent, Pangaea, that existed about 250 million years ago.

Pangaea

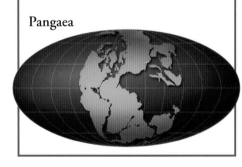

Rising mantle current

FRONTIER ZONES

The boundaries between colliding tectonic plates are the world's most active earthquake zones. They are also lined with chains of volcanoes. Some are more unstable than others—the boundary marked by the Indonesian islands of Sumatra and Java has more than 100 active volcanoes.

◀ FIRE ISLAND
Volcanoes cluster on Java, which has 45 active volcanoes and many dormant ones.

31

Plate boundaries

Since tectonic plates are pulling apart in some places and pushing together in others, different types of boundaries are created between the plates. In places where the plates are ripping apart, new crust is created as molten rock wells up from below. Where they are grinding together, old crust is destroyed. But there are also boundaries where slabs of crust simply slide past each other.

DIVERGENT BOUNDARIES

As heat currents in the mantle rise and divide, they rip apart the brittle crust at spreading rifts known as divergent boundaries. Where plates open up, magma erupts through the rift. The molten rock cools and solidifies, but then the rift opens again, allowing more magma to erupt and build new crust. Most of these rifts are on ocean floors.

Mid-ocean rift

Rising magma

Diverging ocean plate

New oceanic crust

EXPANDING OCEANS

When rifts open, they form valleys that tend to fill with water. In North Africa, this process has created the Red Sea (left). The Atlantic looked like this about 160 million years ago. It has been expanding ever since from the rift of the Mid-Atlantic Ridge at the rate of about 1 in (25 mm) per year.

◀ SPREADING SEA
The Red Sea has formed in the rift where the African Plate and the Arabian Plate are being pulled apart. It is getting steadily wider and will eventually become an ocean.

FACT!
Many rift valleys are filled with long, deep lakes. Among these is Lake Baikal in Russia, which is the deepest lake on Earth and contains a fifth of the world's fresh water.

CONVERGENT BOUNDARIES

At a convergent boundary, where plates are pushing together, the edge of one plate can be subducted, or drawn beneath, the edge of the other. Oceanic crust is always dragged below continental crust because it is heavier. In places where two oceanic plates push together, the one with the oldest, heaviest rock is dragged beneath the newer one.

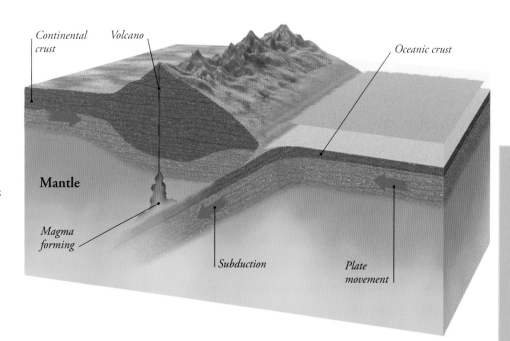

Continental crust
Volcano
Oceanic crust
Mantle
Magma forming
Subduction
Plate movement

OCEAN TRENCHES

Oceanic subduction zones are marked by deep trenches in the ocean floor that follow the edge of the upper plate. On average, the ocean floors lie about 12,500 ft (3,800 m) below the surface, but some of these ocean trenches are at least twice as deep. The deepest part of the Mariana Trench in the western Pacific plunges to nearly 36,000 ft (11,000 m) below sea level, the deepest point on Earth's surface.

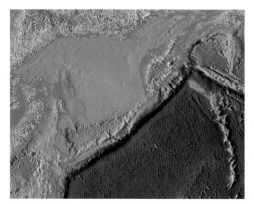

◄ DEEP BLUE
The dark blue line in this image of the northwest Pacific is the Kuril Trench, extending from off northern Japan to the Kamchatka Peninsula in Siberia.

VOLCANIC CHAINS

Subducted oceanic crust melts as it is carried down into the hot mantle. The melted rock may then erupt from volcanoes above the subduction zone. These form chains of volcanic islands along the plate boundary, known as island arcs, such as the Aleutian Islands off Alaska, shown in this satellite image.

SLIDING BOUNDARIES

At transform boundaries, the plates slide past each other without pulling apart or pushing together. This means that there is no new crust created, and no old crust destroyed. Most transform boundaries are on ocean floors, where they allow sections of oceanic crust to move at different rates. But some occur on land—the most famous example is the San Andreas Fault, which runs through California.

▶ FRACTURED LANDSCAPE
Moving plates on either side of the San Andreas Fault have ripped a long seam in the Carrizo Plain of California, and regularly cause earthquakes.

Earthquakes

Most earthquakes occur on the plate boundaries of Earth's crust, where the plates are moving relative to one another. This movement may cause just minor tremors, but if the plates lock together, the strain builds up until something snaps. It is this sudden release of tension that causes a big, destructive earthquake.

EARTHQUAKE ZONES

In the 1960s, the United States used a network of seismometers (instruments that record motions in the ground) to monitor nuclear bomb tests. The instruments also recorded all the earthquakes worldwide, and revealed that most of them (shown in red below) occur in narrow bands along the tectonic plate boundaries.

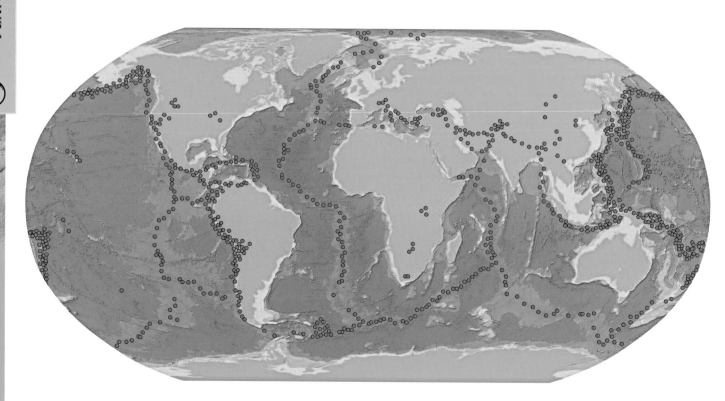

SLIPPING AND SLIDING

The plates of the crust are always moving, but very slowly. As they move, they slip against each other at plate boundaries. When this occurs at a steady rate, it causes gradual creeping movement that can crack road surfaces and move fences out of line. It also triggers frequent small earth tremors—often so small that no one notices them.

◄ MINOR SHIFT
This crack in the road was caused by creeping movement at or near the boundary between two moving plates.

FACT!

During the 1964 Alaska earthquake, the Pacific floor slid 66 ft (20 m) beneath Alaska in just three minutes, and lifted an old shipwreck out of the water.

LOCK AND SNAP

If two plates of Earth's crust lock together at a plate boundary, this doesn't stop them from moving. The edges of the plates just get distorted like giant springs, building up tension. When the boundary finally gives way, the plates spring back and all the movement that might have taken place over many years happens within minutes. The sudden shock is what generates an earthquake.

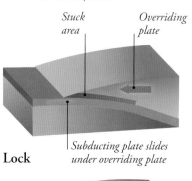

Stuck area
Overriding plate

Subducting plate slides under overriding plate

Lock

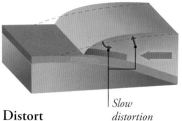

Slow distortion

Distort

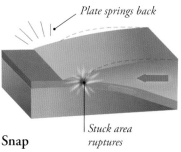

Plate springs back

Stuck area ruptures

Snap

THE RICHTER SCALE

Earthquake waves are picked up and recorded using seismometers or seismographs. They are often measured on the Richter scale of magnitude. Each increase in number represents ten times the shaking force, so a category 7 earthquake is ten times as powerful as a category 6. The earthquake that caused the 2011 tsunami in Japan measured 9.0 on this scale.

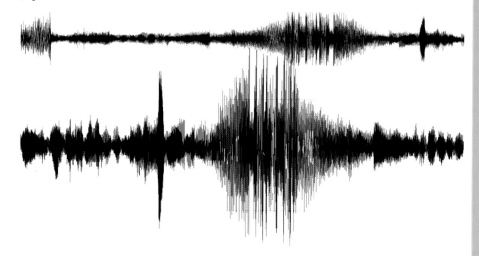

SHOCK WAVES

During an earthquake, radiating shock waves shake the ground like ripples on a pond. Sometimes they liquefy it, just as you can liquefy wet sand on a beach if you paddle it with your foot. This makes it quiver like jelly and then give way beneath tall buildings, making them keel over like capsizing ships.

▼ MAJOR DAMAGE
An earthquake measuring 8.5 on the Richter scale caused this building in Sichuan, China, to collapse in 2008.

FAST FACTS

■ There are roughly half a million earthquakes every year.
■ The biggest earthquake recorded so far hit 9.5 on the Richter scale.
■ A deadly quake killed around 316,000 people in Haiti in 2010. The widespread damage badly hampered rescue efforts.

GROUND SHIFT

An earthquake has ripped apart and uplifted this asphalt road in Italy. The fault movement is often deep underground, but sometimes it is very obviously on the surface. Here, one side of a fault has moved up by well over 3 ft (1 m). The strain would have been building for decades, but when the fault finally gave way, the movement occurred in seconds.

Tsunamis

Earthquakes happen on the ocean floor as well as on land. The shock waves ripple up and out through the water, pushing up enormous waves called tsunamis. Out on the open ocean, they can be quite hard to detect because they are very broad, but when they sweep into shallow water they get much steeper and more destructive.

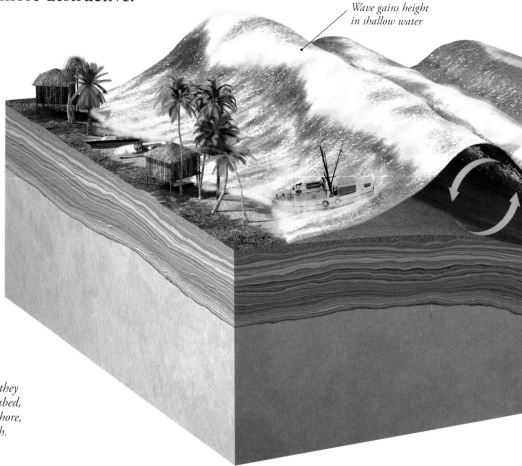

Wave gains height in shallow water

SUBMARINE EARTHQUAKE

When the ocean floor plows beneath another slab of Earth's crust, the moving plates tend to lock together, build up strain, then snap apart to cause ocean-floor earthquakes. As the upper plate springs back up, it pushes the water above it up into a heap. This huge ripple then surges across the ocean at high speed as a series of giant waves that can cause chaos when they strike land.

▶ MONSTER WAVES
If tsunamis drive into shallow water, they slow down due to friction with the seabed, and get much steeper. As they surge ashore, they overwhelm anything in their path.

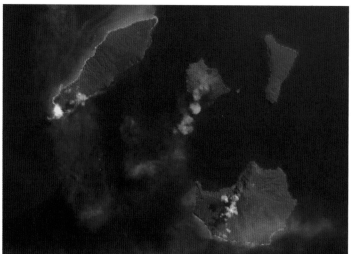

EXPLODING ISLANDS

Tsunamis can be generated by massive landslides that plunge into the sea and push up giant waves. A volcanic island can also trigger a tsunami if it erupts so violently that it blows itself apart. Seawater cascading into the red-hot heart of the shattered island boils instantly and explodes, with a shock wave that turns into a tsunami. This can be just as lethal as the eruption itself.

◀ VOLCANIC BOMB
In 1883, the volcanic island of Krakatoa near Java exploded, causing a deadly tsunami. The dark island in this image is a new volcano erupting from the flooded crater of the old one.

WALL OF WATER

A tsunami is not like a giant version of an ordinary ocean wave. It has a very long wavelength, which means that it takes many minutes to pass, rather than a second or two. It seems to rise like an extra-high tide, and plows ashore like a vast step in the ocean that can completely drown the landscape.

▲ SWEPT AWAY
An offshore earthquake in 2011 caused this vast wave to plow into the eastern shores of Japan.

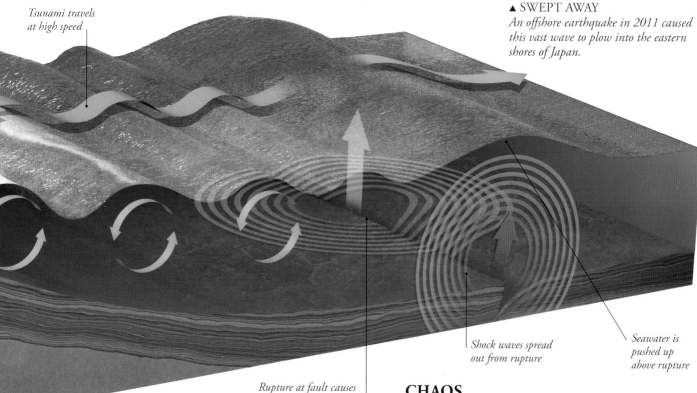

Tsunami travels at high speed

Shock waves spread out from rupture

Seawater is pushed up above rupture

Rupture at fault causes ocean floor to spring up

CHAOS

The waves of a tsunami behave like a colossal fluid bulldozer, trashing everything in their path. The water gets loaded with floating debris that adds to its destructive power and makes it more deadly—any people caught up in the chaos are unlikely to survive.

INTERNATIONAL DISASTERS

Tsunamis can travel vast distances, crossing oceans and devastating communities. In 2004, an earthquake in the Indian Ocean off the west coast of Sumatra, Indonesia, caused a tsunami that killed more than 230,000 people living on the shores of 14 countries.

Before

After

▲ DEVASTATED DISTRICT
This district of the city of Banda Aceh on the Sumatran coast was ripped apart by the devastating tsunami of 2004.

Making mountains

Mountains are built by the same forces that cause earthquakes. Colliding plates crumple continental crust into ranges of fold mountains. When crust is pulled apart, some pieces slip downward, leaving high walls of rock on each side. Molten magma oozing up from below can solidify in great masses of hard rock that may be exposed if softer covering rock is worn away.

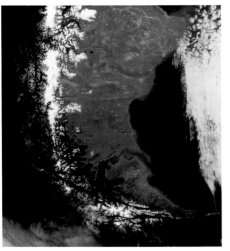

COLLISION ZONES

When oceanic crust plows beneath a slab of continental crust, the edge of the continent crumples into ranges of fold mountains. This is the force that is raising the Andes mountain range in South America. A similar process built the Rocky Mountains of North America more than 35 million years ago.

◄ UPLIFTED
The snow-capped Andes are being pushed up by the Pacific ocean floor grinding eastward beneath the western side of South America.

CRASHING CONTINENTS

If two continents collide, this can cause massive folding and thickening of the crust. This is happening today in Asia, where the Indian Plate is plowing north into the Eurasian Plate at the rate of about 1 in (2.5 cm) per year.

▼ ROOF OF THE WORLD
The collision of the Indian and Eurasian Plates has formed the Himalayas, Earth's highest mountains.

BLOCK MOUNTAINS

Sometimes, shifting plates can pull continents apart. The stretched rocks fracture, forming faults that allow big blocks of crust to slip downward and create rift valleys. The rocks on either side are left as block mountains. The African Great Rift Valley was formed like this.

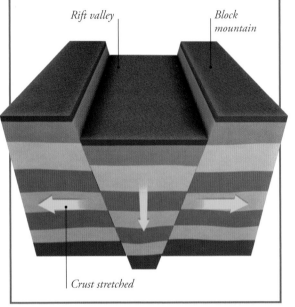

Rift valley

Block mountain

Crust stretched

HARD ROCK

The titanic earth movements that build mountains are often linked to processes that melt the rock beneath the crust. The molten rock seeps upward and slowly solidifies below ground. This creates huge masses of granite and other hard rock. Over time, the softer rock above may be worn away, slowly exposing the hard granite to form spectacular mountains. Similar processes may expose the cores of ancient volcanoes made of solidified lava.

▼ GRANITE GIANT
Half Dome in the Sierra Nevada range of California is a massive lump of exposed granite that originally formed deep below ground.

FADED GLORY

In time, all mountains fade away. They sink under their own weight like heaps of wet sand, and are worn away where the rock is exposed to the weather. If it weren't for the continuing movement of Earth's crust, they would all eventually vanish.

▼ RUGGED SURVIVORS
The once towering mountains of the Scottish Highlands have been gradually reduced to rounded stumps.

FAST FACTS

The "seven summits" are the highest individual peaks on each continent.
- **Asia** Everest: 29,029 ft (8,848 m), Himalayas, Nepal/China
- **South America** Aconcagua: 22,841 ft (6,962 m), Andes, Argentina
- **North America** Mount McKinley: 20,320 ft (6,194 m), Alaska Range, USA
- **Africa** Kilimanjaro: 19,341 ft (5,895 m), Kilimanjaro Range, Tanzania
- **Europe** Mount Elbrus: 18,510 ft (5,642 m), Caucasus, Chechnya, Russia
- **Antarctica** Vinson Massif: 16,500 ft (4,897 m), Ellsworth Mountains
- **Oceania** Puncak Jaya: 16,024 ft (4,884 m), Sudirman Range, New Guinea

Volcanoes

Few things in nature are as dramatic as volcanoes. There are many different types, ranging from simple cracks in Earth's crust to giant cone-shaped mountains built up of many layers of lava and ash. Most volcanoes form at the boundaries where tectonic plates are either coming together or pulling apart.

RIFT VOLCANOES

In the rift zones where tectonic plates pull apart, the pressure that normally keeps the mantle rock solid relaxes, allowing some of it to melt and erupt as fluid basalt lava. These eruptions are frequent and relatively predictable, but often spectacular. Erta Ale volcano in Ethiopia's Rift Valley (above) has contained a churning lake of liquid lava for more than a century.

VOLCANIC LAVA

The rivers of liquid lava erupted by rift and hot spot volcanoes can flow fast over long distances. Other volcanoes such as Mount Etna in Italy erupt stickier lava that does not flow as far. The lava erupted by volcanoes where plates are pushing together is particularly thick, and flows so slowly that it may block the volcano. Pressure then builds up to cause very explosive eruptions.

HOT SPOT VOLCANOES

Some volcanoes erupt away from plate boundaries, over hot spots below Earth's crust. At places where a plate is moving over a hot spot, new volcanoes erupt as older ones fall extinct. This creates long chains of volcanic islands such as those of Hawaii, seen here from space.

▲ ETNA
Lava erupting from Mount Etna in Italy has a temperature of about 1,830°F (1,000°C).

VOLCANO SHAPES

A volcano's shape depends on the material being erupted. Fluid lava can build a low, broad mountain known as a shield volcano. Sticky lava and ash can create a cone-shaped stratovolcano (shown here). The lava of a stratovolcano doesn't flow far, allowing ash to settle on it. Each eruption adds another layer.

Ash cloud

Erupting lava

Layers of old volcanic eruptions

Old lava flow

▶ KILLER CLOUD
A billowing, deadly cloud of hot ash threatens to engulf a truck speeding away from the 1991 eruption of Mount Pinatubo in the Philippines.

PYROCLASTIC FLOWS

Much of the rock and ash blasted into the sky during an explosive eruption falls back down again. It pours down the volcano in an avalanche of searingly hot rock and dust called a pyroclastic flow. This can travel at up to 450 mph (700 km/h) and surge far beyond the volcano, incinerating and often burying everything in its path.

43

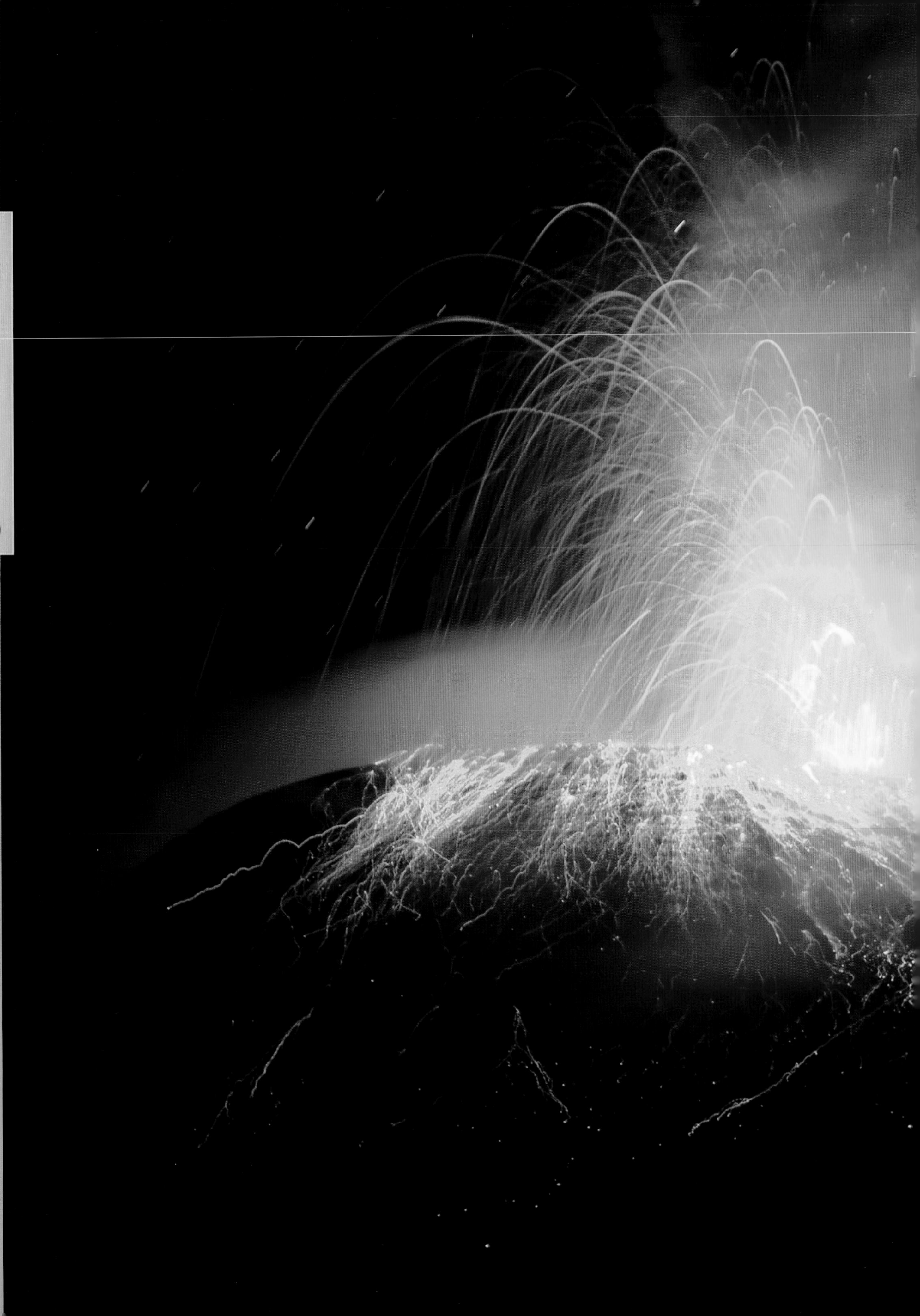

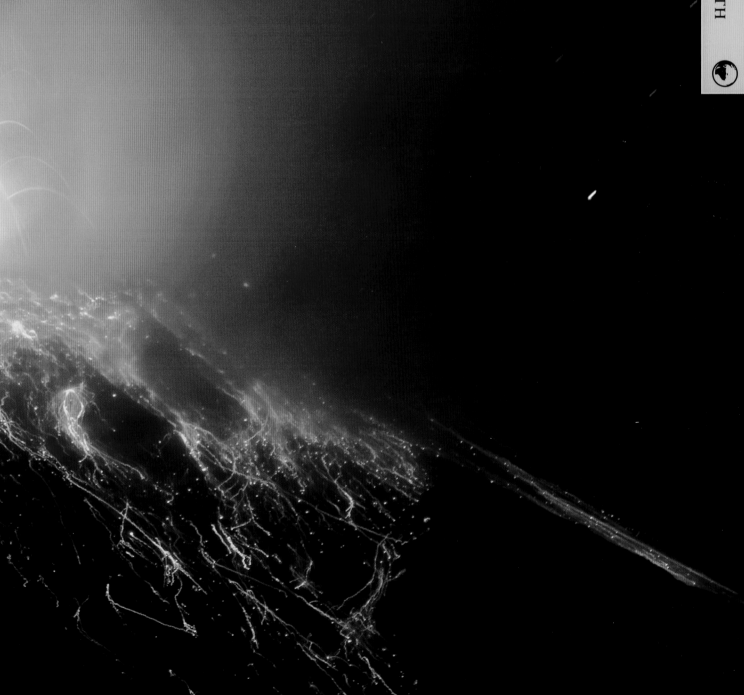

ERUPTION
A volcano can be considered active, rather than dormant, even if it hasn't erupted for 10,000 years. After many years of inactivity, the stratovolcano Tungurahua in Ecuador, South America, entered an eruptive phase in 1999. This eruption in 2010 produced an ash cloud reaching 1.2 miles (2 km) in height.

Cataclysm

Erupting volcanoes have caused some of the worst natural disasters in history. The most dangerous volcanoes are not those that erupt frequently, but the ones that have not erupted for centuries. People start living close by, farming the fertile volcanic soil, and even building great cities. But then the volcano erupts again, with catastrophic results.

Laki
Iceland

Eruption June 1783–Febuary 1784
Features Huge lava flow, gas cloud
Estimated death toll 9,350

Rift volcanoes usually erupt so regularly that people keep away from them. But sometimes there is no escape. In 1783, the Laki rift in Iceland erupted from more than 140 craters over eight months, releasing vast amounts of lava and poisonous gases. A quarter of Iceland's population died from poisoning and starvation, and the effects of the eruption were felt around the world.

▼ LETHAL RIFT
This is just part of the Laki rift system, which erupted over a total length of 16 miles (26 km) in 1783, producing the largest lava flow of modern times.

Krakatoa
Sunda Strait, Indonesia

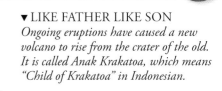

Eruption August 1883
Features Explosion, pyroclastic flows, tsunamis
Estimated death toll 36,417

In 1883, Krakatoa exploded, causing pyroclastic flows and tsunamis that killed thousands of people. The explosion may have been the loudest ever heard.

▼ LIKE FATHER LIKE SON
Ongoing eruptions have caused a new volcano to rise from the crater of the old. It is called Anak Krakatoa, which means "Child of Krakatoa" in Indonesian.

Mount Pinatubo
Luzon, Philippines

Eruption June 1991
Features Ash cloud, pyroclastic flows, mudslides
Estimated death toll 800

The 1991 eruption of Mount Pinatubo blew the top off the volcano and ejected about 2.4 cubic miles (10 cubic km) of ash and rock into the air. This caused a colossal ash cloud and deadly pyroclastic flows. Fine ash smothered the landscape, and created a layer of sulfuric acid haze all around the world.

Tambora
Sumbawa, Indonesia

Eruption April 1815
Features Explosion, tsunamis, global ash cloud
Estimated death toll 60,000

This was the biggest volcanic eruption in recorded history—the explosion was heard from 1,243 miles (2,000 km) away. Gas and ash spread worldwide, dimming the Sun for so long that 1816 became known as "the year without a summer." Crops stopped growing, causing the worst famine of the century.

Mount Pelée
Martinique, West Indies

Eruption May 1902
Features Ash cloud, pyroclastic flows
Estimated death toll 29,500

The city of Saint-Pierre below Mount Pelée was crowded with people when the volcano exploded and a vast cloud of ash poured out. The cloud became a pyroclastic flow that surged toward Saint-Pierre at more than 400 mph (650 km/h), reaching the city in under a minute and completely destroying it. Virtually everyone was killed.

Vesuvius
Naples, Italy

Eruption August 79 CE
Features Ash cloud, pyroclastic flows
Estimated death toll 2,100

The most famous eruption of all time occurred in the year 79 CE, during the Roman Empire. Vesuvius had been dormant for centuries, but then erupted with catastrophic violence. Pyroclastic flows buried the Roman towns of Pompeii and Herculaneum, killing anyone who could not escape.

Santorini
Greek Aegean Islands

Eruption c. 1600 BCE
Features Explosion, ash cloud, tsunami
Estimated death toll Unknown

Many thousands of years ago, this island volcano exploded, creating a huge water-filled crater. A new volcano appeared, and 3,600 years ago it also exploded, causing a gigantic tsunami. Now, the volcano (in the center of the sea-filled crater) is growing again.

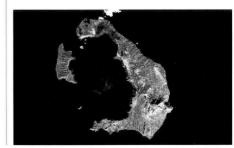

Hot springs and geysers

In some volcanic regions, water seeping into the ground comes into contact with very hot rock. It usually bubbles back to the surface as a hot spring, but it can also erupt as an explosive geyser. In the deep ocean, the same process creates "black smokers" of superheated water.

BOILING UP

Hot springs are found in highly volcanic regions where molten rock lies near the surface. High pressure underground heats water to well above its normal boiling point. It is then forced to the surface, where it forms steaming hot pools. These are often vividly colored by microbes called archaea that can survive in extreme conditions.

▶ WARM GLOW
Dense colonies of microscopic life create a dazzling effect in the Morning Glory Pool, a hot spring in Yellowstone National Park.

DISSOLVED MINERALS

Water that is superheated at high pressure deep below the surface can reach a temperature of 572°F (300°C) or more. This allows it to dissolve minerals from the rocks, but the minerals turn solid again when the water reaches the surface and its temperature drops. This process can result in spectacular terraced deposits of minerals building up in places where the water flows away from the hot spring.

▼ TRAVERTINE TERRACES
Carbonate minerals known as travertine hang like frozen waterfalls from the terraced pools around the Pamukkale hot springs in southwestern Turkey.

MUD AND GAS

The hot water and gas that rise to the surface often react with the rocks, turning them to clay. The mixture of clay and water forms pools of hot liquid mud that pop and bubble with rising gas. Other vents called fumaroles release clouds of steam that often reek of sulfurous volcanic gases—the "rotten egg" smell.

BLACK SMOKERS

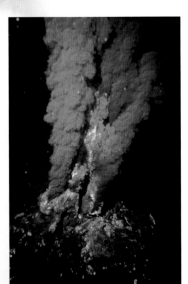

The mid-ocean ridges on deep ocean floors are dotted with hot springs that gush superheated water into the cold, dark ocean. The hot water contains dissolved minerals that solidify into tiny sooty particles as soon as they hit the near-freezing ocean, so the erupting water can look like a cloud of billowing black smoke. The minerals often build up to form dramatic "chimneys" that tower above the vents.

▲ DARK MATTER
Lit up by the powerful lights of a deepwater submersible vehicle, a black smoker belches hot water and mineral particles into the cold ocean.

 HOT BATH

The hot springs of Nagano, Japan, feed a series of pools where the water cools to a comfortable 122°F (50°C) or so. Japanese macaques, or snow monkeys, use them to keep warm in winter, when the air temperature in the region can drop to a numbing 5°F (−15°C). The macaques sit in the steaming pools, basking in the volcanic heat while snow falls on their heads.

PRESSURE COOKER

At a few sites, hot water beneath the ground erupts as geysers. The weight of the water above the heat source increases the pressure on the hot water, and this raises its boiling point. It gets hotter and hotter, and expands until some of the water is pushed up and out of the ground. This reduces the pressure, so the superheated water boils and turns to steam—blowing the remaining water out of the ground as a geyser.

◄ BLOWOUT
A geyser in the Taupo volcanic zone of New Zealand shoots steam and hot water high into the air. Some geysers erupt to heights of well over 330 ft (100 m).

ROCKS AND MINERALS

Glittering mineral crystals have built the rocks that make up planet Earth, its spectacular landscapes, and its treasure trove of precious metals, gems, and fossils.

Elements and minerals

Everything in the Universe is made of substances called elements, each made up of just one type of atom. These elements react or bond with others to form chemical compounds, which include the minerals that form rocks. But some elements, such as gold, do not react with others easily, and are found in their pure state.

STARDUST

The elements were created in the stars. Each star is a giant nuclear reactor that fuses together the nuclei (central parts) of atoms to make new elements. Stars like our Sun fuse hydrogen nuclei to make helium. Larger stars fuse helium nuclei to create carbon, carbon with helium to form oxygen, carbon with carbon to make magnesium, and so on.

ELEMENTS AND COMPOUNDS

Altogether, 88 elements occur naturally on Earth, ranging from hydrogen (the lightest) to plutonium (the heaviest). Some elements occur in pure form, but most combine with other elements in chemical reactions that form chemical compounds. Some of these compounds, such as water, are quite simple. Others are far more complex, containing the atoms of many elements.

▶ MOLECULES
Atoms can bond together into groups called molecules. For example, oxygen and hydrogen atoms are bonded together in a water molecule.

Oxygen atom

Hydrogen atom

FACT!

All the elements were made in the stars. These include the elements that form Earth and everything on it, including every atom in your body.

MINERALS

Some chemical compounds exist as gases such as carbon dioxide, or liquids such as water. Others form solids known as minerals. A mineral is composed of one or more elements in fixed proportions, usually with a distinctive crystal structure. There are more than 4,500 minerals, including silica, a compound of two elements—silicon and oxygen. In its pure form, silica occurs as quartz. Flint, used to make this ancient arrowhead, is made up of fine-grained quartz.

The most abundant element in the Universe is hydrogen.

METALS

The shiny elements known as metals are made of identical atoms and are good conductors of heat and electricity. Most metals react with other elements to form minerals known as metal ores. For example, iron combines with oxygen to form iron oxide, the main ingredient of iron ore—but more familiar to us as rust.

NATURAL PAINT BOX

Many metal-bearing minerals are colorful, such as the green copper compound malachite, and the red mercury-sulfur compound cinnabar. In the past, they were ground up and used as pigments in paints. Some, such as blue lapis lazuli, were rare and highly valued, and used to adorn religious paintings and manuscripts.

MINERALS AND ROCKS

The planet is made largely of rocks, which are all created from combinations of minerals, which in turn are made from elements. This granite is made of the minerals quartz, feldspar, and mica. These contain the metallic elements potassium, sodium, aluminum, iron, and magnesium, plus silicon and oxygen.

Crystals

Many minerals and other chemical compounds naturally form crystals. These glittering geometric structures are often created when molten or dissolved minerals slowly turn solid, giving time for their atoms to form organized structures. Some of the most beautiful crystals may be cut and polished into valuable gems.

CRYSTAL STRUCTURE

The atoms or molecules that form minerals cling to each other by electrical forces. Depending on the elements involved, they form different three-dimensional patterns. For example, common salt is made of chlorine and sodium atoms that bind together in a cubic structure. This defines the shape of salt crystals (right), which are also cubic.

ICE CRYSTALS

Frost is crystallized water, formed as liquid water cools to below its freezing point. The V-shaped, or triangular, water molecules latch onto each other as they cool. They form six-sided patterns that grow into six-sided, or hexagonal, crystals. Many mineral crystals form in the same way, but at higher temperatures. Quartz crystals start to form at about 3,090°F (1,700°C).

▼ WINTER FROST
The ice crystals glittering on this leaf have formed after an overnight frost.

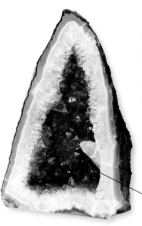

HYDROTHERMAL VEIN

Water deep inside the Earth can become hot enough to dissolve minerals from rocks. If the resulting solution seeps up toward the surface, it cools and deposits the minerals in cracks and cavities. These form narrow veins and crystal-lined cavities known as geodes.

Quartz geode is colored by impurities in the minerals

GLITTERING FACES

The faces of crystals are perfectly flat, because of the way the atoms form the crystal bond. Sometimes the faces have steplike raised surfaces, but each step is perfectly aligned with the others on that face. This is why these galena crystals glitter with reflected light, like miniature mirrors.

Step in face

GEMSTONES

Transparent crystals, such as diamonds, bend light like tiny lenses, so that the crystal appears to sparkle. Gem-cutters enhance this effect by carefully reshaping the crystal. The resulting gemstone is smaller than the original crystal, but far more valuable.

SYMMETRICAL SHAPES

There are seven basic crystal types, which are usually grouped into six "families." Some are very regular, but others seem to have random shapes until you realize that their flat faces always lie at particular angles to each other. This feature is caused by their symmetry.

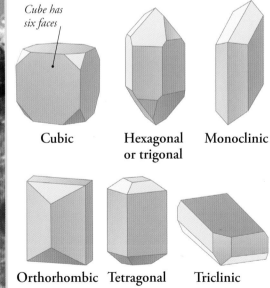

Cube has six faces

Cubic	Hexagonal or trigonal	Monoclinic

Orthorhombic	Tetragonal	Triclinic

Crystal types

There are crystals all around us. Most rocks are made of them, and most sandy beaches are made of billions of broken quartz crystals. Even the sugar and salt in your kitchen are crystals. Some of the most spectacular are mineral crystals that grow in underground cavities, sometimes reaching enormous sizes.

Beryl
Precious emerald

Main ingredients Beryllium, aluminum, silicon, oxygen
Crystal type Hexagonal
Hardness on 1–10 scale 7.5–8

This hard mineral forms crystals in rocks that have been altered deep beneath the ground. Some crystals can grow larger than cars, but the most valuable are smaller green emeralds, as below. Beryl also occurs in a blue-green form called aquamarine.

Quartz
Abundant and beautiful

Main ingredients Silicon, oxygen
Crystal type Trigonal
Hardness on 1–10 scale 7

White quartz is pure silica—the compound of silicon and oxygen that we use to make glass. It is one of the most common minerals in continental rocks, where the crystals often form clusters inside rock cavities. Typical quartz crystals are six-sided columns topped with six-sided pyramids.

▶ AMETHYST
This violet form of quartz owes its beautiful color to impurities in the mineral, including traces of iron.

Olivine
Sea green

Main ingredients Silicon, oxygen, iron, magnesium
Crystal type Orthorhombic
Hardness on 1–10 scale 6.5–7

This is the main ingredient of the basalt bedrock of the ocean floor, and the peridotite that forms the upper mantle below Earth's crust. Large, well-formed crystals are rare, and are highly valued as a gemstone known as peridot.

Fluorite
Eerie glow

Main ingredients Calcium, fluorine
Crystal type Cubic
Hardness on 1–10 scale 4

This simple chemical compound often forms twinned crystals that are like interlocking cubes. They are commonly green or purple. Some varieties of fluorite glow under ultraviolet light—a property known as fluorescence.

Rutile
Titanium ore

Main ingredients Titanium, oxygen
Crystal type Tetragonal
Hardness on 1–10 scale 6–6.5

Rutile is about 60 percent titanium— a light but strong metal that is used for many high-tech purposes including spacecraft. The crystals are often in the shape of long prisms, but also form clusters of slender needles.

Calcite
Soft and soluble

Main ingredients Calcium, carbon, oxygen
Crystal type Trigonal
Hardness on 1–10 scale 3

This common mineral can look like quartz, but it is much softer. Calcite often forms limestones that are gradually dissolved by slightly acid rainwater. The crystals grow in a variety of shapes.

Pyrite
Fool's gold

Main ingredients Iron, sulfur
Crystal type Cubic
Hardness on 1–10 scale 6–6.5

Very common and widespread, pyrite crystals have a glittering golden luster that has fooled many gold prospectors into thinking they have struck it rich. If pyrite is scratched with steel, it gives off sparks.

Tourmaline
Multicolored complexity

Main ingredients Silicon, oxygen, boron, plus various metals
Crystal type Trigonal
Hardness on 1–10 scale 7–7.5

Tourmaline is a complex compound of many elements. It forms long crystals that can be almost any color, and can even be multicolored.

Garnet
Historic gem

Main ingredients Silicon, oxygen, plus two or more metals
Crystal type Cubic
Hardness on 1–10 scale 6.5–7.5

Garnet crystals often occur in rocks that have been altered by intense heat and pressure, and can contain a variety of metals, which give them different colors. Pyrope, a magnesium-rich, blood-red variety, is a prized gem.

THE CRYSTAL CAVE

In 2000, miners working deep below ground in the Naica lead mine of Chihuahua Province, Mexico, broke into a cave containing some of the largest crystals ever found. Some are more than 30 ft (9 m) long. They grew to this size over thousands of years, from minerals dissolved in the hot water that once filled the cave.

Igneous rocks

All rocks are mixtures of different minerals. This is obvious in igneous rocks such as granite, which are visibly made up of different types of crystals. These crystals form when molten magma or lava cools and freezes solid. As the crystals form, they lock together in a rigid mass with no gaps. This makes most igneous rocks extremely hard.

MAGMA AND LAVA

Although it's very hot, most of the mantle rock below Earth's crust is kept solid by intense pressure. However, if this pressure eases, or if the rock's melting point is lowered (by an added substance, such as water), the rock can melt. It becomes magma, which is less dense than solid mantle rock. The magma rises through the mantle and may slowly cool and solidify below ground, or erupt from volcanoes as liquid lava.

◄ MOLTEN ROCK
Red-hot lava spills down the side of a volcano in Hawaii. As it cools, it turns to basalt, one of the most common igneous rocks.

INTERLOCKING CRYSTALS

When a molten rock solidifies, each mineral ingredient forms its own crystals. As these grow, they become tightly interlocked in the very rigid structure that makes most igneous rocks so hard. This is clearly visible in this microscope image.

▲ LIGHT SHOW
Polarized light shining though this thin sample of a crystalline rock reveals the different mineral crystals in vivid colors.

CHANGING NATURES

When rock melts, some minerals may be left behind or added as it rises through the crust. This means that the mineral makeup of magma is different from the solid rock that produced it. In general, heavier elements, such as iron, are left behind. If the molten rock solidifies and then melts again, more changes occur. The heavier elements generally produce minerals that are darker in color, so each new stage is paler than the last. For example, granite, which is lightest in color, is created after basalt and diorite.

Basalt   **Diorite**

Granite

PLUTONIC ROCKS

When magma cools and solidifies deep underground, it forms plutonic rocks. Because it is insulated by surrounding rocks, the cooling can take millions of years, giving the minerals in the molten rock a long time to separate out into crystals. This allows the crystals to grow bigger than they would if the magma cooled quickly, like volcanic lava.

◀ BIG AND SLOW
The giant pink crystals in this granite show that the rock formed deep underground, in a large mass called a pluton.

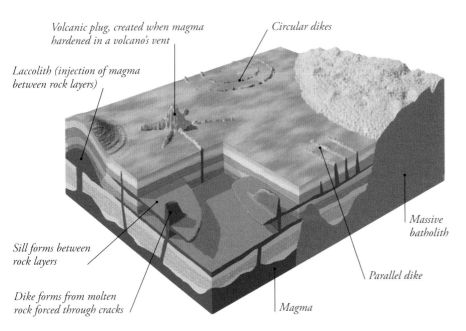

Volcanic plug, created when magma hardened in a volcano's vent

Circular dikes

Laccolith (injection of magma between rock layers)

Sill forms between rock layers

Dike forms from molten rock forced through cracks

Magma

Massive batholith

Parallel dike

IGNEOUS INTRUSIONS

Igneous rocks often solidify underground as huge masses called batholiths—igneous intrusions that can be 60 miles (100 km) or more across. But the molten magma can also push up through cracks in the crust to form dikes, or squeeze between rock layers to create sills. These features are all linked together underground, as shown here, but the rocks of dikes and sills have smaller crystals because they have cooled more quickly.

VOLCANIC ROCKS

Rock that erupts from volcanoes cools quickly, so solidified lava has very small, often invisible crystals. The resulting volcanic rocks have their own names. Rhyolite, for example, is a volcanic form of granite. But while these rocks may have no obvious crystal structure, thick lava flows often crack into distinctive forms as they cool and shrink. Basalt, in particular, splits into natural hexagonal columns.

▼ FRACTURED LAVA
The Giant's Causeway in Northern Ireland is a basalt lava flow that erupted around 55 million years ago and split into about 40,000 basalt columns.

Igneous intrusions

Some of the most spectacular rock formations on Earth have been created from molten rock forced up through the planet's brittle crust. When it cooled, it crystallized into massive batholiths and plutons, volcanic plugs, walllike dikes, and horizontal sills. As soft surrounding rocks have been worn away, these igneous intrusions are left standing proud in the landscape.

Great Dike
Africa

Location Zimbabwe
Intrusion type Lopolith (T-shaped dike)
Rock Serpentinite
Age 2.6 billion years

This colossal intrusion of ancient, altered mantle rock is 3 miles (5 km) wide and 340 miles (550 km) long, which means that it is only really visible from space. As it formed, the molten rock spread out at the top as a lopolith—a dike that is T-shaped in cross-section.

Devil's Tower
North America

Location Wyoming, USA
Intrusion type Plug or pluton
Rock Phonolite
Age 40 million years

This stupendous monolith of solidified magma has split into hexagonal columns, like the basalt of the Giant's Causeway. Scientists believe that it is either a volcanic plug or a pluton—a mass of igneous rock that formed underground from cooled magma.

Sugar Loaf
South America

Location Rio de Janeiro, Brazil
Intrusion type Batholith
Rock Granite
Age 800 million years

Rising dramatically above Guanabara Bay in Rio de Janeiro, Brazil, the Sugar Loaf is part of an enormous granite batholith underlying the whole area. The rock formed from magma that erupted between two overlapping oceanic plates.

Great Karoo
Africa

Location South Africa
Intrusion type Dikes and sills
Rock Dolerite
Age 180 million years

In southern Africa, horizontal layers of shale and sandstone are cracked and split by dikes and sills of dolerite, which is like basalt with bigger crystals. The rock erupted during the breakup of an ancient supercontinent called Gondwana.

Bodmin Moor
Europe

Location Southwest England
Intrusion type Batholith
Rock Granite
Age 300 million years

The southwest tip of Britain lies above an enormous mass of granite that breaks the surface at Bodmin Moor, Dartmoor, Land's End, and the Scilly Isles. Many of the granite outcrops have weathered into strange shapes called tors.

Ship Rock
North America

Location New Mexico
Intrusion type Volcanic plug
Rock Lamprophyre
Age 30 million years

The rugged peak of Ship Rock is the remains of a long-extinct volcano. The volcanic cone, which once rose high above it, eroded away long ago, leaving its core, or plug, of solidified magma rising above the New Mexico desert.

Mount Kinabalu
Southeast Asia

Location Northern Borneo
Intrusion type Pluton
Rock Granodiorite
Age 10 million years

The dramatic peak of Mount Kinabalu in Borneo is made of granodiorite—a rock that is slightly heavier and more metal-rich than granite. It originally solidified deep underground, from a mass of molten rock that pushed up through layers of much older rock.

▶ RUGGED PEAK
Kinabalu's summit is 13,435 ft (4,095 m) high.

63

Weathering

As soon as rock is exposed above sea level, it comes under attack from the weather. Rain is slightly acidic and eats away at all kinds of rocks, from soft limestone to the toughest granite. Acids in the soil or made by plants also contribute to this process. Meanwhile, frost and baking sun gradually loosen fragments that are then carried away by the processes of erosion.

BREAKDOWN

Water vapor dissolves carbon dioxide from the air to form weak carbonic acid that falls as rain. The acid breaks down certain minerals. For example, the feldspar minerals in granite are turned into soft clay, releasing tougher quartz crystals as sand grains. Over time, the rock is weathered on the outside, becoming rounded as the edges crumble away.

ACID ATTACK

Limestone is slowly dissolved by acid rainwater. The water eats away the surface, enlarging cracks to form limestone pavements, such as these in Yorkshire, England. As the water seeps through fissures, it also creates limestone caves. In hot climates, the process is sped up, destroying most of the limestone and leaving a few rocky pinnacles.

MICROBES AND ROOTS

Living things also attack rocks. Microbes break down rocks so they can use their minerals as nutrients—all living things need elements such as iron and potassium, which can be found in rocks. In the same way, the lichens that grow on rocks use acids to dissolve them. Plant roots penetrate rocks and pry them apart as the roots grow—especially tree roots, which become broader with age.

▶ PROBING ROOTS
These tree roots are not just clinging to the rock—they are also dissolving its minerals.

FROST ACTION

In cold places, such as near the poles or high in the mountains, rock is splintered by frost. Water seeps into a crack, then freezes and expands at night, forcing the crack wider. The next day, the ice thaws, allowing more water to enter the crack and freeze the following night. Over time, the crack is wedged apart. Chunks of rock fall away, forming scree slopes at the bases of cliffs.

◄ SCREE SLOPE
Rock splintered from this crag by the freeze-thaw process has built up a mass of broken rubble.

BAKING SUN

Hot sun can make the outer layers of rocks crack away in sheets. This is called exfoliation, and is common in deserts with hot days and cold nights. The rock surface expands by day and shrinks at night, becoming detached from the rock underneath. The Devil's Marbles in northern Australia (below) are granite boulders that were created by this process. The image shows the rock surface flaking away.

FACT!

Solid rock pressed down by heavy layers of ice often expands when the ice melts. This can make it crack along lines of weakness and fall apart.

Sun, wind, and rain can shape granite rocks into spheres.

The dynamic landscape

Rock that has been broken down by weathering is worn away by other forces in a process called erosion. A lump of granite may crumble under the attack of acidified rainwater, but it is erosion that scours away the resulting clay and sand particles. They are carried off by flowing water, moving ice, or even high winds, and deposited somewhere else as various types of sediment. The process of erosion is constantly reshaping the landscape.

SCOURED BY WATER

Most of the particles that crumble from weathered rocks are carried away by flowing water. When this flows over limestone, it gradually dissolves the rock, but usually the erosion is not caused by the water itself. It is caused by hard mineral particles that are suspended in the water. They scour rock faces like sandpaper and carve them away, especially when the water is flowing fast.

▶ SLOT CANYON
Flash flooding in deserts carves through bare rock to create deep, narrow canyons.

SHINGLE, SAND, AND SILT

Rivers carry small particles suspended in the water, and this often makes them look muddy. Their flow bumps bigger, heavier stones along the riverbed, rounding off their sharp corners to form shingle. When a river reaches flatter ground, it slows down and drops first the heaviest stones, then the smaller ones. It carries the small sand grains farther, and may carry the tiniest silt and clay particles all the way to the sea.

SANDBLASTING

Wind alone cannot erode rock, but it can pick up small, hard mineral particles such as quartz sand grains and hurl them through the air. This usually happens in deserts, where there is plenty of loose sand. The tiny quartz grains grind away softer rock, creating rock sculptures called ventifacts. The sand usually stays near ground level, so lower parts of the rock are carved away more quickly.

◄ MUSHROOM ROCKS
Windblown sand has undercut rock to create these unusual shapes in Egypt's White Desert.

ASH CLOUD

Some volcanic eruptions blast rocky debris high into the air. The wind may carry the finest ash particles around the globe, but the bigger rocks fall to the ground, where they settle as a deposit called tephra. The heavier rock falls first, while lighter particles are carried farther away on the wind. Volcanic ash that simply pours down the flank of a volcano settles as a mixture of big and small particles called ignimbrite.

▲ ASH LAYERS
The rocks of the Painted Hills in Oregon are solidified layers of volcanic ash.

WINDSWEPT DUNES

Wind sweeps sand into hills called dunes, especially in deserts and on seashores. The dunes often creep slowly in the direction that the wind is blowing, as sand grains blow up and over the dune crests. This creates sloping layers of sand, which are called dune cross-bedding. The sand grains themselves are smashed together over and over again, giving them a rounded, "frosted" look.

▶ MOVED BY ICE
Tiny mineral particles are mixed with big, sharp-edged rock fragments in this lump of glacial till.

GLACIER ICE

In high mountains and polar regions, slowly moving glacier ice freezes onto the rock that it is flowing over and rips away rock fragments. These become embedded in the moving ice, making it grind away more rock. The glacier carries the mixture of sharp fragments and finely ground "rock flour" within the ice flow, so it is not sorted or rounded off by further erosion. Whenever the ice melts, the rock debris is deposited as a sediment known as till, or boulder clay.

COYOTE BUTTES

Reflections in the water turn layers of rock into abstract art on the arid Colorado Plateau of the southwestern United States. These wind-eroded landforms are carved in sandstones that were originally desert dunes, formed around 250 million years ago. The layers in the rock preserve the cross-bedding patterns created when the dunes were still loose sand.

Sedimentary rocks

When rocks are broken down or dissolved by
weathering, the fragments are carried away
by erosion and laid down as layers of sediment
such as sand or mud. Over time, these layers are
compressed beneath more layers of sediment, and
then cemented together to form sedimentary rocks.
Other sedimentary rocks, including coal and many
limestones, are made from the remains of living
things such as plants or marine organisms.

SANDSTONE

One of the most recognizable types of
sedimentary rock, sandstone is made of
grains of sand that have been cemented
together, or lithified. Some sandstones
form on seabeds. Others, such as this
example in Utah, are lithified sand dunes
made of "frosted" windblown sand laid
down in cross-bedded patterns.

MUDSTONE AND SHALE

Fine sediments may be compressed and cemented together to form
fine-grained mudstone. As they age, these rocks harden into shale.
Mudstone and shale often contain the fossils of extinct plants and animals.
They may also contain the remains of microbes that, over millions
of years, have turned into oil and natural gas.

◀ JURASSIC COAST
*These mudstone cliffs on the shores of southern
England are rich in fossils from the age of
the dinosaurs.*

FACT!

Mud carried into the Bay
of Bengal by the Ganges
River has built up
layers of sediment and
sedimentary rock that
are at least 9.3 miles
(15 km) deep!

CLAY

The finest sediments of all are created from the chemically altered minerals of weathered rocks such as granite. They bind together to form clay, which always contains water. Clay can be molded and then "fired" in a potter's kiln to make rock-hard ceramics.

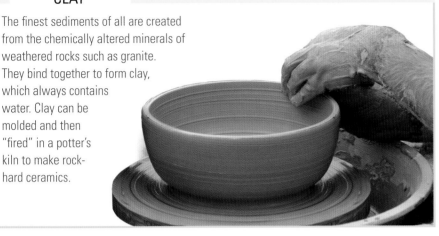

▼ PUDDING STONE
Conglomerates are sometimes called pudding stones because the big stones look like fruit in a pudding.

Large pebble

Fine-grained matrix (cement)

LIMESTONE

Some sedimentary rocks are formed by chemical processes. These include oolitic limestone, which is made up of tiny calcite balls. The balls settled out of warm seawater that was full of dissolved lime. Other limestones are built up from the chalky shells and skeletons of marine life such as plankton that lived and died in ancient oceans.

▼ WHITE CLIFFS
These chalk cliffs on the south coast of England are made from the remains of trillions of tiny organisms that lived more than 65 million years ago.

CONGLOMERATE AND BRECCIA

Sedimentary rocks are usually made of grains of very similar sizes, but conglomerates are made of big, water-rounded pebbles cemented together by much finer-grained material. Many conglomerates are the petrified remains of ancient beaches. A similar rock called breccia contains big stones with sharp edges. These were often transported by ice before being cemented together.

COAL

Waterlogged plant remains that do not decay can build up and turn into peat. If it is buried and compressed for millions of years, peat can turn into coal. Coal is almost pure carbon, which is why it can be burned as a fuel.

Fossils

Some sedimentary rocks contain fossils—the remains or traces of once-living things that died long ago. Fossils are typically bones or shells that have turned into stone. Some are beautifully preserved intact skeletons, and some even retain traces of soft tissue. They allow us to reconstruct extinct life-forms such as dinosaurs—if it were not for fossils, we would have no idea that these organisms had ever existed.

FACT!

Fossils called coprolites are the remains of animal dung. Scientists have found *Tyrannosaurus rex* coprolites, complete with crunched-up bone fragments from the dinosaur's last meal.

FOSSILIZATION

Most fossils are created by a process that starts when an organism dies and its remains are buried in soft, airless mud. This stops animals from eating it, and prevents rapid decay. Over millions of years, the mud hardens to form sedimentary rock, and minerals dissolved in groundwater slowly turn the organic remains to stone.

◄ DEATH AND BURIAL
A fish living in a lake dies and sinks into the mud on the lake bottom.

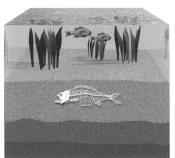

◄ DISSOLVING MINERALS
Over time, more mud settles on top, and minerals start replacing the bones.

◄ DISCOVERY
The mud becomes rock, which erodes to reveal the fossil.

TRACE FOSSILS

Some fossils don't preserve the actual remains of the animal or plant. They preserve something else, such as animals' burrows or footprints. These trace fossils can be very revealing. A line of dinosaur footprints, for example, can tell us about the animal's size, its stride length, and how it moved. In other words, they show us how it lived, rather than how it died.

Trace fossils have helped bring this long-extinct

Barosaurus footprint

dinosaur to life.

ALMOST FOSSILIZED

Any evidence of life that survives the processes of decay and is preserved for 10,000 years or more can be called a fossil. Ice-age plant pollen preserved in peat bogs is a type of fossil; however, since it is not turned to stone, it is sometimes called a "subfossil." The same is true of this fly, which was trapped in sticky tree resin about 20 million years ago and was preserved because the resin hardened to form amber.

GRAPHIC EVIDENCE

The delicate tissues of dead organisms usually decay rapidly or are eaten. This means that most fossils are of scattered shells, bones, and teeth. But some fossils are complete organisms or entire skeletons. This fossil dragonfly was found in fine-grained mudstone at Solnhofen, Germany.

AMAZING SURVIVALS

Although most fossils preserve only shells and bones, some show evidence of soft tissues such as skin, feathers, and even what an animal had for its last meal. The discovery of dinosaur fossils with feathers, such as this *Archaeopteryx*, has proved the link between dinosaurs and modern birds. The microscopic remains of cell structures in fossil feathers are even providing evidence of their color.

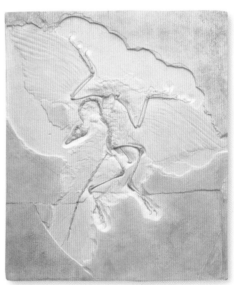

THE FOSSIL RECORD

Fossils tell us how life on Earth has evolved over many millions of years. Some types of fossils, such as marine shellfish, are very common in rocks from particular periods, and are useful "index fossils," which can be used to date rocks. Others, such as dinosaur bones, are much rarer and a whole species may be known from only a few fragments. The fossil record is not complete and has gaps. But scientists discover new fossils every day that help fill these gaps in the story of life.

◄ DELICATE WORK
A scientist in the Gobi Desert, Mongolia, cuts a fossil Protoceratops *skull out of the rock that has protected it for millions of years.*

Ancient life

All fossils preserve evidence of ancient life. They can range from tiny microbes to skeletons of giant dinosaurs. Some are spectacular, while others can only be identified using special equipment. But it is often the smallest fossils that tell us the most, helping us date rocks and identify the positions of ancient continents and oceans.

Trilobite
Armored crawler

Type of organism Marine arthropod
Geological period Cambrian to Permian
Age range 520–252 million years old
Location Worldwide

▼ MASS GRAVE
These fossilized trilobites probably died when their environment dried out.

Resembling modern-day horseshoe crabs, these armored sea creatures were some of the earliest complex life forms to be preserved as fossils. They lived on seabeds, where they probably used their insectlike compound eyes to locate and catch other animals for food.

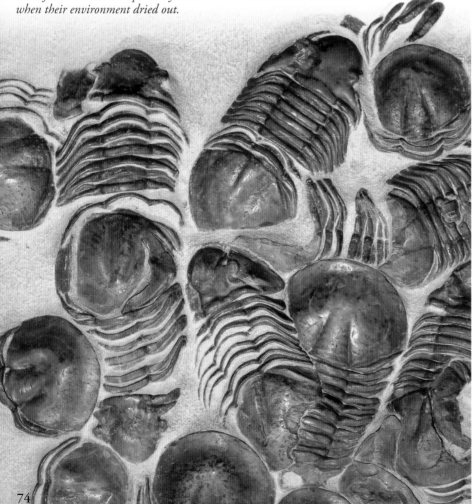

Diplomystus
Freshwater herring

Type of organism Fish
Geological period Eocene
Age range 56–34 million years old
Location North America, South America, Middle East, Africa

This widespread freshwater fish lived in the era that followed the extinction of the giant dinosaurs. It is a distant relative of herrings and sardines, with an upward-facing mouth. It ate small fish and insects living on or near the water surface.

Archaeocidaris
Spiny sea urchin

Type of organism Echinoid
Geological period Late Devonian to Late Permian
Age range 395–300 million years old
Location North Africa, Europe, North America, Russia

This creature had long, sharp spines on its shell. It moved around on flexible "tube feet" like those of starfish. As with many fossils, this specimen has been crushed by the weight of the rock layers above it.

Atrypa
Ancient shellfish

Type of organism
Brachiopod
Geological period
Early Silurian to Late Devonian
Age range 440–372 million years old
Location Worldwide

Brachiopods have a long history, appearing about 500 million years ago and still found alive today. They look like small clams, with two shells hinged together. This ancient brachiopod may have lived attached to the seabed by a fleshy stalk.

Gallimimus
Birdlike reptile

Type of organism
Theropod dinosaur
Geological period
Late Cretaceous
Age range
72–66 million years old
Location Mongolia

This is the skull of an ostrichlike dinosaur. It had a long, blunt, toothless beak that it probably used to prey on small animals, but it may have eaten some plants too. Its big eyes were protected by rings of small bones.

▼ BIG BIRD
Gallimimus *lived in the same era as* Tyrannosaurus rex.

▲ SPIRAL
SHELL
This image shows the fossil shell's chambers.

Ammonite
Shelled squid

Type of organism Cephalopod mollusk
Geological period Devonian to Cretaceous
Age range 420–66 million years old
Location Worldwide

Distantly related to the nautilus that still lives in tropical oceans, ammonites were tentacled mollusks that lived in much the same way as modern cuttlefish. Fossils of their coiled shells are very common, and are a useful "index fossil" for dating rocks. Some were large, with shells that measured 6.5 ft (2 m) across.

Megalodon tooth
Deadly weapon

Type of organism Shark tooth
Geological period Miocene to Pliocene
Age range 23–2.6 million years old
Location Worldwide

This is the tooth of an extinct relative of the great white shark called *Carcharodon megalodon*. The tooth of a great white is up to 2.7 in (7 cm) long, but this is more than twice as big! This huge shark preyed on mammals such as whales and dolphins.

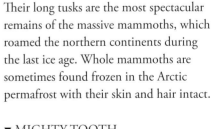

Dicroidium
Fossil leaf

Type of organism
Seed fern
Geological period
Triassic
Age range 252–208 million years old
Location Southern hemisphere

Dicroidium is one of an extinct group of plants that looked like ferns. It bore seeds instead of the simple spores produced by true ferns. It dates from the period when dinosaurs first appeared, and it is likely that this flora formed part of their diet.

Mammoth tusk
Ice-age relic

Type of organism Mammal tooth
Geological period Pliocene to Holocene
Age range 5 million to 3,600 years old
Location North America, northern Eurasia

Their long tusks are the most spectacular remains of the massive mammoths, which roamed the northern continents during the last ice age. Whole mammoths are sometimes found frozen in the Arctic permafrost with their skin and hair intact.

▼ MIGHTY TOOTH
Mammoth tusks were curved. The longest could reach up to 14 ft (4.2 m).

Rock strata

Sedimentary rocks were laid down horizontally to form layers called strata, with the oldest at the bottom. This is the basis of the relative dating system called the geological timescale. But finding the precise age of rock strata was impossible until recently, when scientists found out how to detect radioactive elements. These have enabled scientists to determine not only the age of rocks, but also the age of planet Earth itself.

ROCK RECORD

Wherever rocks are forming today—usually deep beneath lake beds, or on the bottom of the sea—they are being created from soft sediments that settle in horizontal, parallel layers. A new layer may be very similar to the one that it settles on, or it may be visibly different due to some change in the environment. A huge volcanic eruption, for example, might eject ash that settles in a distinctive layer. The oldest layers are at the bottom.

BEND AND TILT

The moving plates of Earth's crust can bend and fold rock strata so they are no longer horizontal. Often, they seem to be tilted, or even vertical, because the folds in the layers are so big that we can see only parts of them. But sometimes the rock strata are so crumpled up by extreme pressure that they form dramatic zigzag patterns.

ORDOVICIAN

First fish appear

SILURIAN

PRECAMBRIAN

SNAP AND SLIP

If rock strata are stretched or squeezed by the movements that cause earthquakes, they may snap. The result is a fault. The strata slip along the line of the fault, relative to each other, so layers that were joined together become offset. However, the nature and thickness of each layer usually enables them to be identified, even if they have slipped over a very long distance.

RADIOMETRIC DATING

Many elements in rocks are unstable. Their atoms decay over time, emitting radiation. Scientists know how long it takes for an element to decay. Uranium, for example, decays into lead at a steady rate. This radioactive dating technique has enabled geologists to put dates to all the eras and periods in the geological timescale.

FOSSIL MARKERS

The sequence of rock strata can be mixed up by folds and faults, so it is not always obvious how old the rocks are. But in the 18th century, geologist William Smith saw that if rocks in different places contained the same fossils, the rocks were the same age. This allowed geologists to create geological maps, such as this one of the Grand Canyon, where each color shows a different rock age.

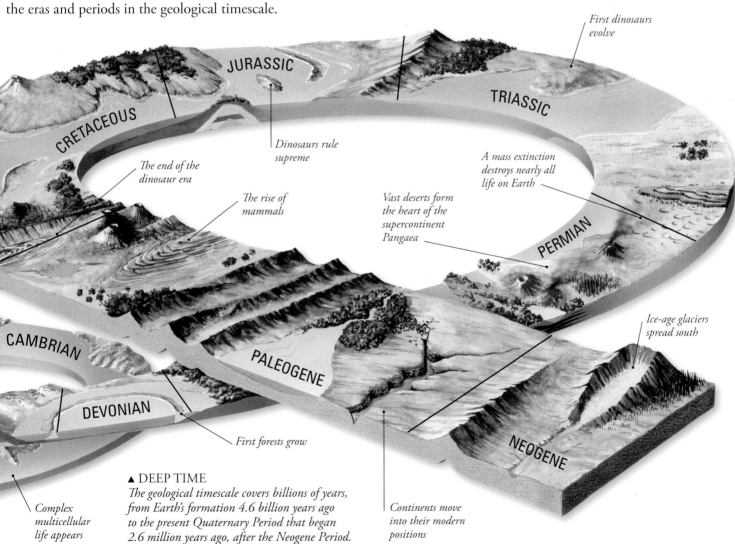

First dinosaurs evolve

JURASSIC

TRIASSIC

CRETACEOUS

Dinosaurs rule supreme

The end of the dinosaur era

A mass extinction destroys nearly all life on Earth

The rise of mammals

Vast deserts form the heart of the supercontinent Pangaea

PERMIAN

Ice-age glaciers spread south

CAMBRIAN

PALEOGENE

DEVONIAN

NEOGENE

First forests grow

▲ DEEP TIME
The geological timescale covers billions of years, from Earth's formation 4.6 billion years ago to the present Quaternary Period that began 2.6 million years ago, after the Neogene Period.

Continents move into their modern positions

Complex multicellular life appears

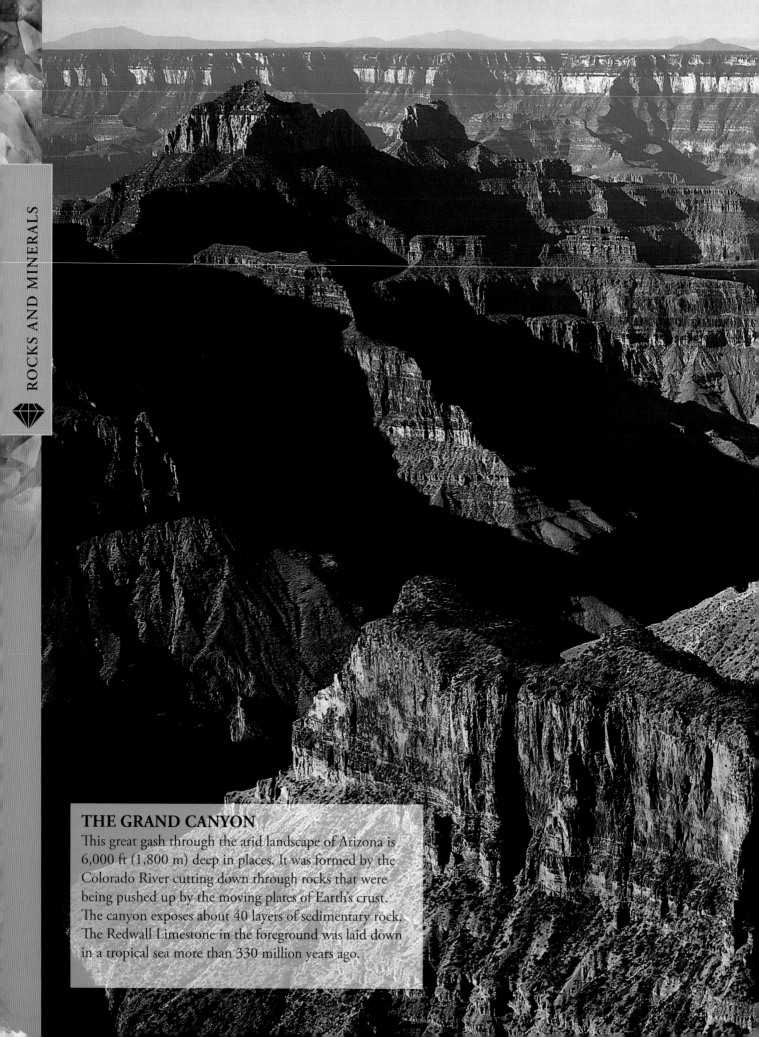

THE GRAND CANYON

This great gash through the arid landscape of Arizona is 6,000 ft (1,800 m) deep in places. It was formed by the Colorado River cutting down through rocks that were being pushed up by the moving plates of Earth's crust. The canyon exposes about 40 layers of sedimentary rock. The Redwall Limestone in the foreground was laid down in a tropical sea more than 330 million years ago.

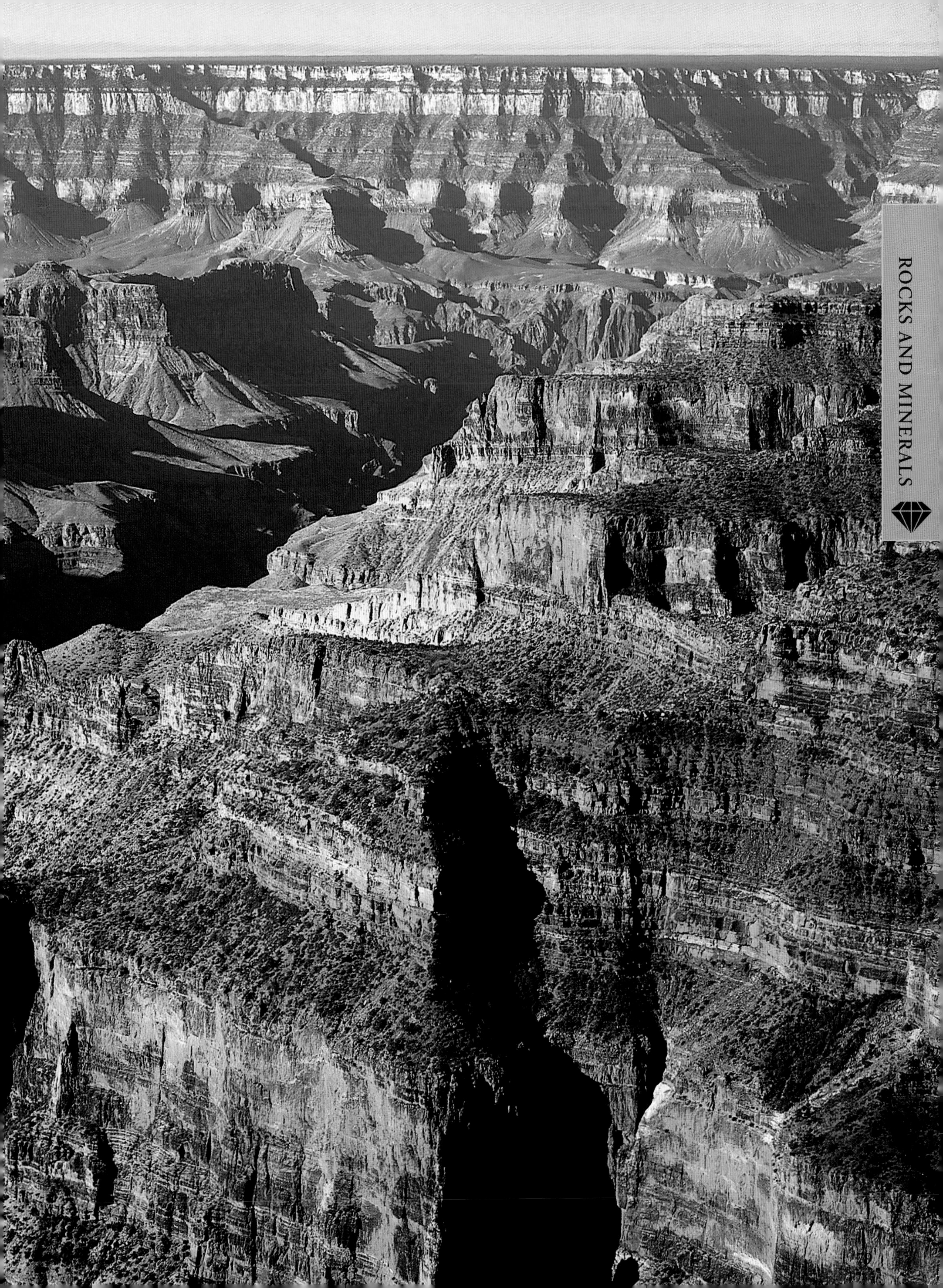

Metamorphic rocks

Extreme pressure or heat can squeeze or cook rocks so much that they change their character, turning into metamorphic rocks. Rocks can be squeezed by tectonic forces, heated by intrusions of molten magma, or both. There are different grades of metamorphism, creating rocks that are harder and more crystalline at each stage.

MOUNTAIN SLATE
The forces that buckle sedimentary strata into mountain ranges also compress the rock itself. They can squeeze soft shale so much that the minerals break down and recrystallize in thin layers. The result is slate—a rock that is harder than shale, but which splits easily along the cleavage planes between layers. This makes it very useful for manufacturing thin, light, weatherproof roofing tiles.

▲ SLATE QUARRY
The mountains of Snowdonia in Wales are an important source of high-quality roofing slate.

SPARKLING SCHIST
Increasing pressure and heat can turn slate and other rocks into a harder metamorphic rock called schist. Like slate, schist contains flattened crystals that are all aligned the same way. This makes the crystal faces glitter with reflected light. Some types of schist also contain garnet crystals that grow from the original rock minerals.

BANDED GNEISS
In the subduction zones that destroy the edges of tectonic plates, intense pressure and extreme heat create a highly compressed metamorphic rock called gneiss. It usually has dark and pale bands of crystals that are crumpled and distorted. The oldest-known rocks on the planet are gneisses that were created almost 4 billion years ago.

ROASTED ROCK

Upwelling magma that cools below ground cooks the rocks around it. The result is hornfels, a hard rock that may be spotted with mineral crystals. The areas where it is found, around igneous intrusions, are known as metamorphic aureoles. They might also contain veins of metal ore yielding copper, lead, and silver.

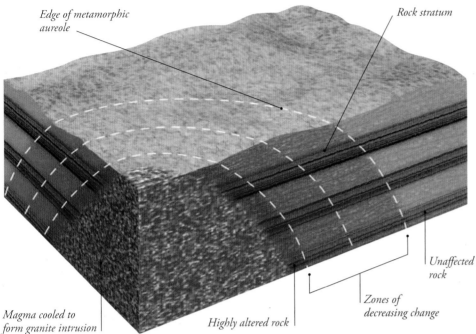

Edge of metamorphic aureole

Rock stratum

Magma cooled to form granite intrusion

Highly altered rock

Zones of decreasing change

Unaffected rock

◄ HEAT TREATMENT
A mass of hot magma pushed up into existing rocks cooks and alters them.

FINE MARBLE

Marble is a metamorphic rock formed from chalk or limestone. The original rock is recrystallized by high temperatures and extreme pressure, often during periods of mountain building. This is why most marble is found in mountain ranges. Marble can be many colors, often with complex patterns, but some marbles, such as the Carrara marble quarried in Tuscany, Italy, are pure brilliant white.

► ARTIST'S STONE
Pure white and excellent for carving, Carrara marble has been used for many famous sculptures.

DEEP HEAT

Before they were changed by heat or pressure, or both, most metamorphic rocks were sedimentary rocks such as shale, sandstone, or limestone. But igneous rocks can undergo the same process. They include the mantle rock peridotite, which can be transformed into serpentinite and eclogite. These form when rock is put under pressure deep in the subduction zones between the colliding plates of Earth's crust.

► MANTLE ROCK
This serpentinite, found in Cyprus, formed from rock in the oceanic crust.

The rock cycle

As soon as igneous rocks are exposed to the air, they start to be eroded, creating sediments. These often form sedimentary rock, which may then be buried and transformed into metamorphic rock. If this is drawn below the crust, it may melt and erupt as lava that undergoes the whole process over again. This is known as the rock cycle.

▼ FIRE FOUNTAIN
Blown into the air by gas pressure, this fountain of lava will cool to form igneous rock.

ERUPTION

Igneous rock is created when volcanic lava erupts and cools on the surface, or when molten magma pushes up between existing rocks and cools underground. Lava is attacked by the weather right away and starts crumbling. Buried intrusions of rocks such as granite must be exposed to the air before they start to break down.

EROSION

As soon as rock is erupted or exposed on the surface of the land, it begins to fall apart. It is dissolved, split, crumbled, and eroded by rain, ice, sunshine, windblown sand, flowing water, and plant roots. The rocky debris, sand, and dissolved minerals are carried away by glaciers, rivers, or the wind.

▲ SWEPT AWAY
Fine sediment eroded from the plains of China is swept out to sea by the Yangtze River.

NEW ROCK

The rock debris eventually settles in beds of sediment that form on seabeds, on the floors of lakes, or in sand dunes. Dissolved minerals gradually harden around the rock fragments, cementing them together to create layers of new sedimentary rocks such as sandstone and shale.

◄ PUSHED UP
The ocean floor grinding beneath the edges of continents crumples the rocks into fold mountains.

UPHEAVAL

The forces of plate tectonics push sedimentary rocks above sea level and buckle them into mountain ranges. As they are pushed up, the rocks are squeezed, hardened, and recrystallized by the processes that create metamorphic slates and schists. Such rocks form many of the world's highest peaks.

SUBDUCTION

While some rocks are pushed up by colliding tectonic plates, others are dragged down into the mantle beneath the crust. Here, they are exposed to extreme pressure and intense heat, which transforms them into metamorphic rocks such as gneiss, migmatite, and eclogite.

MELTDOWN

If subduction drags rocks down far enough, they are likely to melt, forming magma. This wells up toward the surface, and either forms igneous intrusions underground or erupts from volcanoes. This new igneous rock starts to break down as soon as it is exposed to the air, and the cycle starts over again.

◄ EXTREME STRESS
This outcrop of gneiss was formed by intense heat and pressure deep beneath the crust.

Soil

In most parts of the world (except for extreme deserts) the land surface is covered by soil. Most soils are mixtures of crumbling, fragmented rock and decomposing organic material. Soil contains the water that plants need and the substances that they use as nutrients. Most plants could not grow without it, and since land animals cannot survive without plants, soil is vital to life on land.

ORGANIC DECAY

The mineral particles in soil are mixed with decayed organic material, mostly derived from the remains of dead plants and animals. These are broken down by fungi, bacteria, and other organisms to form a dark, crumbly substance called humus. The mixture of soluble minerals and humus provides plants with the nutrients that they need to grow.

ROCK BREAKDOWN

The basis of most soil is the rock beneath it. Weathering breaks down the rock surface into smaller particles, which form the mineral content of the soil above. Soils can also develop on beds of soft sediment such as sand, and on totally organic material such as waterlogged peat that has dried out at the surface.

▲ CRACK AND CRUMBLE
Rainwater seeping into soluble limestone is breaking it up, forming fragments that crumble to powder. This mixes with the organic matter to form a fertile soil.

RICH EARTH

If the mineral and organic ingredients are in the right proportions, they combine to form a fertile, crumbly soil called loam. Such soils are ideal for plant growth because they contain plenty of plant nutrients and rarely become waterlogged.

▲ PLOWLAND
Plowing the land folds plant remains back into the soil, where they decay and add to its fertility.

Acidic layer

Deposited iron

Sandy subsoil

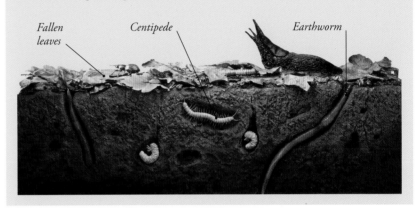

HIDDEN LIFE

Healthy soil is alive with microbes, which support worms and creatures such as burrowing centipedes. These help convert the remains of dead plants and animals into plant nutrients. Earthworms also mix up the soil and allow air to penetrate, which encourages the growth of microbes.

Fallen leaves

Centipede

Earthworm

VITAL MINERALS

Plants need nutrients. They get some from decayed organic matter, but others are minerals released from rocks by weathering. Crumbling volcanic rocks create rich soils, which is why people risk their lives to farm on the flanks of active volcanoes. Here, a vineyard grows on the volcanic slopes of Mount Pico, in the Azores.

RAIN AND SAND

High rainfall or rapid drainage through sand or gravel can make soils less fertile. The water washes soluble plant nutrients and iron out of the topsoil and deposits them lower down. The soil develops distinct layers, with an acidic, infertile layer where the iron has been washed out. Only specialized plants such as heathers thrive in these acid soils.

WATER

Seen from space, Earth is a blue planet—the blue of liquid water. Water fills rivers and oceans, swirls through the air as clouds, and falls on the land as life-giving rain.

The water cycle

The movement of water around Earth is vital to support life on land. Water evaporates from the oceans to form clouds, which are carried over the land by wind. The clouds drop their water in the form of rain and snow, especially on high land near the sea, and the water drains back into the oceans. Some parts of this cycle are quick, but others take centuries.

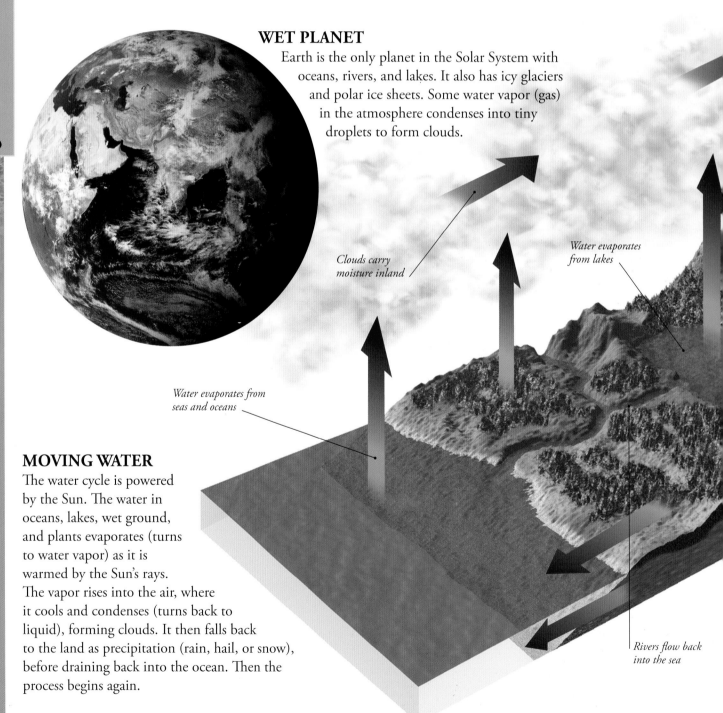

WET PLANET

Earth is the only planet in the Solar System with oceans, rivers, and lakes. It also has icy glaciers and polar ice sheets. Some water vapor (gas) in the atmosphere condenses into tiny droplets to form clouds.

Clouds carry moisture inland

Water evaporates from lakes

Water evaporates from seas and oceans

Rivers flow back into the sea

MOVING WATER

The water cycle is powered by the Sun. The water in oceans, lakes, wet ground, and plants evaporates (turns to water vapor) as it is warmed by the Sun's rays. The vapor rises into the air, where it cools and condenses (turns back to liquid), forming clouds. It then falls back to the land as precipitation (rain, hail, or snow), before draining back into the ocean. Then the process begins again.

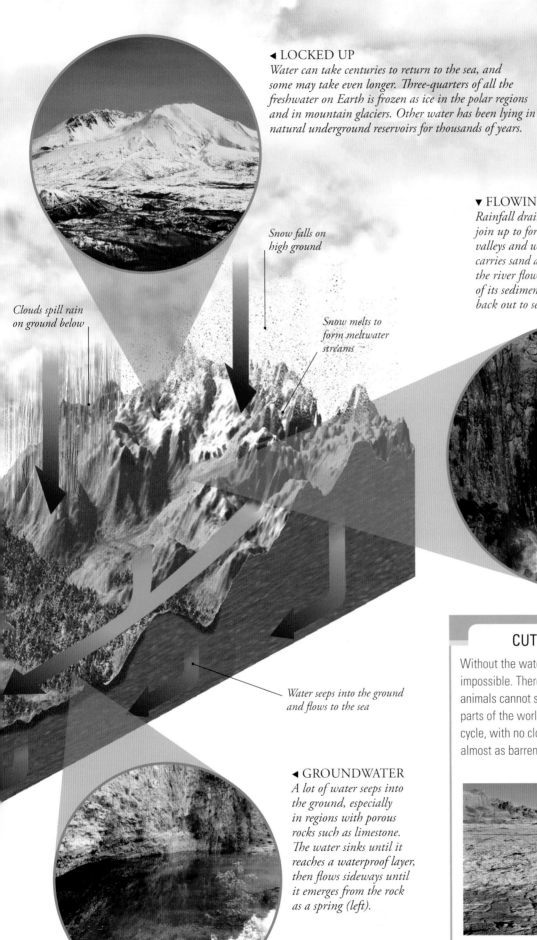

◄ LOCKED UP
Water can take centuries to return to the sea, and some may take even longer. Three-quarters of all the freshwater on Earth is frozen as ice in the polar regions and in mountain glaciers. Other water has been lying in natural underground reservoirs for thousands of years.

Snow falls on high ground

▼ FLOWING STREAMS
Rainfall drains off the land in streams that join up to form rivers. The flowing water cuts valleys and waterfalls into the landscape, and carries sand and silt to lower ground. Here, the river flows more slowly and drops much of its sediment. Eventually, the water flows back out to sea.

Clouds spill rain on ground below

Snow melts to form meltwater streams

Water seeps into the ground and flows to the sea

◄ GROUNDWATER
A lot of water seeps into the ground, especially in regions with porous rocks such as limestone. The water sinks until it reaches a waterproof layer, then flows sideways until it emerges from the rock as a spring (left).

CUT OFF

Without the water cycle, life on land would be impossible. There would be no plants, and animals cannot survive without plants. There are parts of the world that are cut off from the water cycle, with no clouds or rain. These places are almost as barren as the surface of the Moon.

▲ ATACAMA
The Atacama Desert in Chile is one of the driest places on the planet. Few plants survive here.

Rivers and valleys

As water drains off the land, it gradually carves away the uplands, cutting a network of stream and river valleys. The water carries eroded rock, sand, and silt from the uplands to the lowlands, depositing them as sediments. These sediments change the shape of the land and also contain the plant nutrients that make the lowlands so fertile.

FAST FACTS

■ The largest river in the world by volume is the Amazon in South America. It empties 52 million gallons (200,000 cubic meters) of water into the Atlantic Ocean every second.
■ The Nile Delta spreads out across 150 miles (240 km) of the Egyptian coast on the Mediterranean Sea.
■ The Gandaki River in Nepal cuts a gorge through the Himalayan mountains that is 18,000 ft (5,500 m) deeper than the peaks on either side of it.

SPRINGS AND STREAMS

Rainwater drains downhill over hard rock in trickles and rivulets. It also soaks into the ground and seeps through the rock until it emerges at springs. Rivulets and springwater flow together into streams, and these join with other streams to form rivers.

SHAPING THE LAND

Streams flow down hillsides, cutting valleys divided by ridges. Smaller streams flow off these ridges, creating more valleys and ridges. This process builds up patterns of streams and valleys that look like the twigs and branches of trees. The streams carry eroded debris away to the lowlands.

Melting snow feeds upland streams

Streams carve valleys

Lakes form in natural basins

Ridge between main valleys

Rivers flow to lowlands

VALLEYS AND GORGES

Most river valleys in the uplands are winding V-shaped channels, often thick with trees. But some rivers flow though dramatic sheer-sided gorges. These can be created by the collapse of limestone cave systems, or by a river cutting down though a landscape that is slowly being pushed upward by the forces that build mountains.

FERTILE PLAINS

Rivers flowing from hills onto flatter ground can carry vast amounts of sediment. Heavy rain or spring snowmelt swells the rivers until they burst their banks and flood the surrounding landscape. Sediment settles from the slow-moving floodwaters to form broad floodplains with deep, fertile soils that make excellent farmland.

Tributary streams join the river and add to its flow

MEANDERS

A river tends to wind across its floodplain in loops called meanders. The flow cuts away the outside bank of the loop while depositing sediment on the inside bank, so the meanders become steadily more extreme. Eventually, the river may take a shortcut, leaving an isolated lake known as an oxbow.

▲ AMAZON OXBOW
Here, one of the meanders on the Amazon River has become an oxbow lake.

ESTUARIES AND DELTAS

When rivers reach the sea, the freshwater mixes with saltwater. This makes particles suspended in the water clump together and settle in thick layers of mud. These may form a muddy estuary, or fan out to sea in a delta. The river flow over a delta splits into many channels, as seen in this satellite view of the Yukon Delta in Alaska.

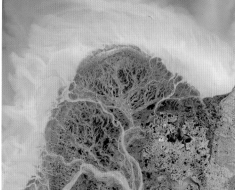

91

▼ ICE CAVE
Meltwater can carve spectacular ice caves beneath glaciers.

Glaciers and ice sheets

In cold climates, snowfall may not melt, even in summer. It builds up in layers that turn into ice, forming glaciers. These flow slowly downhill until they either melt or reach the sea. In polar regions, huge glaciers form thick ice sheets that smother the landscape and even extend over the ocean as ice shelves.

SNOW TO ICE

High in the mountains, some of the snow that falls in winter stays frozen throughout the summer. When winter sets in again, more snow falls on top of it. Over time, the snow builds up. Its weight compresses the lower layers, expelling most of the air and turning the snow into solid blue ice.

CREEPING GLACIERS

Ice made from compacted snow in the mountains builds up and creeps downhill as glaciers. The moving ice carves away the landscape, creating deep U-shaped valleys. It also carries rock debris away in long heaps of rubble on the glacier edges, or in the middle where two glaciers have joined. These are called moraines.

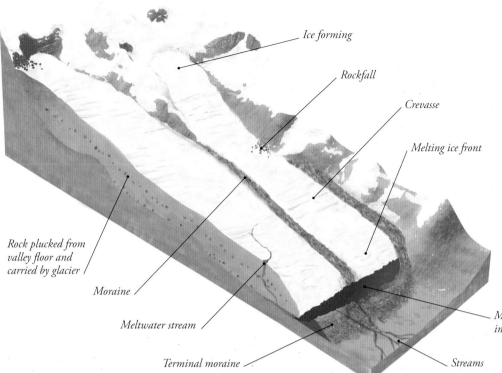

Ice forming

Rockfall

Crevasse

Melting ice front

Rock plucked from valley floor and carried by glacier

Moraine

Meltwater stream

Terminal moraine

Meltwater seeps into ground

Streams

THE ICE FRONT

A mountain glacier flows downhill until it reaches a lower altitude where the air temperature is warm enough to melt it. If the climate is stable, the ice melts as fast as the glacier moves forward, so the ice front stays in the same place. It is marked by deep crevasses (large cracks) in the ice, and a terminal (end) moraine of rock debris.

ICE SHEETS

Antarctica and Greenland are covered by incredibly deep ice sheets. The East Antarctic Ice Sheet forms a huge dome up to 2.8 miles (4.5 km) thick, and its weight has made the rock beneath it sink as much as 0.6 miles (1 km) into Earth's crust. Parts of the Antarctic ice sheets extend over the sea as floating ice shelves.

ICE SHELF ▶
The sheer cliffs of the Antarctic ice shelves are up to 160 ft (50 m) high.

RETREATING GLACIERS

Global warming is making most of the world's glaciers melt away. The lower stretches of many mountain glaciers have disappeared, so they seem to have retreated uphill. These satellite images show how the front of the Helheim Glacier in Greenland retreated 4.2 miles (7.5 km) between 2001 and 2005 (in each image, the glacier is on the left). Some coastal glaciers are breaking up, including several Antarctic ice shelves, and all the extra ice tumbling into the ocean is raising sea levels.

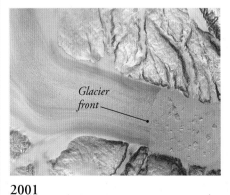

Glacier front

2001

2003

Icebergs fill space left by glacier

2005

ICEBERG

When a glacier flows all the way to the coast, its floating front, or snout, extends over the water. Great chunks of ice break off from the front and float away as icebergs. Some icebergs are vast—tens or even hundreds of miles across. But they slowly melt away, adding more water to the oceans and depositing rocky debris on the ocean floor.

Rivers of ice

Glaciers are found on high mountain ranges all over the world, even on the equator. This is because the higher you climb, the colder it gets. If it is cold enough for snow to survive all year round, it can form a glacier. Some glaciers, called ice caps, cover huge highland areas.

Aletsch Glacier
Bernese Alps

Location Southwest Switzerland
Type Valley glacier
Length 15.3 miles (24.7 km)
Area 33.5 sq miles (86.7 sq km)

The Aletsch is one of the longest Alpine glaciers. It descends from an altitude of 13,583 ft (4,140 m) near the Jungfrau peak, is joined by two more glaciers, and extends south for almost 15.5 miles (25 km) toward the valley of the Rhône.

Khumbu Glacier
Himalayas

Location Nepal
Type Valley glacier
Length 7.5 miles (12 km)
Area 18 sq miles (45 sq km)

This Himalayan glacier has become famous as part of the southern route to Mount Everest. Climbers leaving base camp have to negotiate its steep, deeply crevassed upper section, the Khumbu Icefall, on their way to Everest's summit.

Franz Josef Glacier
New Zealand

Location Southern Alps, South Island
Type Valley glacier
Length 6.4 miles (10.3 km)
Area 12.6 sq miles (32.6 sq km)

The climate in New Zealand's Southern Alps allows the Franz Josef Glacier to descend into lush green forests near sea level. Since 2008, it has been retreating rapidly, exposing large areas of barren rock in a valley that was once packed with deep ice.

Vatnajökull
Iceland

Location Southeast Iceland
Type Ice cap
Area 3,127 sq miles (8,100 sq km)

This massive sheet of ice is the biggest glacier in Europe. It forms a frozen dome over almost a tenth of Iceland, including several volcanoes. Heat from these volcanoes melts the ice to create lakes underneath the glacier. In 1996, an eruption of Grímsvötn, the most active volcano, caused a dramatic flood of glacial meltwater.

▶ DEEP FREEZE
The ice of Vatnajökull in Iceland is 1,300 ft (400 m) thick on average, and overflows into several channels called outlet glaciers.

Perito Moreno Glacier
Southern Andes

Location Patagonia
Type Outlet glacier
Length 18.6 miles (30 km)
Area 99.6 sq miles (258 sq km)

The Southern Patagonian Ice Field is a vast area of glacial ice in the southern Andes of South America, and has dozens of outlet glaciers—streams of ice extending from an ice cap. The Perito Moreno is one of the most dramatic, descending from the mountains to form a broad lobe of ice that breaks up into icebergs floating on a large freshwater lake.

Kilimanjaro
East Africa

Location Northeast Tanzania
Type Ice cap
Area Less than 1 sq mile (2 sq km)

Despite lying close to the equator, the summit of Kilimanjaro is so high at 19,341 ft (5,895 m) that for centuries it was covered by a thick mass of ice known as an ice cap. Climate change has melted most of the ice, leaving just a few fragments at the volcano's summit. The ice may soon vanish altogether.

▼ TROPICAL GIANT
A dormant volcano, Kilimanjaro is the highest mountain in Africa.

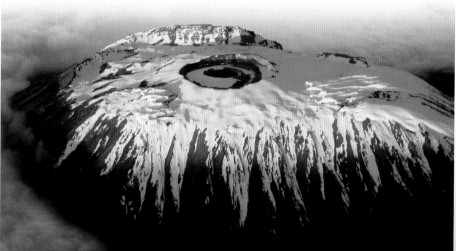

WATER

Earth has experienced several ice ages, when the climate was icy cold over large areas. Each ice age has had warm and cold periods. Right now, we are in a warm period of an ice age. During the last cold period, glaciers extended across much of northern Europe and North America. Today, there are still permanent ice sheets in Greenland and Antarctica.

ORBITAL CYCLES

Ice ages are caused by continental drift, which moves land into colder parts of the globe, and by variations in Earth's orbit around the Sun. There are three orbital cycles. The first, a 100,000-year cycle, causes Earth's orbit to change from circular to elliptical. The second, a 42,000-year cycle, affects the tilt of Earth's axis. The third, a 25,800-year cycle, causes Earth to wobble on its axis. Sometimes these cycles combine and chill the planet enough to make the ice sheets start growing.

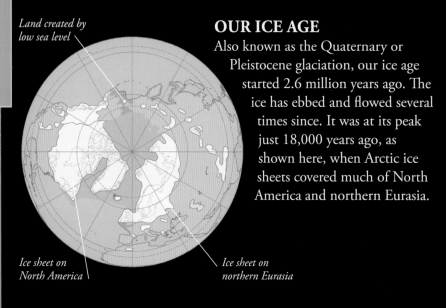

Land created by low sea level

Ice sheet on North America

Ice sheet on northern Eurasia

OUR ICE AGE

Also known as the Quaternary or Pleistocene glaciation, our ice age started 2.6 million years ago. The ice has ebbed and flowed several times since. It was at its peak just 18,000 years ago, as shown here, when Arctic ice sheets covered much of North America and northern Eurasia.

MAMMOTH STEPPE

Although ice sheets covered vast areas during the last big freeze, 18,000 years ago, there were also large areas of snowy tundra and open grassland in northern Europe and Asia. These grasslands, known as mammoth steppe, supported herds of animals such as mammoths. The herds were hunted by powerful predators, including saber-toothed cats, and also humans, who painted images of their prey on cave walls.

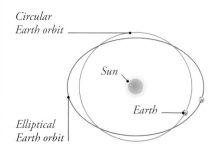

Circular Earth orbit

Sun

Earth

Elliptical Earth orbit

Orbit shape: 100,000-year cycle

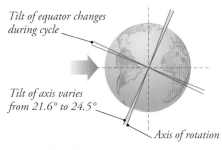

Tilt of equator changes during cycle

Tilt of axis varies from 21.6° to 24.5°

Axis of rotation

Tilt: 42,000-year cycle

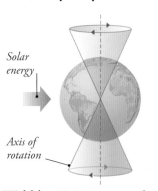

Solar energy

Axis of rotation

Wobble: 25,800-year cycle

◀ CAVE CREATURES
This image of a horse was painted on a cave wall in Lascaux, France, around 13,000–15,000 BCE during the last cold period of the ice age.

During the last cold period, so much water was locked up as ice that global sea levels fell by 330 ft (100 m). Shallow coastal seas dried out, including the Bering Strait between Siberia and Alaska. This allowed animals and people to migrate between Asia and America. By 11,000 years ago, rising temperatures had melted much of the ice and the seas filled up again. They also led to many species dying out.

▲ SABER TEETH
The fearsome saber-toothed cat became extinct when climate change caused the ice sheets to melt.

ICE-SCOURED LANDSCAPE

When the ice sheets and glaciers melted at the end of the last big freeze, they left their mark on the landscape. The glaciers had gouged deep U-shaped valleys (above). When these extended to the coast, they filled with water to become steep-walled fjords.

SNOWBALL EARTH

Throughout its history, Earth has experienced many ice ages. The most dramatic may have occurred about 650 million years ago. Clues in the rocks suggest that the entire planet was frozen, with land at the equator as cold as Antarctica is now. This "Snowball Earth" idea is disputed by many scientists, because it would have had a catastrophic effect on the evolution of life.

▶ ICY WORLD
If the Snowball Earth event really happened, our planet may have looked like ice-covered Europa, one of the moons of Jupiter.

99

Underground water

Much of the rain that falls from the sky sinks into the ground. Some is immediately soaked up by plants, while some seeps down into porous (water-holding) rocks. It flows gradually downhill beneath the ground, where it forms natural reservoirs that we can access by digging wells. The water can also reappear at springs or in temporary lakes.

THE WATER TABLE

Rainwater drains through soil, sand, and porous rock until it reaches a layer of impermeable (waterproof) rock such as granite. This stops it from sinking any farther, so the ground above fills with water like a bucket of wet sand. The top of this saturated zone is called the water table. If you dig deep enough to pass this point, the bottom of the hole fills with water to form a well.

◀ DEEP WELL
A bucket lowered down a well brings cool, fresh water to the surface.

CHANGING LEVELS

In a wet season, the level of the water table on low-lying land can be very close to the surface, saturating the soil and creating a marsh or swamp. If the rain keeps falling, the water table rises above ground level, causing the land to flood. In a drought, the water table can sink so far below ground that lakes and rivers dry up, leaving dry, cracked earth.

FACT!

Dragon's Breath Cave in Namibia contains the largest underground lake in the world. It lies about 330 ft (100 m) below the surface, and covers 5 acres (2 hectares).

AQUIFERS

Porous rocks that contain water are called aquifers. The water usually flows very slowly downhill over impermeable rock below. If an aquifer is capped with more impermeable rock, it can completely fill with water. However, if there is a fault (a gap or break) in the rock, water can seep to the surface.

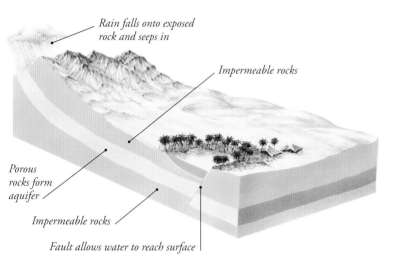

Rain falls onto exposed rock and seeps in

Impermeable rocks

Porous rocks form aquifer

Impermeable rocks

Fault allows water to reach surface

ANCIENT WATER

Some deserts conceal vast underground water reservoirs formed thousands of years ago. One beneath the eastern Sahara contains about 36,000 cubic miles (150,000 cubic km) of water. These ancient water reserves are capped by layers of waterproof rock, but wind erosion can strip away the rock to expose the water and create an oasis (below).

SPRINGS

Impermeable rock strata often outcrop (come to the surface) on hillsides, so the water stored above them flows out at this level as a spring. Usually, a whole layer of rock outcrops in this way, and a row of springs marks its position. Springwater is normally very pure because the porous rock it passes through acts as a filter.

PERMAFROST

On Arctic tundra, water seeping into the soil freezes solid. It thaws near the surface in summer, but stays frozen below ground. This permafrost layer stops the summer meltwater from draining away, so it forms vast areas of swamp. Repeated freezing and thawing opens cracks that fill with stones, creating a strange effect called patterned ground.

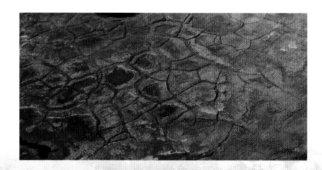

Caves

Rainwater seeping into the ground in areas with porous limestone can create elaborate networks of caves with spectacular natural rock sculptures. Acid in the water dissolves the rock, seeping into cracks and gradually enlarging them into potholes and caves. Some of these are open to the air, but most are hidden deep underground.

UNDERGROUND WORLD

In limestone regions, most of the surface water flows into hollows called sinkholes. It cuts down through the limestone, creating hidden canyons, until it reaches the water table. Then it starts flowing horizontally through tunnels and caves. If the water drains farther down through the rock, the caves dry out.

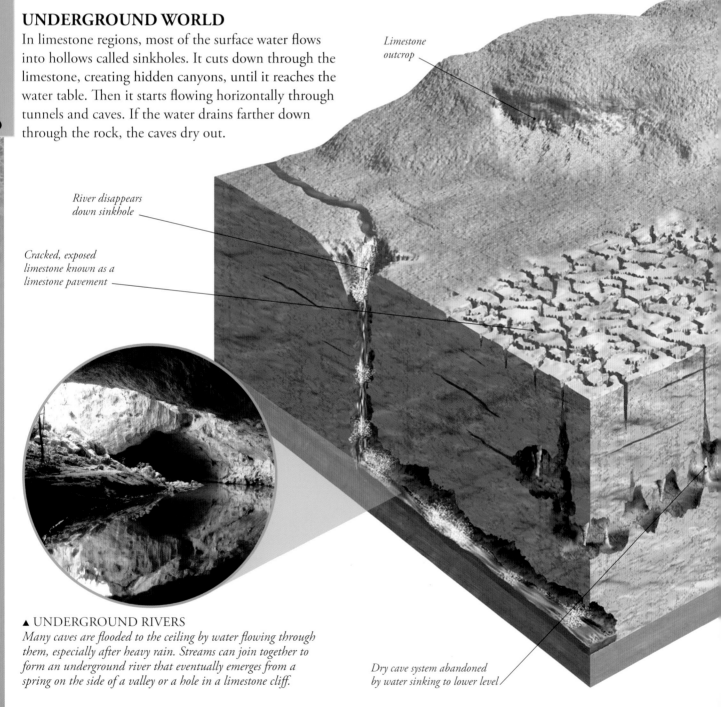

Limestone
outcrop

River disappears
down sinkhole

Cracked, exposed
limestone known as a
limestone pavement

Dry cave system abandoned
by water sinking to lower level

▲ UNDERGROUND RIVERS
Many caves are flooded to the ceiling by water flowing through them, especially after heavy rain. Streams can join together to form an underground river that eventually emerges from a spring on the side of a valley or a hole in a limestone cliff.

► INTO THE VOID

Rainwater often just sinks into the ground, but if it flows over impermeable rock first, it may form a stream. When this stream flows onto limestone, it soon finds a weak point and enlarges it into a vertical shaft, or sinkhole. All the water cascades into the hole and down into the dark void below.

CAVERNS

Water flows through flooded tunnels in the lower parts of the cave network. But if it finds an even lower route, it will abandon the tunnels, which then become dry caves. Sometimes a cave ceiling collapses, enlarging it into a cavern with a broad arching roof. Caverns can be colossal, with ceilings more than 650 ft (200 m) high.

MEXICAN CENOTES

On the Yucatán Peninsula in Mexico, rainwater draining into limestone has created a vast network of caves. Many have collapsed and are open to the sky, revealing pools of clear water known as cenotes. These were once a vital source of water for the local Maya people.

▲ CAVE DIVERS
Specially equipped divers explore a beautiful cenote in Mexico's Yucatán Peninsula.

◄ DRIPPING WATER
The water seeping through the rock is full of dissolved lime (calcium bicarbonate). When it drips into a cave, the dissolved lime is exposed to air and turns to solid calcite. Over centuries, the calcite builds up at drip points to form stalactites and other rock sculptures.

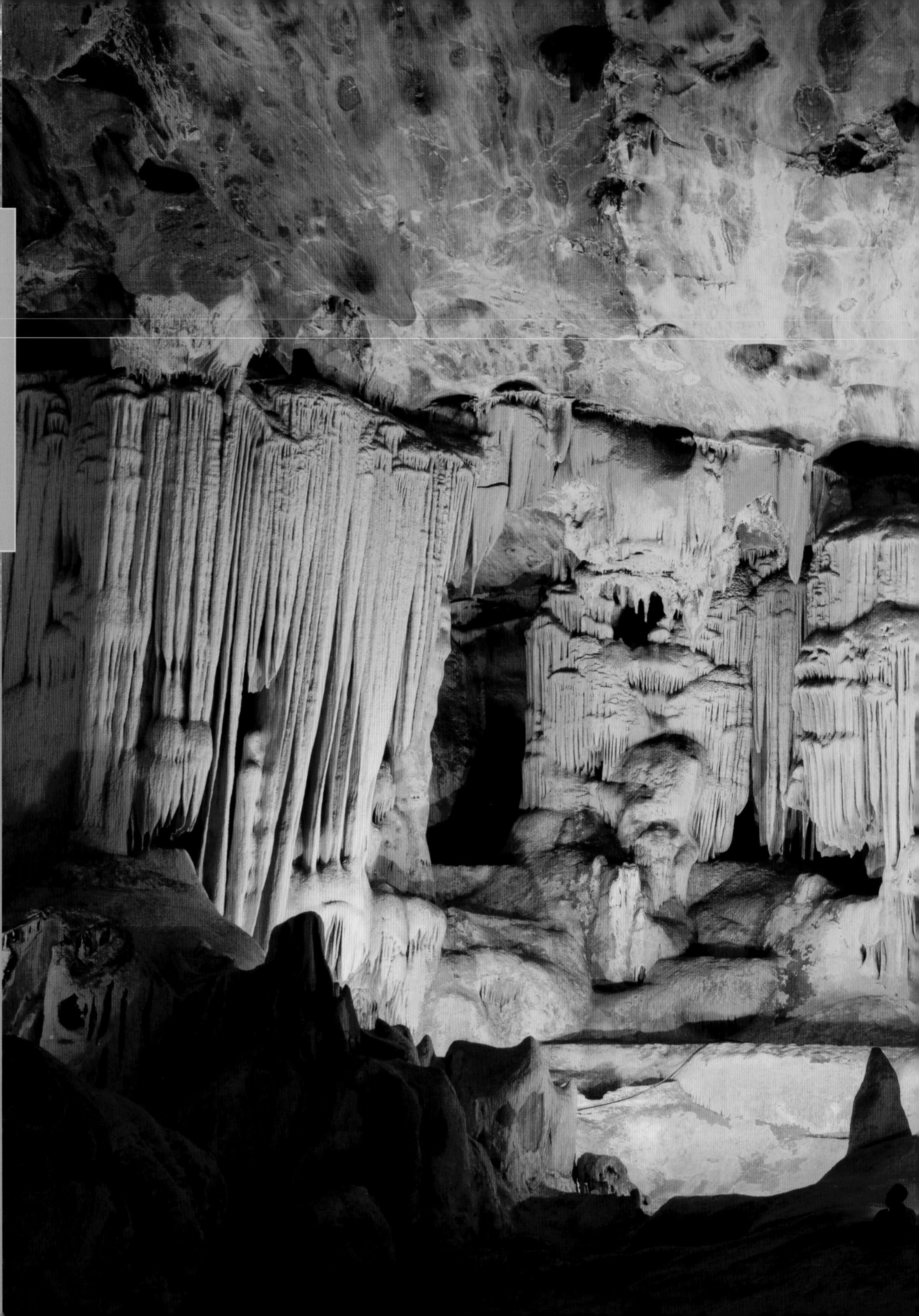

SCULPTED IN STONE

Over thousands of years, lime-saturated water dripping into this limestone cave has created an astonishing gallery of natural rock sculptures. They include clusters of long, slender stalactites hanging from the cave ceiling, stalagmites that have grown up from the cave floor, and strange sheets of calcite called flowstones.

WATER

Lakes

Lakes are big pools of water that form in natural hollows. Some are basins of impermeable rock that are fed by streams, while others are filled by water seeping up from below. They may be rich in life or almost barren. The more plant nutrients a lake contains, the more quickly it becomes overgrown and turns into a marsh or swamp.

FLOODED BASINS

Many lakes are scooped out of hard, impermeable rock by the moving ice of glaciers. Others occupy long cracks in Earth's crust or form in volcanic craters. Many were once stretches of river that have been cut off from the main flow, while some were once parts of the sea.

▼ GLACIAL LAKE
This lake, high in the Carpathian Mountains in Bulgaria, has formed in a hollow made by a glacier.

EBB AND FLOW

Some lakes are like hollows in a wet sponge, filling with water from below. As the level of the underground water table rises and falls, so does the level of the lake. Some fill rapidly, then empty almost overnight. These lakes are most common in limestone landscapes such as western Ireland, below.

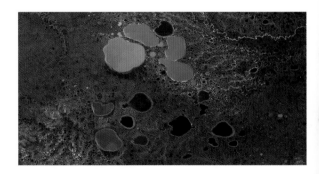

KETTLE LAKES

Regions that were deep-frozen during a past ice age are often dotted with lakes. The ones in this satellite image of land near the Gulf of Ob in northern Russia are kettle lakes, formed as blocks of ice sank into soft ground and then melted.

LAKE WATER

Cool upland lake water contains very few dissolved minerals that could feed plants. This keeps the lakes clear and almost weed-free (as above). Lowland lake water is usually warmer and rich in nutrients. It supports large numbers of microscopic plankton, which make the water appear cloudy.

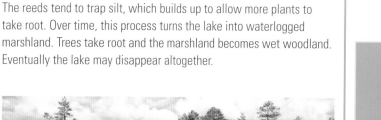

LAKE EVOLUTION

Lowland lakes with nutrient-rich water support a wide range of plant life, including plants such as reeds that grow in the muddy lake fringes. The reeds tend to trap silt, which builds up to allow more plants to take root. Over time, this process turns the lake into waterlogged marshland. Trees take root and the marshland becomes wet woodland. Eventually the lake may disappear altogether.

▲ DISAPPEARING LAKE
Reeds and trees are gradually taking over this small lake.

SALT AND SODA LAKES

Lake water contains salty minerals that have been carried into it by streams. Normally, the minerals are carried out of the lake by streams that flow to the sea. However, in hot climates, the water evaporates as fast as the lake fills. As the water evaporates, it leaves the minerals behind, where they form crystals on rocks (below) and make the water very salty. The result is a salt or soda lake, depending on the minerals.

▼ SALT LAKE
The water in the Dead Sea in the Jordan Rift Valley is so salty that no plants or animals can survive in it.

Salt crystals

Lakes of the world

There are lakes on every continent, even in high mountain ranges and deep underground. Some lakes are little more than shallow, salty pools that may dry out altogether in summer. Others are vast inland seas, or deep rifts in Earth's crust that are filled with cold, dark water.

Lake Baikal
Southern Siberia

Location Russian Federation
Area 12,160 sq miles (31,500 sq km)
Maximum depth 5,716 ft (1,741 m)
Elevation 1,500 ft (456 m) above sea level

Long and narrow, Lake Baikal occupies the deepest rift in Earth's continental crust. It was formed 25 million years ago and is the world's oldest lake. The water is four times as deep as New York's Empire State Building, and the lake bed lies above a very deep layer of sediment that is about 4.3 miles (7 km) thick.

Caspian Sea
Central Asia

Location Longest border is with Kazakhstan
Area 143,000 sq miles (371,000 sq km)
Maximum depth 3,120 ft (950 m)
Elevation 100 ft (30 m) below sea level

Once part of the Mediterranean Sea, the Caspian Sea was cut off when sea levels fell during the last ice age. Its water is still salty, and in places much saltier than the oceans. This is because it has no outflow, so the salty minerals carried into it by the Volga and Ural Rivers have nowhere to go. Northern areas of the sea freeze in winter.

▼ INLAND SEA
The Caspian Sea is shallowest in the north, where it forms part of Kazakhstan's coastline.

Lake Superior
North America

Location US-Canada border
Area 51,159 sq miles (82,367 sq km)
Maximum depth 1,333 ft (406 m)
Elevation 600 ft (183 m) above sea level

Lake Superior is the largest freshwater lake on Earth—so large that it is like an ocean. It is one of the five Great Lakes of North America, created by ice hollowing out the landscape during the last ice age. The Great Lakes were once one lake, but when the heavy mass of ice melted, the land rose up and divided them.

Lake Nakuru
East Central Africa

Location Kenya
Area 15 sq miles (40 sq km)
Maximum depth 10 ft (3 m)
Elevation 5,780 ft (1,760 m) above sea level

This shallow lake lies in Africa's Great Rift Valley, where the heat constantly evaporates the water, concentrating dissolved minerals to create a soda lake with a high level of sodium carbonate. The very alkaline water supports specialized microbes that are eaten by dazzling flocks of flamingos. It is one of several lakes that lie in the Rift Valley, including the very deep Lake Malawi.

▶ PINK FLOCKS
Colored proteins in their diet of plankton give flamingos their beautiful pink plumage.

Crater Lake
North America

Location Oregon
Area 21 sq miles (53 sq km)
Maximum depth 1,934 ft (589 m)
Elevation 8,159 ft (2,847 m) above sea level

Famous for its clear, deep blue water, Crater Lake lies within a dormant volcano called Mount Mazama. After an eruption about 7,700 years ago, the peak collapsed into the empty magma chamber to form a broad caldera. This is flooded with rainwater, and is very pure because there are no streams carrying impurities into the lake.

Lake Titicaca
Andes, South America

Location Bolivia-Peru border
Area 3,386 sq miles (8,772 sq km)
Maximum depth 923 ft (281 m)
Elevation 12,516 ft (3,812 m) above sea level

Lying high in the Andes between Bolivia and Peru, this is the highest large lake in the world and the largest lake in South America. It is fed by more than 20 rivers flowing off the surrounding mountains. Some parts of the shore have dense beds of totora reeds, which the local people use to make boats and even floating villages.

▼ FLOATING VILLAGE
Titicaca has more than 40 islands. Some of them are artificial, built using the totora reed.

Oceans and seas

Oceans are the vast expanses of water filling the areas of low-lying oceanic crust that separate the continents. The shallow edges of the oceans form coastal seas. About 97 percent of the world's water is contained in the oceans. It has been made salty over time by minerals washed off the land by rivers.

THE GLOBAL OCEAN

The earliest ocean probably covered the whole globe. Most of its water was originally contained in the rock that formed the planet. Heat turned this water into gas, which erupted as vapor from volcanoes more than 4 billion years ago. As the planet cooled, the vapor turned to rain, which poured down for millions of years, filling the ocean.

▼ DEEP STEAM
Volcanoes, such as this one on the island of Java in Indonesia, still erupt vast amounts of water vapor from deep within the planet.

SALTWATER

After the first continents were formed, rain pouring down on the land weathered the rocks and carried dissolved minerals into the seas. The minerals included sodium chloride, which makes seawater taste salty. This process is still happening today, although the level of salt in the oceans is stable because the extra salt is locked up in ocean-floor rocks.

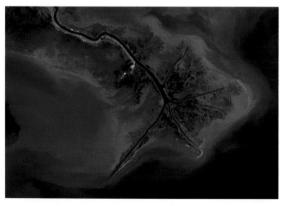

◄ MINERAL FLOW
This satellite view of the Mississippi Delta shows brown river sediment rich in minerals pouring into the Gulf of Mexico.

OCEAN FLOOR

The ocean floors are far from featureless. Many are dotted with submerged extinct volcanoes known as seamounts, which sometimes form long chains. Other volcanoes erupt from mid-ocean ridges, producing the molten basalt that forms the ocean floors. Deep trenches mark areas where old oceanic crust is being drawn into the mantle

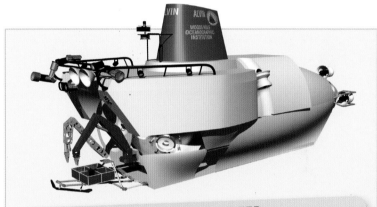

▼ SEA CRATERS
This sonar image shows a chain of Pacific seamounts.

Crater in flat volcano summit

False colors show elevation

Apron of debris extends away from the volcanoes

LIGHT AND HEAT

Scientists divide the ocean into vertical zones, depending on how much sunlight they receive. Near the surface is the sunlit zone, which is bright enough for photosynthesis to take place. Most ocean life is found here. Below 660 ft (200 m) is the twilight zone, where there is only blue light and the water is colder. Many of the animals here rise to the surface at night to feed on plankton. Below 3,300 ft (1,000 m) is the dark zone, where there is no sunlight and the water is close to freezing. Most animals here feed on dead organisms that have drifted down from above.

Sunlit zone

Twilight zone

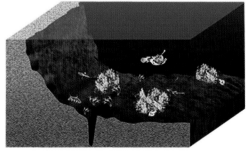

Dark zone

EXPLORING THE DEEP

Most of what we know about the deep ocean floors has been discovered through remote sensing—using devices at the surface to detect what lies beneath. Scientists can also use submersibles—underwater craft, such as the one above—but the difficulty of reaching the ocean floors means that only a tiny fraction has been explored.

SUBMARINE CANYONS

On average, the oceans are almost 2.5 miles (4 km) deep, but their fringes are much shallower. This is because the seabed near the shore is the submerged edge of a continent called a continental shelf. Rivers flowing into the sea can cut deep canyons in the sea beds of the continental shelves.

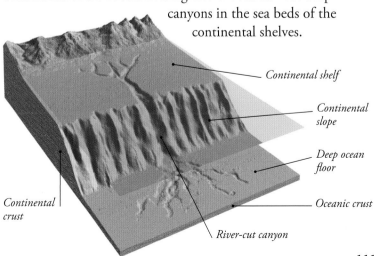

Continental shelf

Continental slope

Deep ocean floor

Oceanic crust

Continental crust

River-cut canyon

111

World oceans

The oceans of the world occupy more than two-thirds of the globe and contain a colossal volume of water, so there is far more ocean than land on planet Earth. They extend from the equator to the polar regions, and range from the warm, shallow coral seas of the tropics to the icebound waters of the Arctic and Antarctic.

Arctic Ocean
Shrinking ice

Area 5.4 million sq miles (14 million sq km)
Average depth 3,953 ft (1,205 m)
Maximum depth 15,305 ft (4,665 m) in Eurasia Basin

The Arctic is a frozen ocean surrounded by continents. In winter, the entire surface is covered by floating ice, but much of this melts away in summer, leaving an area of permanent ice around the North Pole. However, this permanent summer ice is dwindling each year as the effects of climate change warm the planet.

▼ FLOATING ICE
Small icebergs that have cracked away from glaciers float among the fractured sea ice of the Arctic Ocean.

Atlantic Ocean
Spreading sea floor

Area 29.7 million sq miles (77 million sq km)
Average depth 10,950 ft (3,926 m)
Maximum depth 28,230 ft (8,605 m) in Puerto Rico Trench

The Atlantic accounts for 29 percent of Earth's ocean area. It began forming 130 million years ago, and is still getting wider as the tectonic plate boundary that runs down its middle gradually pushes apart. The Atlantic is linked to the Mediterranean and Baltic Seas in the east, and the Caribbean and Gulf of Mexico in the west.

▼ MIGRATING TURTLE
This turtle migrates between the North Atlantic and its Caribbean nesting site.

Southern Ocean
Frozen fringe

Area 7.8 million sq miles (20 million sq km)
Average depth 14,763 ft (4,500 m)
Maximum depth 23,735 ft (7,235 m) in South Sandwich Trench

Unlike the other oceans, this ocean has no real boundary, because its northern frontier is just a line of latitude on a map (60°S). It forms the fringe of ocean around Antarctica, and much of it freezes in winter. When the ice melts in summer, the water teems with new marine life, which provides a feast for animals such as the humpback whale above.

Indian Ocean
Tropical waters

Area 26.5 million sq miles (69 million sq km)
Average depth 13,002 ft (3,963 m)
Maximum depth 23,812 ft (7,258 m) in Java Trench

The Indian Ocean lies between Africa, India, and Australia. Although its southern waters border the icy Southern Ocean, much of it is tropical, with coral reefs and atolls like these in the Maldives near India. It is the warmest of the oceans, and its warmth generates many tropical storms during the summer months.

Pacific Ocean
Coral seas

Area 60 million sq miles (156 million sq km)
Average depth 15,215 ft (4,028 m)
Maximum depth 35,840 ft (10,924 m) in Mariana Trench

Although it is by far the largest ocean, the movement of Earth's tectonic plates means that the Pacific is shrinking at the same rate that the Atlantic is expanding. It is dotted with so many islands that they have been given the collective name Oceania. The coral reefs that fringe the South Pacific islands are famous for their rich marine life.

▲ DESERT ISLAND
Many Pacific islands, like this one near Fiji, are uninhabited.

Waves and currents

Oceanic winds whip up waves on the ocean surface, and drive currents that swirl around the oceans in vast whirlpools called gyres. These surface currents are linked to deepwater currents. Together, they form a system that carries ocean water all around the world.

RIPPLES AND WAVES

As the wind blows over the ocean, it creates ripples that grow into waves. The farther waves travel, the bigger they get, so strong winds can generate huge waves that get steeper as they push into shallow coastal water. But even though waves travel over the water quite fast, the water itself stays in roughly the same place, moving very slightly forward as each wave passes.

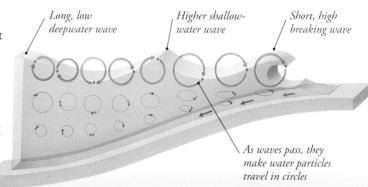

Long, low deepwater wave

Higher shallow-water wave

Short, high breaking wave

As waves pass, they make water particles travel in circles

SHIP SINKERS

In some places, opposing waves may meet head-on. They can either cancel each other out or combine to create huge "rogue waves" up to 100 ft (30 m) high— big enough to break right over ships and even sink them. Several big ships that have disappeared at sea were probably hit by such waves.

SURFACE CURRENTS

Winds over oceans usually blow steadily from a particular direction. These prevailing winds drive the surface water of the oceans in five huge gyres (right) that swirl clockwise in the Northern Hemisphere, and counterclockwise in the Southern Hemisphere. They carry warm tropical water (red arrows) toward the poles, and cold polar water (blue arrows) toward the tropics.

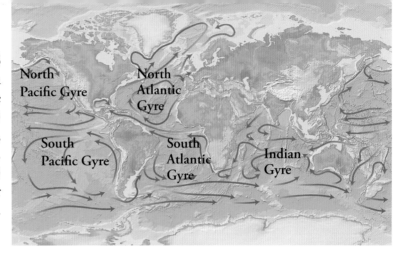

North Pacific Gyre

North Atlantic Gyre

South Pacific Gyre

South Atlantic Gyre

Indian Gyre

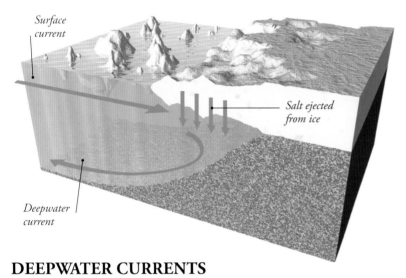

Surface current

Salt ejected from ice

Deepwater current

DEEPWATER CURRENTS

In cold oceans, the water surface freezes and ejects salt. The salt and icy cold make the water below the ice denser and heavier, so it sinks toward the ocean floor. This cold, dense ocean water then flows very slowly beneath warmer, less dense water, and gradually mixes with it until it reappears at the surface.

UPWELLING ZONES

When surface water is driven away from coasts by the wind, deeper water rises to take its place. It comes up loaded with minerals, fueling the growth of plankton—as seen here off southwest Africa. The plankton supports dense populations of animals, so these upwelling zones teem with marine life.

Namibia

▲ PLANKTON BLOOM
Blooms of plankton, such as this one off Namibia, can be many miles across.

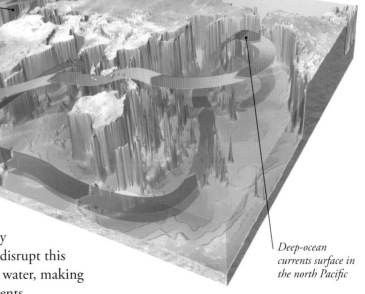

Ocean water sinks in the north Atlantic

— Cold deep-ocean current

— Warm surface current

Deep-ocean currents surface in the north Pacific

THE OCEAN CONVEYOR

The surface and deepwater currents are linked together in a "conveyor belt" of water that flows through all the oceans. Over centuries, this transports every drop of seawater around the world. Climate change could disrupt this circulation—melting glaciers add freshwater to cold ocean water, making it less salty, and less likely to sink and drive deepwater currents.

MAKING WAVES

As waves sweep into coastal water, they are slowed down by the shallow seabed. This causes the crests of the waves to push together, making the waves steeper and steeper. Eventually each wave gets so steep that its crest topples forward in a spectacular breaker. All the energy that built the wave is suddenly released in a cascade of tumbling, crashing white water.

Tides

Most seashores on Earth experience rising and falling sea levels, known as tides, caused by the gravity of the orbiting Moon. The difference between high and low tide level varies from day to day, and from place to place. As the tides rise and fall, they also make the water flow along coasts in strong currents, first one way and then the other.

SPRING TIDES

The Moon's gravity is the main cause of the tides, but the Sun's gravity also has an effect. When the Sun and Moon are in line, their gravitational pulls combine to create an extra-big tidal rise and fall. This is called a spring tide, and it happens twice a month—on the full Moon and the new Moon. During the twice-monthly half Moons, the gravity of the Sun pulls in a different direction, causing the much smaller neap tide.

TIDAL STREAMS

As the tide rises and falls, it shifts water along coasts in tidal streams. On the rising tide the streams flow one way, and on the falling tide they flow the other way. This makes water travel difficult, because a boat crossing a tidal stream may be carried sideways as fast as it moves forward. It has to be steered in a different direction to compensate for this.

LUNAR INFLUENCE

As the Moon orbits Earth, its gravity pulls water toward it in a tidal bulge. But Earth is also orbiting the Moon very slightly, and this slings water towards the other side of the world to create a second tidal bulge. As Earth spins, most shores pass in and out of both bulges each day, causing two high tides and two low tides.

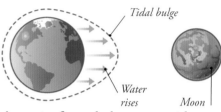

Tidal bulge

Water rises

Moon

Moon's gravity forms bulge on one side

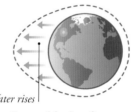

Water rises

Second bulge forms on other side

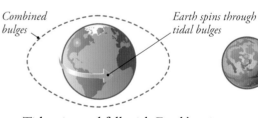

Combined bulges

Earth spins through tidal bulges

Tides rise and fall with Earth's spin

▼ USING THE TIDE
Tidal streams can flow as fast as a boat like this can sail, so it's vital to make the trip when they are flowing in the right direction.

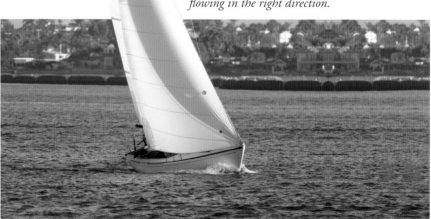

LOCAL TIDES

The shape of a coastline can make a big difference to the tidal rise and fall. In some places, such as here in Cornwall, England, it acts like a funnel, concentrating the tidal streams so they cause a very big tidal range—rising very high and falling very low. But other shores have very small tidal ranges, and some have just one tide a day.

RACES AND WHIRLPOOLS

On some coasts, the ebb and flow of the tides can create dangerously fast local currents. This usually happens when the tidal stream has to force its way through a tight gap or around a prominent headland, creating the steep, dangerous waves of a tidal race. Sometimes the flow can swirl back on itself to cause a whirlpool.

◄ SWIRLING WATER
Whirlpools form when opposing currents meet. Large, powerful whirlpools are known as maelstroms.

TIDAL RIVERS

Rising tides also force water up river estuaries. This stops the river flow and may even reverse it. As the river water stops moving, suspended particles settle on the riverbed to form the mudflats that are exposed along many river estuaries at low tide. In some places, a very powerful rising tide can drive a wave of water upriver in a tidal bore. This can be high enough to surf on, and may reach speeds of up to 15 mph (25 km/h).

▶ GLEAMING MUD
As the tide level falls in this river estuary, water draining away down a winding creek exposes a tidal mudflat.

Coasts

Waves smashing against exposed rocky shores gradually erode the rock to create caves, cliffs, or reefs. The sea sweeps the debris along the coast to more sheltered shores, where it forms shingle banks and sandy beaches. This process is always changing the shape of the coast, carving it away in some places and building it up in others.

▼ COASTLINE
Waves have shaped Byron Bay in eastern Australia into a series of headlands and sandy coves.

WAVE ENERGY
Breaking waves force water into cracks in coastal rocks. This exerts so much pressure that the rocks can be blown apart. Big chunks fall away near sea level, and this undercuts the rock above so that it eventually collapses into the sea.

SHINGLE AND SAND
The rocks torn away by the waves are tossed around and broken up. The corners are knocked off, creating rounded boulders and shingle. Small fragments become sand and the moving water carries all this debris away. Big, heavy stones are dumped on exposed shores, while fine sand is swept into sheltered bays.

EXTENDING THE LAND

When waves break on a beach at an angle, they loosen sand and stones so that they roll into the sea. The waves pick them up and toss them back on the beach farther down the shore, so the sand and stones are steadily moved down the coast. Over time, this process can build long beaches that extend out to sea as spits.

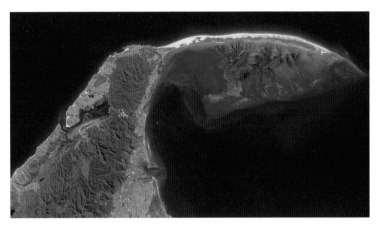

CONSTRUCTION SITE ▶
Waves have pushed beach material from left to right along this shore in South Island, New Zealand, extending it into a long, curving sand spit.

CLIFFS, CAVES, STACKS

On some coasts, the shoreline is cut back at a steady rate to create sheer cliffs. These rise above flat platforms of rock that extend far out to sea beneath the waves. But often the coast is made of different types of rock, and the waves cut these away at different rates. The weaker rocks may then collapse while others survive, creating caves, rock arches, and isolated stacks.

▲ CARVED AWAY
Soft rock tends to crumble, creating cliffs (top). Harder rock survives undercutting to form caves and arches (middle), which often collapse to leave stacks (bottom).

BAYS AND HEADLANDS

Soft rocks erode faster than hard ones, creating bays that lie between headlands of harder rock. The headlands shelter the bays, helping to prevent further erosion. The sheltered water also deposits any sand to form crescent beaches between the headlands. Some shorelines with near-vertical rock strata are made up of many headlands, separated by small sandy beaches.

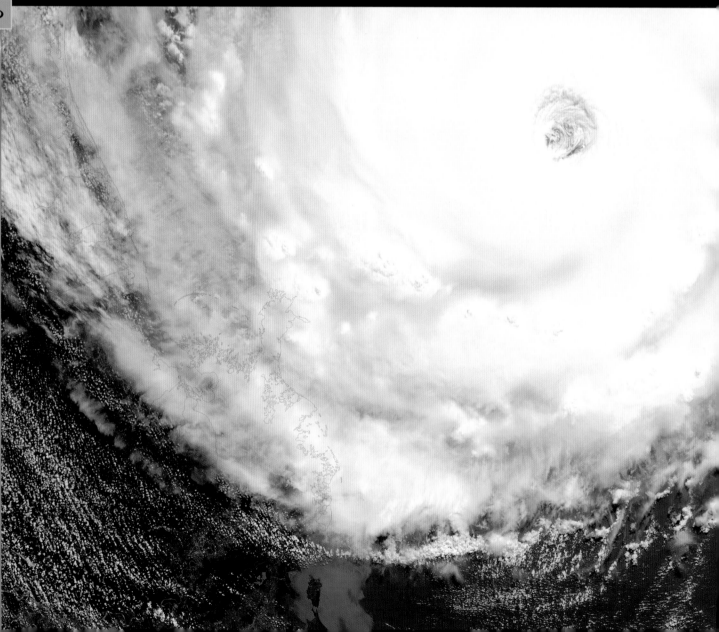

CLIMATE AND WEATHER

The heat of the Sun drives currents in the atmosphere that constantly carry air and moisture around the globe. This creates the climates and weather of the world.

The atmosphere

Earth is surrounded by a blanket of air called the atmosphere. This acts as a sunscreen by day, protecting us from the Sun's ultraviolet radiation. At night, it retains heat, keeping us warm. Air currents in the lowest level of the atmosphere carry heat around the globe, allowing life to flourish almost everywhere.

LAYERS OF AIR

The atmosphere is made up of a series of layers. These are formed by temperature changes that stop the air from moving from one layer to another. The lowest layer is called the troposphere. Above that lies the stratosphere, containing the ozone that shields us from harmful ultraviolet radiation. Above that are the mesosphere and the thermosphere.

ATMOSPHERIC GASES

Viewed from space, our atmosphere forms a glowing blue envelope around the planet. About three-quarters of it is made up of nitrogen. Most of the rest is oxygen. The air also contains argon and a small amount of carbon dioxide. Other gases include neon, helium, methane, krypton, hydrogen, nitrous oxide, and xenon, along with water vapor and ozone.

Thermosphere
The outermost, and deepest, layer starts at around 50 miles (80 km) and extends up to 300 miles (500 km), fading into the vacuum of space.

Mesosphere
The top of this layer, which extends from 30 to 50 miles (50–80 km), is the coldest part of the atmosphere, with temperatures plunging to -112°F (-80°C).

Stratosphere
Extending from 10 to 30 miles (16–50 km), this layer gets hotter with altitude, unlike the troposphere where the opposite happens.

Troposphere
The lowest layer is also the shallowest, up to 10 miles (16 km) deep.

THIN AIR

Four-fifths of the gas that forms the atmosphere, including nearly all its water vapor, is concentrated in the troposphere. The higher you go, the thinner the air gets. If you were to travel just 6 miles (10 km) up, you would not find enough air to keep you alive, which is why mountain climbers and high-altitude skydivers carry their own air supplies.

Nearly all the oxygen in the atmosphere was created more than two billion years ago by tiny microbes called cyanobacteria. They used energy from sunlight to turn carbon dioxide and water into sugar and oxygen in a process called photosynthesis. Green plants use the same process today, releasing oxygen into the atmosphere.

▲ GREEN LEAVES
Chlorophyll, a green-colored compound used in photosynthesis, gives leaves their color.

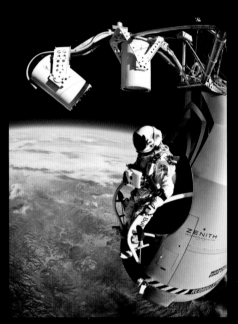

▲ HIGH JUMP
In 2012, skydiver Felix Baumgartner jumped from a record altitude of 24 miles (39 km). He fell faster than the speed of sound, because there was almost no air to slow him down.

BURN OUT

In the upper atmosphere, the air is very thin. However, there is enough air to slow down small rocky meteors as they hurtle toward Earth's surface. Friction with air molecules makes the meteors heat up and burn. They appear as "shooting stars" in the night sky, fading out as the last solid fragment is vaporized.

TOP OF THE WEATHER

Earth's weather takes place in the troposphere—the lowest layer of the atmosphere. This is because a change in air temperature in the stratosphere stops warm air from rising into it. Instead, the air spreads sideways, taking the weather with it. You can see this happening when big thunderclouds grow tall enough to reach the edge of the stratosphere and flatten out.

◀ BLUE GLOW
Viewed from an orbiting spacecraft, Earth's atmosphere appears blue because gas molecules scatter blue light, while the light of other colors passes straight through.

Air currents

The Sun's warmth causes air in the lowest layer of the atmosphere to circulate in currents. But the Sun does not heat Earth's surface evenly. Areas near the equator (the imaginary line that divides the Northern and Southern Hemispheres) receive far more heat than the poles. The warm air from the equator rises and flows north and south, then cools and sinks, creating systems of circulating air.

TROPICAL CIRCULATION

The regions nearest the equator are known as the tropics. Sunlight hits these regions more directly than it strikes the rest of the world, concentrating its energy, which is why the tropics are warmer than the poles. Over the warm oceans, the moist air rises and cools. As it cools, the moisture condenses to form tall storm clouds, which can generate torrential rain. This warmth and rain fuels the growth of lush rainforests.

CONVECTION CELLS

The Sun-warmed ground heats the air above it. This air expands, becoming less dense, and starts to float upward though cooler, denser air—just like the heated air in this paper lantern. Expansion eventually makes the air cool down to the point where it stops rising and starts to sink. This process creates circulating currents of air called convection cells.

Cold air is shown in blue

Warm air is shown in red

High-level air in Ferrel cell flows south

Low-level air flows north

Tropical air flows north in Hadley cell

Dry, desert air flows south

Warm, moist air rises

Polar cell

Ferrel cell

Hadley cell

Hadley cell

CIRCULATING AIR CELLS

As warm air rises, it cools and starts to sink, circulating in a convection cell. In the tropics, air flows north and south in two loops called Hadley cells. Two loops called Polar cells circulate air in the polar regions. There, chilled air sinks down to near ground level, flows back towards the equator, rises again as it warms, and then flows back toward the pole. Each pair of Polar and Hadley cells combines to drive a Ferrel cell, which circulates in the opposite direction.

SPIN AND SWERVE

Air moving north or south is pushed off course by Earth's spin. North of the equator it swerves right, while south of the equator it swerves left. This means that the high-level air flowing away from the tropics in each Hadley cell veers east, but when it flows back toward the equator at low level it is pushed west. As a result, the airflow in each circulation cell spirals around the globe.

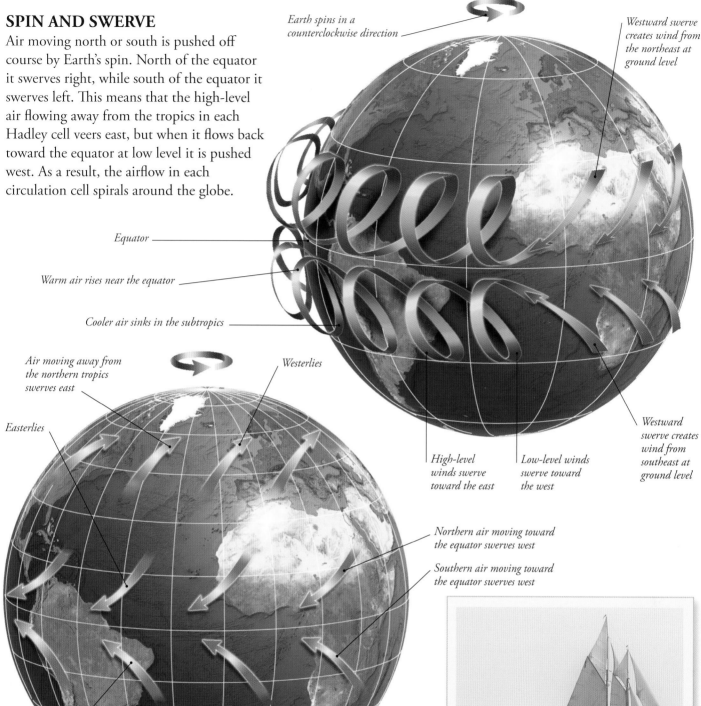

Earth spins in a counterclockwise direction

Westward swerve creates wind from the northeast at ground level

Equator

Warm air rises near the equator

Cooler air sinks in the subtropics

High-level winds swerve toward the east

Low-level winds swerve toward the west

Westward swerve creates wind from southeast at ground level

Air moving away from the northern tropics swerves east

Westerlies

Easterlies

Northern air moving toward the equator swerves west

Southern air moving toward the equator swerves west

Easterlies

Westerlies

Air moving away from the southern tropics swerves east

PREVAILING WINDS

In different parts of the world, winds usually blow from a particular direction. These are called prevailing winds. In each Hadley cell, for example, air moving toward the equator at low altitude swerves west, and this drives the prevailing winds in the tropics, known as the trade winds, or easterlies (because they blow from the east). Prevailing winds blow most reliably over oceans. Land tends to disrupt prevailing winds, creating seasonal, local winds.

WIND AND WAVE

The trade winds get their name from the sailing ships that used them to carry goods across the oceans. Atlantic traders would sail west to America on the trade winds, then return east using the westerlies farther north. Ships sailed around the world using the powerful westerly winds in the Southern Ocean, and racing sailors still follow the same route.

Climate zones

As air currents carry heat away from the tropics, they create warm, wet climate zones near the equator and hot, dry deserts farther north and south. Farther away from the tropics lie the cooler midlatitudes, which are often affected by powerful prevailing winds. The polar regions are cold and dry.

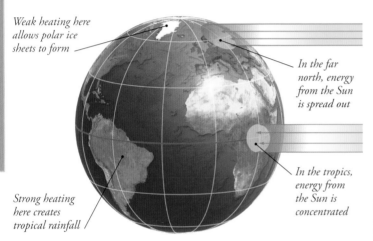

Weak heating here allows polar ice sheets to form

In the far north, energy from the Sun is spread out

In the tropics, energy from the Sun is concentrated

Strong heating here creates tropical rainfall

SOLAR ENERGY

Weather is powered by the Sun's energy. This energy is concentrated in the tropics but spreads out over a larger area near the poles. As a result, sunlight becomes less intense as you move away from the equator, which is why Scandinavia is so much cooler than Kenya. The temperature difference drives the global air currents that control rainfall and wind direction.

FAST FACTS

- In the Amazon Rainforest, it rains about 250 days a year.
- It is said that parts of the Atacama Desert in South America have had no rain at all in living memory.
- The average temperature at the North Pole ranges from -17°F (-27°C) in winter to 73°F (23°C) in summer.
- Winds in Antarctica can reach 199 mph (327 km/h).

TROPICAL RAIN

Rising warm, moist air near the equator creates the biggest storm clouds in the world. They may be 10 miles (16 km) high, and are loaded with moisture that falls as heavy tropical rain. The combination of regular rain and year-round warmth is ideal for trees, which form dense rainforests.

SUBTROPICAL DROUGHT

Having lost all its moisture over the tropical forests, high-level air flows north and south, cools, and sinks over the subtropics—the areas just north and south of the tropics. The sinking dry air stops clouds from forming, so there is little rain and lots of sunshine. This creates hot deserts such as the Sahara.

Some sand dunes in the Sahara are more than 600 ft (180 m) tall.

STORMY WINDS

The winds generated by global air currents become stronger toward the poles. For example, the westerly winds that blow at latitudes of 40–60° north are much stronger than the tropical trade winds. In the Southern Ocean around Antarctica, this effect generates the powerful winds known as the Roaring Forties, Furious Fifties, and Shrieking Sixties.

▲ FAST AND FURIOUS
The fierce winds of the Furious Fifties make the ocean off the southern tip of South America the roughest in the world.

THE POLAR FRONT

At the polar front (the boundary between a Polar cell and a Ferrel cell), cold polar air pushes beneath the warm air of the Ferrel cell, generating storms that are swept along on the prevailing wind. The northern polar front passes over northern Eurasia and North America, but its position is always changing. When it is north of a particular region, that region enjoys warm, dry weather. When it shifts south, it can bring floods, like these in Slovenia in 2010.

ICY DESERTS

In the polar regions, ice chills the air, making it denser. The dense air sinks and this keeps clouds from forming, so it very rarely snows. In Antarctica and northern Greenland, most of the snow lying on the ground has been there for decades. In the heart of Antarctica, the snow never melts, so there is no liquid water at all, making it the driest desert on Earth.

▼ FREEZE-DRIED
The snow-free Dry Valleys in Antarctica are drier than the Sahara Desert.

The seasons

Earth spins as it orbits the Sun. However, it doesn't spin in an upright position, but on an axis tilted 23.5 degrees from the vertical. It is this tilt that causes the seasons. Over a year, different parts of Earth will be closer to or farther away from the Sun and will receive more or less sunlight, giving rise to summers and winters, and wet and dry seasons in the tropics.

ORBITING EARTH

In June, Earth's northern half faces the Sun. It enjoys long, warm summer days when the Sun rises high in the sky. Meanwhile, the southern half has short, cold winter days when the Sun stays low. In December, the southern half faces the Sun, so it is summer there, but winter in the north. The polar regions have 24-hour daylight in summer and permanent darkness in winter.

THROUGH THE YEAR

In the zone between the tropics and the polar regions, each year consists of spring, summer, autumn, and winter seasons. In spring, trees start growing and often sprout new leaves. They keep growing all summer, then slow down in autumn. In the chill of winter, many plants lie dormant, waiting for spring.

Spring   Summer

Autumn   Winter

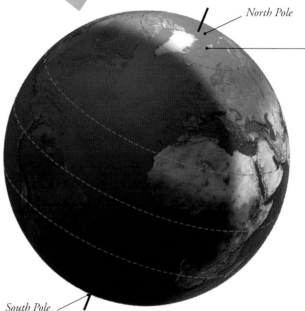

▲ MARCH
Days are the same length in both the north (where it is spring) and the south (where it is autumn).

Sun

North Pole

The Arctic enjoys 24-hour daylight in summer

◀ JUNE
At this point in Earth's orbit, the north is facing the Sun, so it receives more sunlight than the south and enjoys more hours of daylight.

South Pole

SHORT AND LONG DAYS

The shortest and longest days of the year, known as solstices, happen when Earth's tilt is either directly facing, or directly facing away from, the Sun. On the shortest day, the winter solstice, the Sun is at its lowest point in the sky, while on the longest day, the summer solstice, it is at its highest. The ancient stone circle of Stonehenge in England (right) may have been designed to mark the winter solstice.

The Arctic is in constant darkness

▶ DECEMBER
At this point in Earth's orbit, the north is facing away from the Sun, so it receives less sunlight than the south and has fewer hours of daylight.

Arctic Circle

▶ SEPTEMBER
The north and south are heated equally.

Tropic of Cancer

Equator

Tropic of Capricorn

MIDNIGHT SUN

In midwinter, the polar regions get no sunlight at all. It remains dark all day and temperatures plummet to below freezing. But summer brings continuous sunlight, even at midnight, as seen below in Norway. The Arctic and Antarctic circles mark the areas that have 24 hours of darkness on the winter solstice and 24 hours of sunlight on the summer solstice.

DELUGE AND DROUGHT

In the tropics, the zone where the sunlight is most intense moves north and south over the year, as the half of Earth tilted toward the Sun changes. This draws the tropical rain belt—an area of wet weather encircling Earth around the equator—north and south too, causing wet and dry seasons.

▶ SAVANNA LANDSCAPES
The African savanna is drenched by heavy rain in the wet season (near right) but it is parched to the burning point in the dry season (far right).

131

Oceans and continents

Continents warm up and cool down faster than oceans. This is because land has a lower heat capacity (the amount of energy it takes to change something's temperature) than water. Continental climates are therefore far more extreme than oceanic ones. These temperature differences also create local air currents, causing dramatic seasonal changes known as monsoons.

SLOW REACTION

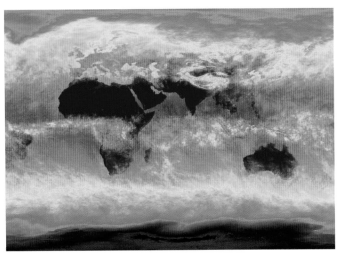

Continents can get much hotter than oceans, as demonstrated in North Africa, Arabia, India, and Australia (all shown in dark red) on this satellite image, taken in April. The oceans never get quite as hot as this, nor as cold as the northern continents in winter. The oceans also stay warm for longer than the continents after the summer has ended, and stay cool for longer in spring.

Temperature °F (°C)

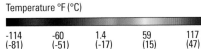

| -114 (-81) | -60 (-51) | 1.4 (-17) | 59 (15) | 117 (47) |

COOL OR WARM WATERS

The coldest ocean water has a temperature of just below 32°F (0°C), and the sea ice at the North Pole is not much colder. By contrast, the continental ice of Antarctica can be colder than -58°F (-50°C). At the other end of the scale, tropical seas rarely get warmer than 86°F (30°C), but desert temperatures can soar above 140°F (60°C).

▼ WINTER SWIM
The water is much warmer than the air in the cold Russian winter. However, the water is still a bracing 32°F (0°C).

OCEANIC CLIMATES

Coastal regions have relatively mild climates because the nearby ocean keeps them from getting too hot or too cold. They also tend to get plenty of rain, but only if the prevailing wind blows from the ocean. Western Europe has a milder, wetter climate than the eastern United States because the prevailing wind blows from west to east over the Atlantic.

OCEAN CURRENTS

The effect of the ocean on climate is changed by currents that flow from other parts of the world. In the eastern Pacific, the cold Humboldt Current flowing north from Antarctica cools the Galápagos Islands, which is why penguins live there. By contrast, northern Europe is warmed by the Gulf Stream flowing up from the Gulf of Mexico.

CONTINENTAL CLIMATES

Regions in the middle of continents have extreme seasons. For example, in central Siberia, north Asia, temperatures rise to 86°F (30°C) in summer, but plunge to well below -22°F (-30°C) in winter. Verkhoyansk, Siberia (left), has seen temperatures of -90°F (-68°C), which is colder than the North Pole.

MONSOONS

Low ground temperatures in winter cool the air over the continents, so it sinks and pushes dry continental air out toward the oceans. In summer, the opposite happens, and rising warm air over the continents draws in moist oceanic air. In India, this seasonal wind change brings a winter drought and a summer deluge—a pattern known as a monsoon climate.

133

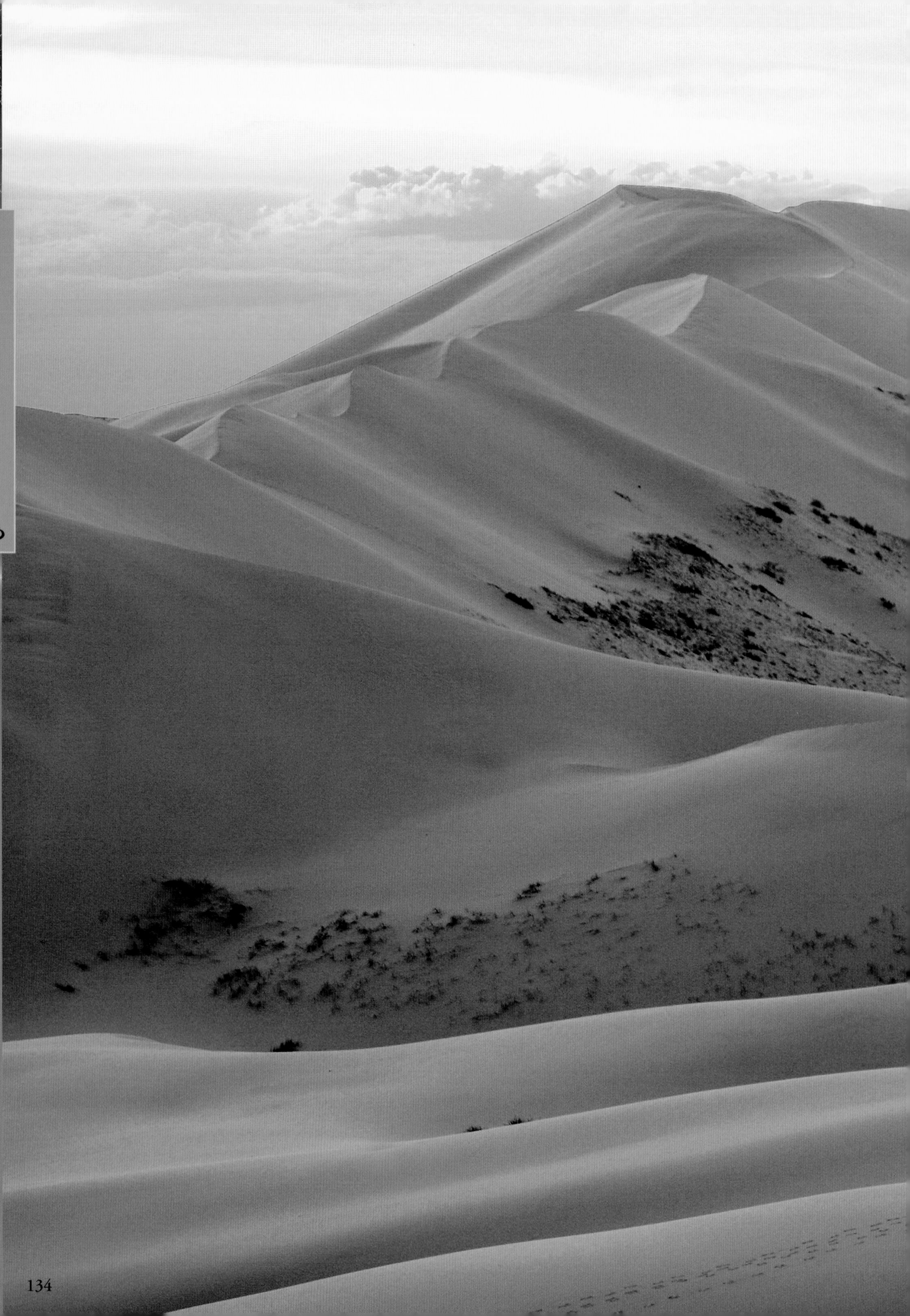

COLD DESERT
The Gobi Desert in central Asia looks like the Sahara, but the Gobi is much colder. It is one of the driest places on Earth because it lies in the heart of a vast, cold continent. It gets so cold in winter that the air above it behaves like the air above Antarctica. Chilled by the land, it cools and sinks; this stops rain clouds from forming, so there is no rain.

Climate types

Humans live all over the planet, in climates ranging from tropical rainforests to cold deserts. Most of us live in areas that have good climates for growing food, but modern technology allows people to survive even in inhospitable climates, such as Antarctica. The cities and settlements featured here represent most of the climates of the world.

Paris, France
Temperate oceanic climate

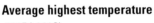

Average highest temperature 78°F (26°C)
Average lowest temperature 35°F (2°C)
Total annual rainfall 24.4 in (620 mm)
Rainfall (wettest month) 2.7 in (69 mm)
Rainfall (driest month) 1.4 in (37 mm)

Although it has suffered some serious heat waves, Paris generally has the oceanic climate typical of western Europe, with rain throughout the year, mild winters, and warm summers. The urban area is mostly residential and commercial, but the surrounding countryside is ideal for growing food.

Sydney, Australia
Temperate oceanic climate

Average highest temperature 81°F (27°C)
Average lowest temperature 47°F (8°C)
Total annual rainfall 39 in (986 mm)
Rainfall (wettest month) 4.3 in (110 mm)
Rainfall (driest month) 1.9 in (48 mm)

Sydney lies in the path of the trade winds that blow from the southeast in the southern hemisphere. The winds blow off the ocean, which gives the city an oceanic climate, with lots of rain, mild winters, and cooler summers than the rest of Australia.

Winnipeg, Canada
Continental climate

Average highest temperature 78°F (26°C)
Average lowest temperature -9°F (-23°C)
Total annual rainfall 21.8 in (555 mm)
Rainfall (wettest month) 3.5 in (88 mm)
Rainfall (driest month) 0.7 in (18 mm)

Located in the heart of Canada, Winnipeg has a continental climate, with less rain than oceanic regions, hot summers, and very cold winters. In 1879, the temperature plunged to a numbing -54°F (-47.8°C).

Vostock Station, Antarctica
Polar desert climate

Average highest temperature
-26°F (-32°C)
Average lowest temperature
-90°F (-68°C)
Total annual rainfall 0.2 in (5 mm)
Rainfall (wettest month) 0.03 in (1 mm)
Rainfall (driest month) 0 in (0 mm)

On July 21, 1983, scientists at Vostock Station at the heart of the east Antarctic ice sheet recorded a temperature of -128.6°F (-89.2°C), the lowest ever recorded anywhere on Earth. This is also one of the driest places on the planet.

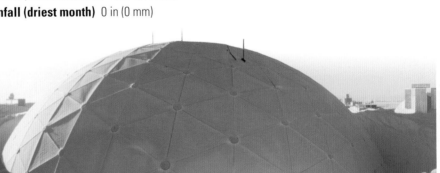

Khartoum, Sudan
Hot arid climate

Average highest temperature 108°F (42°C)
Average lowest temperature 59°F (15°C)
Total annual rainfall 5.2 in (132 mm)
Rainfall (wettest month) 1.7 in (44 mm)
Rainfall (driest month) 0 in (0 mm)

Khartoum is a desert city on the eastern fringe of the Sahara Desert. For much of the year, it doesn't rain at all, and the only significant rain falls in July and August. It is very hot, with temperatures rising above 100°F (38°C) for six months of the year.

Yinchuan, China
Cold arid climate

Average highest temperature
86°F (30°C)
Average lowest temperature
8°F (-13°C)
Total annual rainfall 7.2 in (182 mm)
Rainfall (wettest month) 2.1 in (52 mm)
Rainfall (driest month) 0.04 in (1 mm)

Yinchuan lies to the south of the Gobi Desert in central China. It has a cold desert climate, with low rainfall. Temperatures drop well below freezing in winter.

Iquitos, Peru
Tropical rainforest climate

Average highest temperature 91°F (33°C)
Average lowest temperature 69°F (21°C)
Total annual rainfall 111 in (2,819 mm)
Rainfall (wettest month) 12.9 in (328 mm)
Rainfall (driest month) 5.7 in (144 mm)

Built on the northern bank of the Amazon River in eastern Peru, Iquitos has a tropical rainforest climate, with high temperatures and heavy rain all year round. There is no dry season, but the rain does ease off a little from June to September.

La Paz, Bolivia
Subtropical highland climate

Average highest temperature 66°F (19°C)
Average lowest temperature 34°F (1°C)
Total annual rainfall 22.6 in (575 mm)
Rainfall (wettest month) 4.5 in (114 mm)
Rainfall (driest month) 0.3 in (8 mm)

La Paz is perched at an altitude of 11,975 ft (3,650 m), high in the Andes Mountains of South America. Its height gives it a cool, dry climate, with cold nights. Nearly all the rain falls in the slightly warmer summer months from November to March.

▼ HAZY SKIES
Although Los Angeles has a very pleasant climate, the city is often shrouded in an orange smog caused by air pollution.

Los Angeles, United States
Mediterranean climate

Average highest temperature
78°F (25°C)
Average lowest temperature
49°F (9°C)
Total annual rainfall 15.3 in (388 mm)
Rainfall (wettest month) 4.1 in (104 mm)
Rainfall (driest month) 0.004 in (0.1 mm)

Los Angeles has a warm, dry climate similar to that of the Mediterranean region in Europe. Most of the rain falls in winter. On average, the city has only 35 rainy days and more than 3,000 hours of sunshine each year.

Weather systems

The weather can change dramatically from day to day, and even hour to hour. It changes very fast in cool oceanic regions such as northern Europe, where weather systems are carried in from the ocean. These bring rapid sequences of clouds, rain, storm winds, sunshine, and showers, making weather forecasting very difficult.

HIGHS AND LOWS

As air warms up, it expands, becomes less dense, and rises. This rising air reduces its weight, or pressure, at sea level. By contrast, cool air is denser and sinks, exerting more pressure. Pressure is measured by a barometer like this one—high pressure brings fine weather, but low pressure brings clouds, rain, storms, and snow.

FROM HIGH TO LOW

The atmospheric pressure in a zone of sinking cold air is higher than in a zone of rising warm air. This difference in pressure makes low-level air flow out of high-pressure zones into nearby low-pressure zones. The air is drawn upward as it reaches the center of the low-pressure zone, allowing more air to flow in behind it. We experience this flow of air as wind.

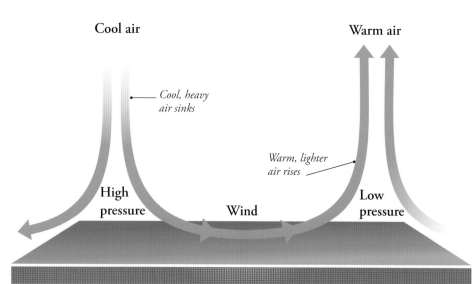

Cool air

Warm air

Cool, heavy air sinks

Warm, lighter air rises

High pressure

Wind

Low pressure

WIND STRENGTH

The bigger the pressure difference between neighboring highs and lows, the stronger the wind that blows between them. The strength of the wind is described using the Beaufort scale of wind force, which rises from 0 for a still day to 12 for hurricane force. It becomes difficult to use an umbrella around scale number 6.

WEATHER FRONTS

When warm air and cold air meet, the warm air rises above the colder, denser air at a boundary called a front. At a warm front, warm air slides up over cold air. At a steeper cold front, cold air pushes beneath warm air. At both kinds of front, warm air is forced upward, making it cooler. Any water vapor in the air turns to clouds and rain.

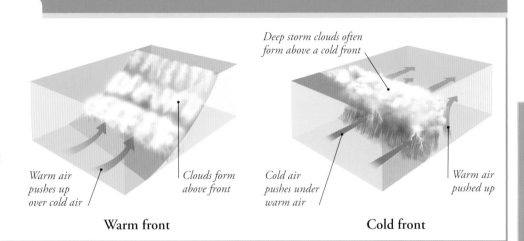

Deep storm clouds often form above a cold front

Warm air pushes up over cold air

Clouds form above front

Cold air pushes under warm air

Warm air pushed up

Warm front

Cold front

CYCLONES AND ANTICYCLONES

Earth's spin makes rising or sinking air spiral up or down. A rising, low-pressure spiral is called a cyclone. It carries warm, often moist air to higher altitudes, where it forms clouds like these. A cool, sinking, high-pressure spiral is called an anticyclone. The sinking air stops clouds from forming, leading to clear skies and dry weather.

FAST FACTS

■ Cyclones swirl counterclockwise north of the equator, and clockwise south of the equator.
■ Anticyclones spiral clockwise in the north, and counterclockwise in the south.
■ If a fast-moving cold front overtakes a warm front, it lifts the warm air off the ground to form an occluded front.

UNDER THE WEATHER

Weather fronts are major features of the moving cyclones that bring bad weather to many parts of the world. A warm front arrives ahead of a cyclone. It causes falling atmospheric pressure, thickening clouds, and then rain. A cold front marks the end of the cyclone. It often brings sharp showers, but then the atmospheric pressure rises, the skies clear, and the Sun comes out.

Clouds and fog

When air containing water vapor rises into the sky, it cools. Since cold air cannot carry as much water vapor as warm air, its water content condenses into a mass of tiny water droplets, which we see as a cloud. If the air at ground level is already saturated with water vapor, the vapor may condense to form low-level clouds known as fog.

WATER VAPOR

Water is always evaporating and rising into the air as an invisible gas, or vapor. Evaporation absorbs heat from the surrounding water, and if the vapor then turns back into liquid water, this heat is released. When water vapor condenses into the tiny droplets that form clouds, the heat is released into the air, warming it so that it rises and builds the clouds higher and higher.

CLOUD DROPLETS

Cloud droplets condense around microscopic particles, such as dust or salt tossed into the air by ocean waves. The cloud droplets are so tiny that it takes a million of them to form one average raindrop. At high, cold altitudes, clouds are formed from microscopic ice crystals instead.

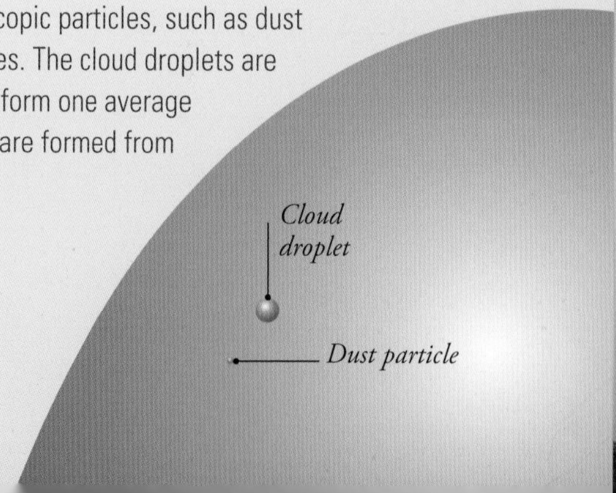

Cloud droplet

Dust particle

▶ DROPS AND DROPLETS
The quarter circle represents part of a normal raindrop—a million times bigger than a cloud droplet.

MIST AND FOG

Clouds can develop at ground or sea level, filling the air with microscopic water droplets to form a veil of mist or fog, as seen here in San Francisco. This often happens when warm, moist air moves over a cold surface such as the sea. The air is cooled to a point at which some of the water vapor in it condenses.

CLOUD FORMATION

Clouds form when moist air is cooled, often because the air rises and gets colder. There are three main reasons why this can happen, shown below.

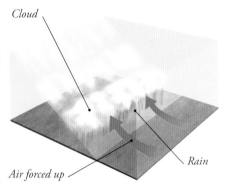

Cloud

Air forced up

Rain

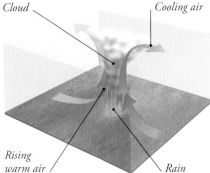

Cloud

Cooling air

Rising warm air

Rain

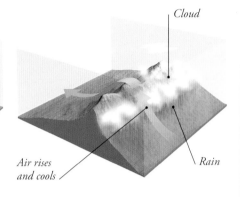

Cloud

Air rises and cools

Rain

▲ FRONTAL CLOUDS
Clouds form when warm, moist air is pushed up over cold air at a weather front. As the rising air cools, the water vapor condenses into clouds.

▲ CONVECTIVE CLOUDS
When the Sun warms the ground or sea, this warms the air above it. The warm air rises and cools, water vapor condenses, and clouds form.

▲ OROGRAPHIC CLOUDS
If moist air is driven over high ground, it is forced upward. This cools any water vapor in the air, making it condense into clouds.

FAIR WEATHER CLOUDS

When air is warmed, the air molecules move apart so the air gets less dense. This makes the air rise. As it rises and cools, its molecules move closer together, making it denser, so that it stops rising. This point is often marked by a layer of fluffy "fair weather" clouds.

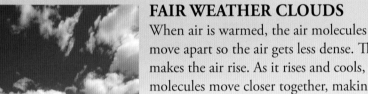

▲ SEA FOG
Fog rolling in from the Pacific Ocean shrouds the Golden Gate Bridge over San Francisco Bay in California.

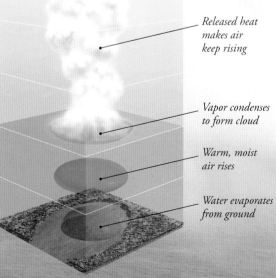

Released heat makes air keep rising

Vapor condenses to form cloud

Warm, moist air rises

Water evaporates from ground

STORMY WEATHER

When hot sunshine creates a lot of water vapor and warm air, the mixture expands, rises, and cools. The vapor condenses into big convective clouds. This releases heat, warming the air and making it rise higher, carrying more water vapor with it. This then condenses, releasing more heat. This process can create huge cumulonimbus storm clouds that are up to 10 miles (16 km) high.

Cloud types

There are ten basic types of clouds. Their names reflect how they look or behave, combining words such as *cirrus* (hair), *stratus* (layer), *cumulus* (heap), and *nimbus* (rain). The cloud types are usually grouped as low-, medium-, and high-level clouds.

Cirrus

Cirrostratus

Cirrocumulus

High-level clouds

20,000 ft (6,000 m)

Altocumulus

Medium-level clouds

Altostratus

Stratocumulus

6,500 ft (2,000 m)

Stratus

Low-level clouds

Cumulus

Nimbostratus

Cumulonimbus

High-level clouds

Cirrus, cirrocumulus, cirrostratus

When water vapor rises to altitudes of 20,000 ft (6,000 m) or more, it condenses into tiny ice crystals. High-level winds often comb the crystals into long, wispy cirrus clouds that look like silver hair. Sometimes, the cloud extends across the sky in a thin sheet of cirrostratus. This is often a sign that bad weather is on the way. Air movements can make this cloud rise and sink in waves, which breaks it up into the small cloudlets of cirrocumulus.

Cirrus

Cirrostratus

Cirrocumulus

Medium-level clouds

Altostratus, altocumulus

The clouds that form at altitudes of 6,500–20,000 ft (2,000–6,000 m) are mostly made of liquid cloud droplets. The extensive flat sheets of altostratus at this level often mark the arrival of a warm front. These can break up into altocumulus, which sometimes forms parallel bands of cloud across the sky. Dark, rainy nimbostratus can sometimes occur at this level as well as nearer to the ground, but it is usually classified as low-level cloud.

Altostratus

Altocumulus

Low-level clouds

Cumulonimbus, cumulus, stratocumulus, stratus, nimbostratus

All clouds that grow below 6,500 ft (2,000 m) are classified as low-level clouds. They include the fluffy cumulus clouds that drift across blue skies in summer and the sheets of gray stratus that spread to the horizon in winter. Cumulus turns into stratocumulus if the clouds merge together. Cumulus can also build higher and higher and turn into colossal cumulonimbus clouds, which rise all the way to the base of the stratosphere. Stratus may thicken into dark, rainy nimbostratus.

Cumulonimbus

Cumulus

Stratocumulus

Rain and snow

Tiny water droplets in clouds can join together to form bigger drops that are heavy enough to fall toward the ground. Ice crystals in high-altitude clouds may do the same, joining together into snowflakes. Before reaching the ground, small water drops may evaporate and snowflakes may melt. Where they do reach ground level, they fall as rain and snow.

THREATENING CLOUDS

You know that it's likely to rain when you see dark clouds approaching. They're dark because they're full of big water droplets that block out the light that makes other clouds look white. You may even be able to see rain falling out of the clouds, forming a gray curtain that hangs down from the base of the cloud.

RAIN AND SHOWERS

The sheets of shallow cloud that form in cyclones produce light, persistent rain. The clouds are not deep enough to allow big raindrops to form, and the drops that do fall often evaporate before they reach the ground. Deep convection clouds cause intense, localized showers. The depth of the cloud allows the raindrops to grow much bigger, and they often fall in dramatic cloudbursts.

RAINDROPS

As cloudy air rises, the water droplets grow steadily bigger. The largest droplets then start to fall back through the cloud. They collide with each other and join together to form even bigger, heavier droplets. When they reach a diameter of about .02 in (0.5 mm), they are heavy enough to fall out of the sky as rain.

Raindrop

Large cloud droplet

▼ RAINY MOOR
On high moorland, sheets of shallow cloud can produce a widespread drizzle that lasts all day.

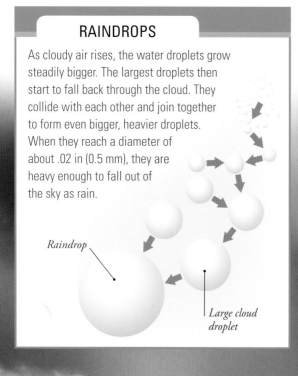

SIX-SIDED SNOWFLAKES

High-level cirrus clouds and the tops of very tall cumulonimbus clouds are made of microscopic six-sided ice crystals. The crystals are attracted to each other, and may become welded together as snowflakes. The crystals join together to create bigger and bigger six-sided structures, and this creates the snowflake's beautiful hexagonal (sixfold) symmetry. Each snowflake has its own unique shape.

SNOW AND SLEET

In very cold weather, lacy snowflakes fall as showers of powder snow. In warmer temperatures close to 32°F (0°C), snowflakes join up to form big, fluffy clumps of "wet snow." In even warmer conditions, the snow may partially melt as it falls, creating a mixture of snow and rain called sleet.

BLIZZARDS AND SNOWDRIFTS

High winds can pick up fallen snow and carry it in a blizzard. This is most common in very cold conditions where the snow is loose powder. When the snow-laden wind passes over or around an obstruction, the snow builds up in deep snowdrifts.

▶ SNOWDRIFT
Wind-blown snow has created a snowdrift alongside this car. The snow has settled on the side that is sheltered from the wind.

145

Storms and hail

Deep cyclones can create very high winds that cause massive damage. They also bring widespread rain, but the biggest cloudbursts are produced by giant cumulonimbus clouds that are built up by intense heat and evaporation. Air currents inside the clouds create hail and thunderstorms.

CLOUDBURSTS

Tall cumulonimbus clouds suck up vast amounts of moisture. The water droplets grow larger and larger until they fall from the cloud. A single cloudburst can release up to 300,000 tons (275,00 metric tons) of water, deluging the land and causing flash flooding.

FRONTAL STORMS

When warm and cold air masses meet at the polar fronts, deep cyclones can build up over the oceans, especially in early autumn when the sea is still warm. The warm, moist, rising air at the center of the cyclone acts like a vacuum cleaner, sucking in low-level air. This creates powerful winds that swirl toward the middle of the cyclone. When one of these major storms moves over land, it can be powerful enough to bring down trees.

HAILSTORMS

Ice crystals form near the tops of cumulonimbus clouds. They then fall through the cloud, picking up water. Powerful updrafts hurl the crystals back up, and the water freezes onto them, making them bigger. They do this many times until they are heavy enough to fall to the ground as hailstones, which can become as large as tennis balls.

SUPERCHARGED

When ice particles are hurled up and down inside a cloud, they rub against each other. This generates electricity, charging up the cloud like a giant battery. The bottom of the cloud becomes negatively charged, while the top and the ground underneath become positively charged. If the charges grow big enough, lightning arcs from the cloud to the ground.

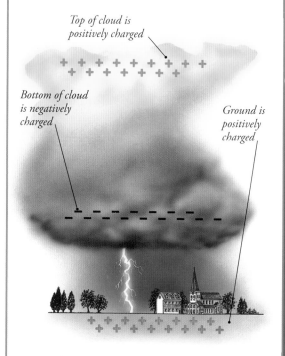

Top of cloud is positively charged

Bottom of cloud is negatively charged

Ground is positively charged

▲ ELECTRIFIED CLOUD
The negative charge at the base of a thundercloud creates a positive charge in the ground below. This difference in charge causes lightning.

LIGHTNING STRIKES

A lightning strike starts when a highly charged, branched "leader" threads its way through the air to the ground. When it touches the ground, a huge charge shoots back up the leader in a bright flash. Within a few thousandths of a second, the air in the path of the lightning is heated to 54,000°F (30,000°C). This makes the air expand explosively, causing the shock wave that we hear as thunder.

▶ FLASHBACK
One of the branched leaders of this lightning strike has touched the ground, triggering a dazzling return flash.

BOLT FROM THE BLUE

The intense heat generated by lightning often starts fires, which can spread to destroy forests and buildings. Tree trunks may have long scars burned in them from top to bottom by lightning. When desert sand is struck by lightning, the heat can melt the sand, fusing it together into a natural form of glass called a fulgurite.

▶ SOLID LIGHTNING
Lightning striking sand often forms tube-shaped fulgurites, like this one.

TORNADO

The biggest cumulonimbus clouds can become massive rotating thunderclouds known as supercells. These often develop spinning funnel clouds that grow down toward the ground to become tornadoes. Inside a tornado, low air pressure creates updrafts of up to 150 mph (240 km/h), which leave trails of destruction wherever they strike.

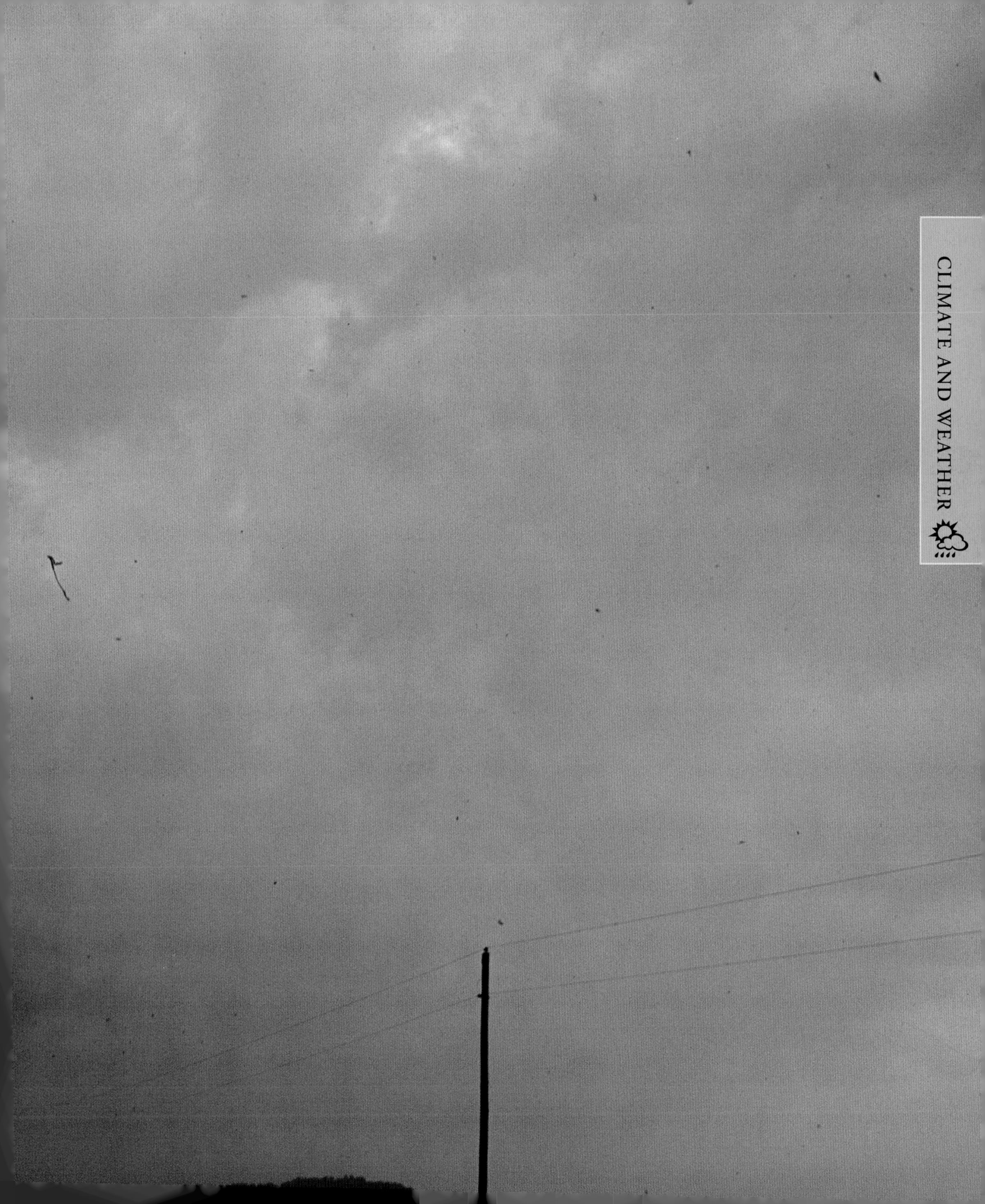

Hurricanes

In the tropics, the intense heat evaporates vast quantities of ocean water. This builds up colossal cloud systems centered on a zone of very low air pressure. Air swirls into the low-pressure zone and sets the cloud mass spinning, creating a tropical revolving storm, or hurricane.

HURRICANE BELT

Hurricanes build up over tropical oceans with surface temperatures of 80°F (27°C) or more. They generally move west, driven by the tropical trade winds, until they hit land and veer off in a new direction. This satellite image shows Hurricane Irene approaching Florida in August 2011.

INSIDE A HURRICANE

At the core of a hurricane, very low pressure makes the surrounding air and storm clouds spiral inward. The wind speeds up as the spiral tightens. A strong updraft around the calm eye of the storm builds the tallest clouds, which produce heavy rain. They are topped by high cirrus clouds that spill out in the opposite direction.

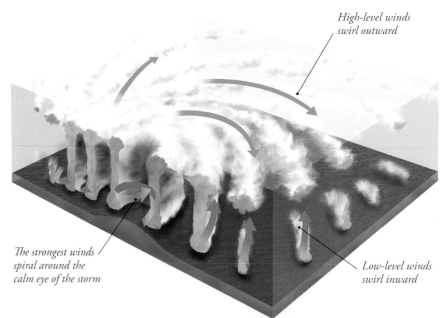

High-level winds swirl outward

The strongest winds spiral around the calm eye of the storm

Low-level winds swirl inward

▶ REVOLVING STORM
The main hurricane-force winds (red) spiral into the eye of the storm, which itself is calm. High-altitude winds (blue) spiral outward.

150

HOWLING WINDS

A hurricane may be up to 300 miles (500 km) across, and can generate 190 mph (300 km/h) winds that leave a trail of destruction. Once it moves over a large landmass, a hurricane loses the supply of water vapor that fuels it, and it blows itself out.

▶ WINDSWEPT
A hurricane blows most powerfully over the ocean, and any island lying in its path is hit by the full force of the storm.

FAST FACTS

The Saffir–Simpson scale classifies storms by their wind speed. Hurricane Irene (shown opposite) peaked at Category 3 off the Bahamas in 2011. Six years earlier, Hurricane Katrina reached Category 5 over the Gulf of Mexico before going on to devastate the city of New Orleans.

CATEGORY 1	74–95 mph (119–153 km/h)
CATEGORY 2	96–110 mph (154–177 km/h)
CATEGORY 3	111–129 mph (178–208 km/h)
CATEGORY 4	130–156 mph (209–251 km/h)
CATEGORY 5	more than 157 mph (252 km/h)

STORM SURGE

The higher air pressure surrounding a hurricane pushes seawater up in a heap inside the low-pressure storm area. This heaped-up water is known as a storm surge. As a hurricane approaches the coast, the storm surge within it builds up in a colossal wave that sweeps over low-lying land, destroying any buildings in its path.

Before the storm surge

After the storm surge

▲ STORM DESTRUCTION
This neighborhood in Crystal Beach, Texas, was washed away by a storm surge in 2008.

DELUGE

Within a few hours, a hurricane can deluge the landscape with more rain than it would normally get in months. The rainwater can overwhelm rivers and trigger flash floods. It may also cause deadly mudslides. This one buried the village of Panabaj in Guatemala when it was hit by Hurricane Stan in 2005.

LIFE ON EARTH

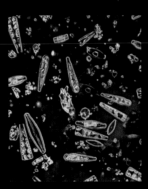

Most of the universe is made up of gas, dust, and barren rock, drifting in the vastness of space. But our planet enjoys something very special—the gift of life.

A living planet

The existence of complex life is what makes Earth unique in the Solar System. A combination of lucky accidents gave the planet the right conditions for life, and a series of chemical reactions created the first microscopic living things. From a slow start, life evolved into a dazzling diversity of forms that live all over the globe.

WATER OF LIFE

Liquid water is essential for life. Luckily for us, Earth's distance from the Sun, along with the insulating effect of its atmosphere, gives it an average temperature of about 59°F (15°C). This allows liquid water to flow almost everywhere on the planet. By contrast, all the other planets in the Solar System are either much too hot or much too cold.

▼ VITAL SUPPLY
Liquid water is the one thing all life forms need, from the smallest microbe to the tallest trees of this tropical forest.

CHEMISTRY OF LIFE

Water is vital because it mixes with so many other substances to make the right chemistry for life. This chemistry takes place inside cells—microscopic bags of fluid that turn chemicals into complex molecules such as proteins.

ORIGINS

Life began about 3.8 billion years ago, possibly when a chance chemical reaction created special molecules called amino acids. This may have been triggered by a lightning strike. Another theory is that these molecules fell to Earth from space. Animo acids link together to form proteins—the basis of all living things.

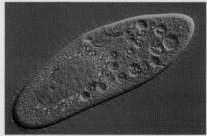

▲ LIVING CELL
This Paramecium *is a microscopic single-celled organism. Plants and animals are made up of many cells.*

THE EARLIEST LIFE

For more than a billion years, the only life forms were single-celled bacteria that lived in pools of water around hot springs. But then new types of bacteria appeared that could use the energy of sunlight to turn water and carbon dioxide into sugar, releasing oxygen. Over about 2 billion years, these cyanobacteria created nearly all the oxygen in the atmosphere.

▲ BACTERIAL COLONIES
Colonies of cyanobacteria form rocklike clumps known as stromatolites, which are made of trapped sediment. These ones are in Shark Bay, Western Australia.

ANIMALS AND PLANTS

About 2.2 billion years ago, some single-celled organisms developed special structures that performed different tasks. These organisms are known as protists. In time, some formed colonies that eventually developed into multicelled creatures similar to this jellyfish—the earliest oceanic animals. Life moved onto land about 470 million years ago, leading to the evolution of the first plants, land animals, and fungi.

DAZZLING VARIETY

Over 800 million years, multicelled life has evolved into an amazing diversity of forms. Many have become extinct, including the largest and most spectacular life-forms of all, the dinosaurs. But there are still nearly 2 million different species of animals, plants, and fungi known to science—370,000 of which are species of beetles, including this yellow-spotted fungus beetle.

EVOLUTION AND EXTINCTION

Each generation of a species is slightly different from the previous one. Sometimes this helps them survive, but sometimes it does not. The survivors prosper and breed, while the others die out and disappear. Over time, this mechanism of natural selection leads to the evolution of new species and the extinction of old ones. The ancestors of the modern elephant all evolved in this way, and eventually died out.

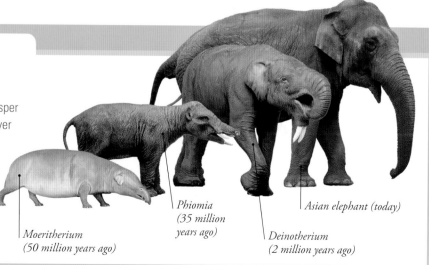

Moeritherium (50 million years ago)

Phiomia (35 million years ago)

Deinotherium (2 million years ago)

Asian elephant (today)

Kingdoms of life

Living things are divided into six kingdoms. Three of these are the animals, plants, and fungi—the relatively large, visible life forms that we notice all around us. The other three are the archaea, bacteria, and protists. These are microscopic organisms that are too small to see with the naked eye, yet they are vital to the web of life on Earth.

Bacteria and archaea

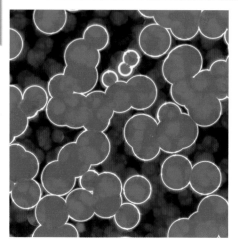

Number of known species 36,000
Habitat Wet places
Size range Microscopic to 0.03 in (0.75 mm)

Archaea and bacteria are simple, single-celled organisms. Though similar in many ways, they have different biochemistry, which shows that they have evolved separately over the billions of years since life first appeared. Because of this, they are now classified as separate kingdoms. Some of these organisms cause diseases, but many more are vital to the other four kingdoms of life.

Fungi

Number of known species 100,000
Habitat Land
Size range Microscopic to about 3.5 sq miles (9 sq km)

Fungi feed on organic matter such as dead plants. They are most familiar as the mushrooms and toadstools that spring up almost overnight in damp places, but these are only the visible parts of much larger root networks that spread over large areas. The largest known example is a honey fungus that covers almost 3.5 sq miles (9 sq km) of forest in Oregon. Other fungi, known as yeasts, are tiny, single-celled microbes.

Protists

Number of known species 115,000
Habitat Water
Size range Microscopic to about 150 ft (45 m)

These are mostly single-celled organisms, but each cell has a nucleus—a central part containing genetic material. Some, such as the phytoplankton that drift in oceans and lakes, live like plants by using the energy of sunlight to make food. Others, such as *Paramecium*, behave like tiny animals. Many live in colonies, and a few, such as seaweed, are truly multicellular organisms.

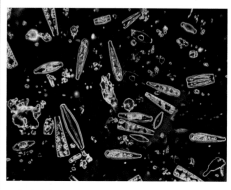

▲ PHYTOPLANKTON
Tiny, single-celled algae drift in water, making food in the same way as plants.

Plants

Number of known species 310,000
Habitat Land and water
Size range Less than 0.04 in (1 mm) to about 280 ft (85 m)

These multicellular organisms nearly all use the energy of sunlight to turn carbon dioxide and water into sugar—a process called photosynthesis. They include primitive mosses and ferns, such as this one, and more complex plants, ranging from grasses to giant, long-lived trees.

Animals

Number of known species 1,367,555
Habitat Land and water
Size range Less than 0.04 in (1 mm) to about 110 ft (33 m)

Animals cannot make foods such as sugar from raw chemicals, as plants do, so they have to find it ready-made. They survive by eating other living things, or things that were once alive. Some aquatic animals live out their adult lives rooted to one spot, and rely on the water to bring food within reach. But most animals—including all the ones that live on land—have various means of moving around so they can search for food. These include fins, legs, and wings, although many animals have other ways of moving, such as gliding on trails of slime like slugs, stretching and contracting their soft bodies like worms, or wriggling like snakes. Animals include a huge variety of creatures, from microscopic worms to giant whales. Many aquatic animals, such as corals and sea anemones, look like plants because of the flowerlike shapes of their bodies. But most animals have distinct heads and tails, with sensory organs such as eyes, nostrils, and ears clustered on their heads. These help them find their way around and identify food. It is animals' ability to make decisions about where to go and why that makes them so different from plants and fungi.

Invertebrates

More than 95 percent of the animal species currently known to science are invertebrates—animals that do not have backbones and jointed internal skeletons. They include creatures such as insects, worms, snails, clams, crabs, jellyfish, and sea urchins.

Vertebrates

A very small proportion of all the animal species on Earth are vertebrates with internal skeletons. They are the fish, amphibians, reptiles, birds, and mammals. They include the largest animals, such as elephants, crocodiles, and whales.

▼ LITTLE AND LARGE
Animals take many forms. Here, a caiman— a type of crocodilian—provides a perch for tropical butterflies.

Ecosystems

Living things interact with each other to form communities called ecosystems. Each ecosystem has a particular character formed by factors such as the climate, geology, and the species that live in it. As plants grow, animals eat the plants, and other animals eat those animals, energy is passed from species to species in a food chain.

ENERGY AND NUTRIENTS

Every ecosystem needs energy and a supply of the nutrients that living things use to build tissue. Most of the energy comes from sunlight, which trees and microbes in this forest soak up and use to fuel their growth. The nutrients include water, carbon, and nitrates (nitrogen and oxygen), along with other chemical compounds that have been dissolved from the rocks by water in the soil or sea.

PRODUCERS AND CONSUMERS

Green plants and many microbes are food producers. They use photosynthesis to turn carbon dioxide and water into carbohydrates such as sugar. They use other raw nutrients to make proteins. Animals eat plants and other living things, and use the digested carbohydrates and proteins to build their own bodies—so they are consumers. The interaction between producers and consumers is the basis of all ecosystems.

▼ FOOD FACTORY
This caterpillar is consuming a leaf that the plant has made from raw chemicals.

DECAY AND RECYCLING

When organisms die and decay, they are recycled by decomposers—fungi and bacteria. These break organisms down into nutrients—substances that can feed living plants. The decomposers are a vital part of any ecosystem, because without them the plants would run out of nutrients. This fallen apple is being decomposed by fungi.

FOOD PYRAMIDS

Any ecosystem has many producers, such as oceanic phytoplankton, fewer consumers, such as zooplankton (microscopic animals), and even fewer secondary consumers, such as fish. This is because some of the energy at each level is turned into activity rather than food. It takes a vast weight of phytoplankton to support one polar bear.

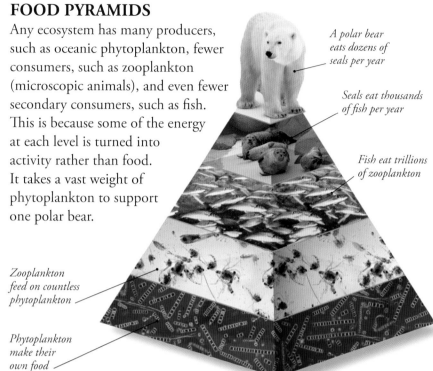

A polar bear eats dozens of seals per year

Seals eat thousands of fish per year

Fish eat trillions of zooplankton

Zooplankton feed on countless phytoplankton

Phytoplankton make their own food

SUCCESSION

Most ecosystems become more complex as they develop over time— a process known as succession. This lone plant growing on the scorched slope of a volcano may be pioneering the way for a more complex ecosystem.

WORLD BIOMES

The world is divided into several large ecosystems called biomes. These include the oceans and vast swaths of landscape such as deserts, grasslands, and forests. Each biome has its own special features, which in most cases are shaped by the climate. Together, these biomes make up the biosphere—the ecosystem of the entire planet.

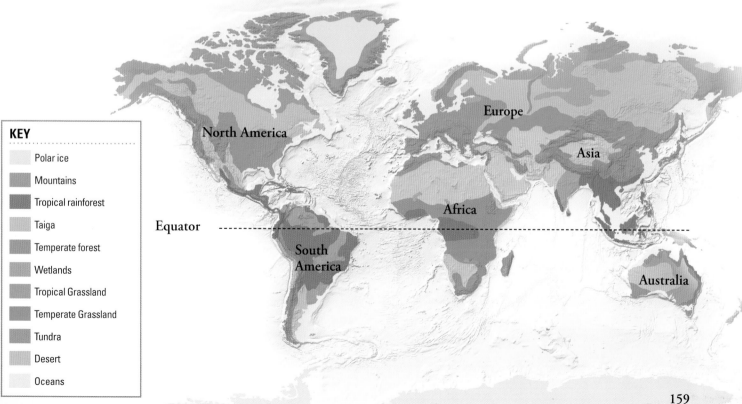

KEY

- Polar ice
- Mountains
- Tropical rainforest
- Taiga
- Temperate forest
- Wetlands
- Tropical Grassland
- Temperate Grassland
- Tundra
- Desert
- Oceans

North America

Europe

Asia

Africa

Equator

South America

Australia

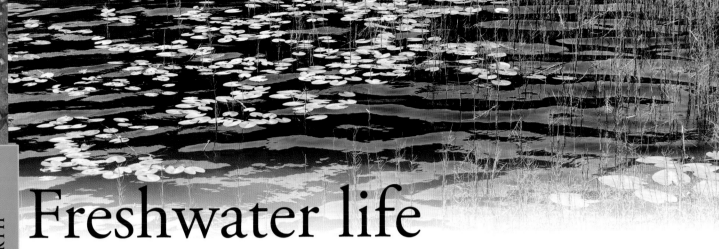

Freshwater life

Most ecosystems are complex, but freshwater habitats, such as rivers, lakes, and marshes, are often easy to understand. In a lake, for example, plants and algae are the producers, while zooplankton, insects, fish, and large, fish-eating animals are the consumers. But the particular species in each ecosystem depend on whether the water is flowing or still, warm or cold, and so on.

RICH AND POOR

The water of upland lakes and streams is often almost pure, with few dissolved nutrients. This limits the growth of plankton, but the cool water is often rich in oxygen, which suits insects and fish. Lowland waters, such as this lake, have more nutrients, which encourages plankton. But the warmer water contains less oxygen, which can be a problem for animals.

DRIFTING SWARMS

The algae drifting in fresh water are eaten by the tiny animals of the zooplankton—creatures such as water fleas and copepods—as well as various aquatic insects. These include the young of winged insects, such as mayflies, which emerge as flying adults in spring. In some regions, mayflies gather over the water in spectacular swarms.

VITAL ALGAE

On land, the primary producers are plants, which capture sunlight and use it to turn air and water into food. In rivers and lakes, this is the job of microscopic single-celled algae that drift in the water as plankton. These live in all freshwaters that contain enough nutrients to support them. They are the first link in the aquatic food chain.

▲ MICROORGANISMS
Although they are not plants, these microscopic freshwater algae make food in the same way.

HUNTERS AND HUNTED

Small aquatic animals such as insects are eaten by fish and frogs, which are preyed upon by larger fish, and diving birds such as cormorants and grebes. The large fish are targeted by powerful hunters—herons, fish eagles, crocodiles, river dolphins, otters like this one, and even grizzly bears, which wade into Alaskan rivers to catch salmon.

FLOWING WATER

Fast-flowing water causes problems for freshwater life. Drifting plankton cannot survive, which means that there is little food. Despite this, some small animals cling to rocks or streambeds, providing prey for other animals. Fish such as these salmon deliberately swim upstream to breed in these waters, partly because there are fewer predators.

LIVING WITH EXTREMES

Some lakes are not really freshwater habitats at all because they are full of dissolved salt or soda. This makes them hostile to many forms of life. However, a few organisms have evolved ways of surviving. These include the microscopic algae called spirulina that flourish in the soda lakes of the African Rift Valley, and are sifted from the chemical-rich water by flocks of lesser flamingos.

Tropical forest

A tropical climate is perfect for plants, because it is always warm and there is no shortage of water. This means that plants grow fast all year, especially large, evergreen trees. The year-round production of leaves and fruit supports an amazing variety of animal species. This makes tropical rainforests the richest of all ecosystems.

WARM AND WET
Tropical rainforests lie in the hottest parts of the world—in Amazonia, Central America, Central Africa, Southeast Asia, New Guinea, and northeast Australia. The climate is always warm and wet, thanks to the strong sunlight and the huge storm clouds that are built up by the heat.

FOREST LAYERS

A rainforest is a multilayered habitat, with two or three distinct layers of tree canopy above the ground. These are the understory, the main canopy, and the very tall emergent trees that rise high above the others. Each layer has its own wildlife.

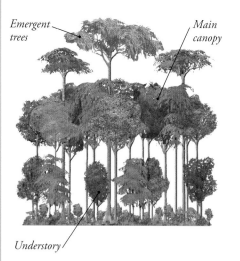

Emergent trees

Main canopy

Understory

▲ FOREST ROOF
The main tree canopy in a rainforest forms an almost continuous layer of foliage.

RAINFOREST
These forests are dominated by tall, broad-leaved hardwood trees such as mahogany, rosewood, and ebony. The dense foliage stops most light from reaching the forest floor, so many of the smaller plants survive as creepers that climb up the trees into the sunlight. Others, such as ferns and orchids, take root in the treetops. Any sunlit areas of ground are smothered by dense undergrowth.

HIGH LIFE

The very tall emergent trees attract colorful birds such as these toucans. Predators, including the South American harpy eagle, prey on the monkeys and sloths that live in the main canopy—the most populated layer. Around the world, this layer is also the home of parrots, birds-of-paradise, gibbons, fruit bats, lizards, and tree snakes. The air rings with the calls of birds and tree frogs.

TREETOP NURSERIES

In the forests of Central and South America, tiny poison-dart frogs are protected from predators by their highly toxic skin. Their vivid colors warn enemies to leave them alone. Some raise their tadpoles in the tiny pools that form in plants growing at the tops of trees, and feed each tadpole on spare, unfertilized eggs.

INSECT HEAVEN

Tropical rainforests are alive with insects such as butterflies and moths, bees, wasps, termites, and an astonishing variety of beetles—most of them still not scientifically described. In one study, scientists discovered 600 new beetle species living on just one type of rainforest tree.

▲ FOREST BEAUTY
Flowers open all year round in tropical rainforests, making life easy for nectar-feeding butterflies.

▲ BREEDING POOL
This poison-dart frog has claimed a pool in a bromeliad plant, high above the forest floor.

THE FOREST FLOOR

In all tropical forests, the floor is the home of larger animals, including tapirs, peccaries, forest elephants, gorillas, and spectacular jungle pheasants. Predators such as big cats, snakes, giant spiders, and army ants prowl through the undergrowth or lie in ambush for victims.

▶ HUNGRY HUNTER
A jaguar scents prey in the tropical forest of Amazonia. This beautifully marked cat is the South American equivalent of the leopard.

Temperate forest

Away from the tropics, climates are cooler with distinct winters and summers. Temperate regions with short, mild winters and regular rainfall are naturally covered by woodland, mostly made up of deciduous trees, which lose their leaves in winter and grow new ones in spring. This creates a seasonal habitat with most of the plant and animal activity taking place during the warmer months of the year.

FOREST ZONES

Temperate forests grow in places with mild oceanic climates. The warmest, wettest regions, such as New Zealand and Oregon, have temperate rainforests of evergreen trees. But cooler areas, such as northern Europe and New England, have deciduous woodland that stops growing in winter.

DECIDUOUS TREES

Leaves soak up sunlight to make food. The broad evergreen leaves of tropical trees are very good at this, but cannot survive frost. The tougher leaves of trees such as holly survive, but are less efficient. By contrast, deciduous trees, like this one, have broad, thin leaves that make all the food the tree needs in just a few months, and are then discarded and replaced.

SPRING FLOWERS

Since deciduous trees have no leaves in winter, the forest floor is flooded with light in early spring. Plants such as these bluebells grow fast and burst into bloom, soaking up the sun to make their seeds before the new tree foliage creates too much shade. These plants vanish in winter, but their bulbs stay alive below ground, insulated from the cold by a blanket of fallen leaves.

◄ FLOWER SHOW
Bluebells carpet an English woodland in May, as new leaves appear on the beech trees overhead.

BREEDING BIRDS

New spring leaves feed swarms of caterpillars, which hatch from eggs laid before the winter. Caterpillars make ideal food for baby birds, so the woods become very busy as birds, such as this nightingale, compete for nesting sites and gather food for their young.

LEAF FALL

As temperatures drop in autumn, deciduous trees lose their leaves. These form a layer of leaf litter, which is rotted down by fungi, bacteria, and other organisms. The decay process releases vital nutrients into the soil. Mushrooms, the fruiting bodies of fungi, push up from beneath the leaf litter to release their spores.

▼ POKING THROUGH
Bright red fly agaric fungi sprout from root systems that feed on the carpet of fallen leaves.

WINTER CHILL

As winter sets in, most of the insects die off. This forces many insect-eating birds to fly to warmer regions, where they stay until the next breeding season. Other birds feast on seeds, berries, and nuts to build up fat reserves for the winter, as do squirrels and bears. Many animals spend much of the winter asleep, but others stay active, providing prey for hungry hunters like this fox.

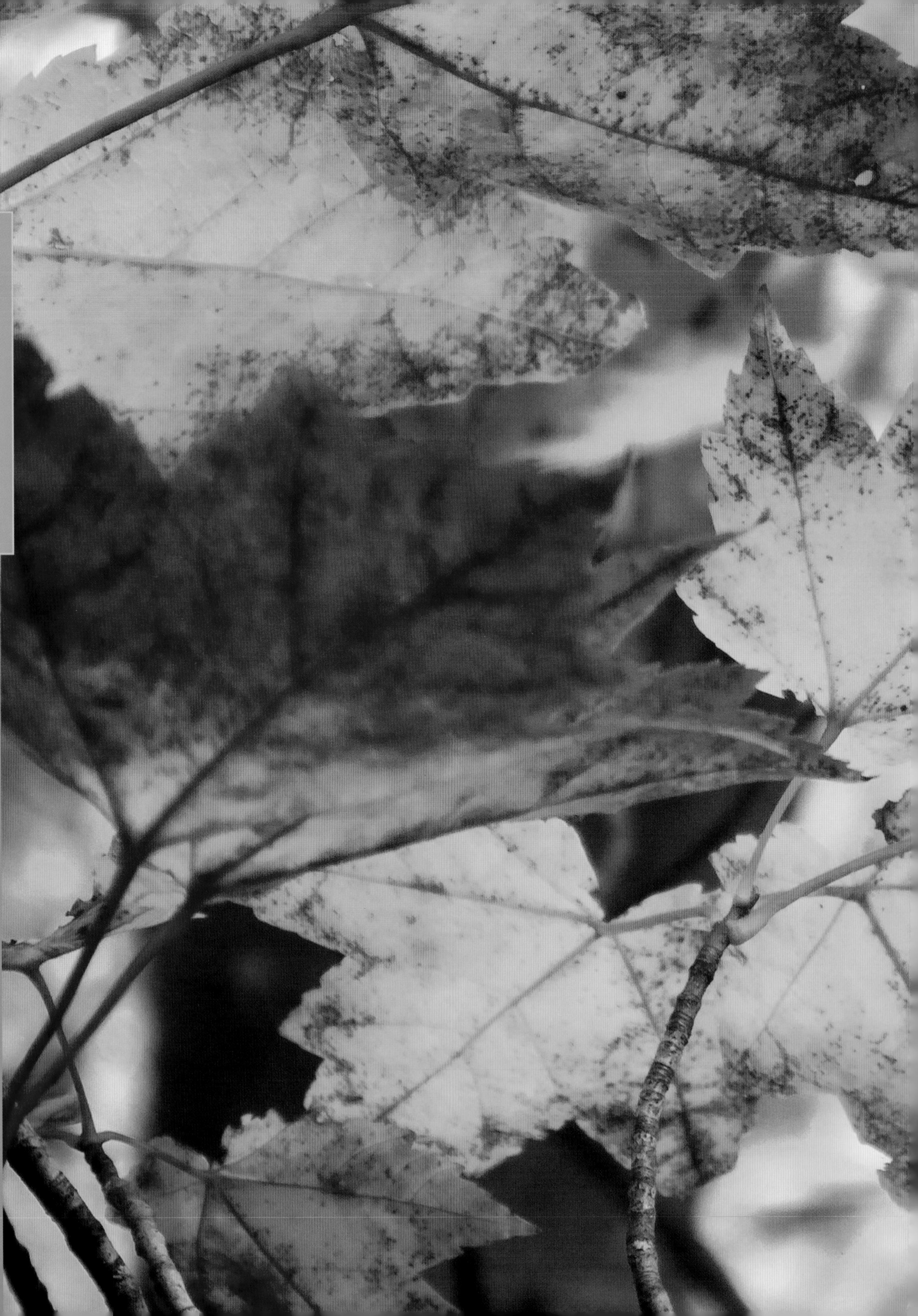

AUTUMN COLOR

A deciduous tree drops its leaves at the end of each year's growing season. But before they fall off, the tree first recycles the leaves' chlorophyll—the green chemical that uses sunlight to make sugar. As the tree draws the green chlorophyll back into its twigs, the leaves change color, creating spectacular seasonal shows of red, yellow, and gold.

Northern forest

In the cold north, the summers are so short that most deciduous trees cannot make enough food to survive. But evergreen conifer trees have tough leaves that make the most of every minute of daylight. These trees form the vast taiga, or boreal forests, that grow all around the globe just south of the northern polar regions.

THE BOREAL ZONE
The northern forests extend in a broad band through Scandinavia, northern Russia, Alaska, and Canada. They are very cold in winter, and have only around two frost-free months a year. There is not a lot of snowfall or rain, but the low temperatures mean that the ground never dries out.

▼ FROZEN FORESTS
Winter temperatures in the forest can drop below -58°F (-50°C) in parts of Siberia and Canada.

FROST-PROOF TREES
The waxy, needle-shaped leaves of conifer trees can survive months of freezing temperatures. Many tree species have a conical shape, which helps them shed heavy snow. They can also grow well on the acidic, infertile soils that are typical of these regions.

BOGGY GROUND
The cold ground beneath the forest trees is often waterlogged. This slows the normal processes of decay, creating thick layers of acidic peat dotted with bog pools. The peaty soil is colonized by spongy moss and acid-loving plants such as bilberry, blueberry, and red cranberry.

TOUGH SURVIVORS

The animals that live all year round in the northern forests have to be tough to survive the cold. Only a few species are hardy enough. All the mammals have thick fur coats and spend the worst part of the winter asleep in their dens to conserve energy. Others stay active, including beavers, who dam streams to form pools around their homes. The pools freeze over, but the beavers gather food from beneath the ice.

FUR COAT ▶
Thick fur helps this grizzly bear and her cubs keep warm, although they spend much of the winter asleep.

PROWLING PREDATORS

Hunters such as weasels, foxes, wolves, and this Eurasian lynx can usually find enough prey to see them through the cold winter. Bears too may hunt other animals, but they mainly eat berries and nuts in the autumn before finding snug dens where they can sleep until spring.

HARD TIMES

Around 300 bird species breed in the Eurasian taiga forest in summer, but only 30 of these stay for the winter. They include scavengers and hunters such as ravens, eagles, and this great gray owl. Seed-eaters such as grouse and crossbills may also stay. Most of the other birds fly south to spend the winter in warmer regions, returning to breed in the spring.

Moorland and heath

In cool, wet, hilly regions made up of hard rock such as granite, the wild landscape is often dominated by heather moors and acidic peat bogs. These bleak moorlands resemble the lowland heaths that form on infertile, sandy, or stony soils in milder climates. Other types of heath develop in warmer regions where the climate is too arid or dry for trees.

COLD RAIN
Rugged uplands are often made of hard rock covered with thin, acidic soil. In cool oceanic regions, heavy rain washes soluble plant nutrients out of the soil, so only a few types of tough, low-growing plants can survive. They cover huge areas, creating bleak moorland with few trees.

▼ HEATHER MOOR
Purple-flowering heather makes a splash of color beneath the rain-swept skies of Glencoe in the Scottish Highlands.

DARK PEAT
Waterlogged moorland is taken over by sphagnum moss, which soaks up the water like a sponge. As the moss dies off, it does not decay, but builds up in thick layers of peat. On the wet uplands, this process forms blanket bogs that cover vast areas of the landscape, dotted with dark bog pools that swarm with mosquitoes in summer.

LOWLAND HEATHS

In milder climates, rainwater seeping down through fast-draining sand or gravel carries away dissolved nutrients to create thin, acidic soils, much like moorland soil. The effect on plants is similar, forming low-growing, heather-dominated landscapes called heaths. But the warmer climate allows a wider variety of plants to grow, and heaths attract reptiles including lizards and snakes, as well as insects such as dragonflies and butterflies.

▲ SUMMER FLOWERS
This coastal heath is bright with the flowers of yellow gorse and different types of heather.

KILLER PLANTS

Plant nutrients, particularly nitrates, are scarce on peat bogs. Some plants get around this by catching insects and digesting them to extract their nitrogen. This Venus flytrap has leaves that snap shut on insects that land on them and brush against their tiny trigger hairs. Pitcher plants drown their insect prey in pools of digestive fluid.

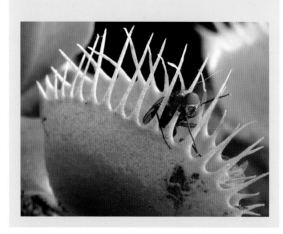

ARID SCRUB

Scrub made up of low-lying bushes and plants is the natural vegetation of many warm, dry regions. It has different names in different parts of the world—South African fynbos, California chaparral, Mediterranean maquis, and Australian mallee. The pincushion protea seen here being visited by a nectar-feeding sunbird is a fynbos plant.

FIRE!

We think of fire as destructive, but natural fires are a key feature of heathlands and arid scrub. In many of these habitats, fire triggers the release and growth of seeds from certain specialized plants. It also destroys trees and other plants that compete with the new seedlings for space. The heathland plants rely on fire for their survival—and without it, these habitats would simply disappear.

Temperate grassland

Many continental regions are too dry for trees to form dense forests. Instead, the wild landscape is dominated by grassland. In the temperate regions, these grasslands are known as prairie, steppe, and pampas. The grasses can build up deep, fertile soils. As a result, much of this grassland has been used to grow crops, but some wild areas survive.

STEPPE AND PRAIRIE

Temperate grasslands develop in places where the climate is almost dry enough to create deserts. They often form in the heart of continents, beyond mountains that catch most of the rain. In North America, for example, the prairies lie beyond the Rocky Mountains. In Central Asia, the steppe forms a broad band across the center of the continent. Such places have continental climates with hot summers and cold winters.

▲ TREELESS STEPPE
Despite the clouds in the sky, little rain falls on the open steppe of Central Asia, and trees are very scarce.

THE TOUGHEST PLANT

Grass is a survivor. It can recover from freezing, drought, fire, and, in particular, intense grazing. It grows from near or below ground level, so if its leaves are chewed off, it just grows more. It is also studded with microscopic shards of glassy silica that wear away the grazers' teeth.

GRAZING HERDS

Grass is hard on teeth and hard to digest. But it is so abundant that many animals have evolved ways of eating and digesting it. They include antelope, wild horses, and these American bison, which live in herds for mutual defense from predators such as wolves. Bison once roamed the American prairies by the millions, before being hunted to near-extinction in the 19th century.

A big bull bison eats up to 33 lb (15 kg) of grass every day.

BURROWING SQUIRRELS

The grazing herds are the most obvious grassland animals, but they are outnumbered by small burrowing mammals such as ground squirrels and mole rats. Other burrowers include rattlesnakes, armadillos, foxes, weasels, and polecats. Even owls nest underground on the American prairies.

◄ LOWLIFE
Ground squirrels such as this prairie dog spend most of their time underground.

DUST BOWLS

Temperate grasslands can make excellent farmland. But the soil of prairies and steppes tends to dry out, and if there is not enough natural vegetation to hold it together, it can turn to dust and blow away. This happened in the American Midwest in the 1930s, creating a large barren area known as the Dust Bowl. It also took place over a far longer period in China, where the windblown soil has formed thick drifts that cover huge areas.

FACT!

American prairie dogs live in underground colonies called towns. In the past, these could be huge—one found in 1900 was home to an estimated 400 million prairie dogs.

NIBBLING TEETH

Although many grasslands have been destroyed by farming, others have been created. As farm animals like these sheep nibble the vegetation, they kill off many plants, especially trees. But the grass keeps growing, and gradually takes over the landscape. Large areas of wild-looking grassland have been created like this, and if the sheep are taken off the land, the trees grow back.

▲ LOESS PLATEAU
In Shanxi Province, China, an area almost the size of Texas is covered by a thick layer of windblown soil known as loess.

173

Tropical grassland

Often known as savanna, tropical grassland develops in hot parts of the world that have distinct wet and dry seasons. The contrast is dramatic, creating lush green grass for half the year and parched dust for the other half. The rain allows some trees to grow, but only if they can cope with months of drought.

WINTER FIRES

Most savannas lie between the tropical rainforests and the subtropical deserts of Africa, South America, and Australia. As the zone of most intense sunshine moves north and south through the year, it drags storm systems with it, so the rainy season is in summer. But the rest of the year is still very hot, so the grass dries out and often catches fire.

PRECIOUS WATER

Seasonal rain allows many of the savanna grasses to grow very tall. It also fuels the growth of scattered, drought-resistant trees such as eucalyptus and the spiny acacia (shown here). The baobab tree soaks up water during the rainy season and stores it in its swollen trunk.

MASS MIGRATIONS

The Serengeti plains in East Africa are famous for the vast herds of zebras, wildebeests, and gazelles that make long journeys to find new pasture when the dry season stops the grass from growing. The herds trek west and then north to the lush grassland around the Mara River, then move back when the rains return.

DANGER ZONE ▶
Migrating wildebeests have to cross the Mara River, where they risk being swept away or attacked by the crocodiles that lie in ambush for them.

SWARMING HORDES

The big animals of the savanna are massively outnumbered by insects. These include dung beetles that recycle the droppings of the grazing herds, and termites that live in large earth mounds that rise above the plains. Sometimes, swarms of locusts descend on the savanna trees, stripping them of every leaf.

▶ FOOD RECYCLERS
Dung beetles eat half-digested animal waste, and also store it underground as food for their young.

▼ SUPERCHARGERS
Cheetahs can sprint at an astonishing 75 mph (120 km/h) in short bursts—faster than any other land animal.

POWERFUL PREDATORS

On the African plains, the grazing animals are preyed upon by fast, powerful hunters. These include lions, leopards, cheetahs, wild dogs, and spotted hyenas. This is why many of the grazers, such as zebras and gazelles, have evolved the ability to run fast. The plains also support scavengers, including jackals and vultures, who feed on the remains of dead animals.

Desert

Few deserts are completely barren. Most support life of some kind. Highly specialized plants manage to stay alive between occasional rainstorms. These provide food for plant-eating animals, which are preyed upon by a variety of hunters. Many of the small animals that live in hot deserts survive the heat of the day by hiding underground, only emerging at night.

DRY AS DUST

Deserts are created by cloudless skies and drought. Many are hot, but some are very cold. Even in hot deserts, the nights are often cold because there is no cloud cover to stop heat from escaping into space. Rain does fall, usually as infrequent storms, and some coastal deserts are moistened by oceanic fog. The water that does reach the ground soon evaporates unless it is absorbed by desert plants.

GREEN SURVIVORS

Some desert plants survive months or even years of drought as seeds, and only spring to life after rainstorms. Others are long-lived shrubs that have very deep or wide root systems for soaking up water, and small leathery leaves to reduce moisture loss. Many, like cacti and this euphorbia, have juicy water-storing flesh, and most are spiny to discourage hungry or thirsty animals from eating them.

CREEPING KILLERS

The most numerous desert animals are insects, scorpions, and spiders. They can survive on relatively little food, making them well adapted to life in deserts. Many scorpions and spiders are highly venomous. This gives them an advantage when they do find prey—a single sting or bite makes escape impossible, and ensures that the hunter gets a meal.

NIGHTLIFE

Small animals such as mice, gerbils, ground squirrels, and kangaroo rats spend the hot days below ground, where the air is cooler and contains more moisture. They emerge at night to forage for food such as seeds, but have to avoid hunters such as foxes.

▲ MOUSE DETECTORS
The huge ears of the African fennec fox help it locate prey in the dark.

SIDE-WINDING

Reptiles can go for long periods without eating, and their scaly skins stop them from drying out. Many have very efficient ways of moving over soft sand. For instance, the side-winding motion of this desert viper helps it grip the loose surface.

HEAT PROTECTION

A few large mammals, such as camels, donkeys, and gazelles, manage to survive in deserts. Camels have special adaptations for dealing with the heat and drought. They can go for long periods without water, rarely sweat, and have humps on their backs where they store fat.

▼ NATURAL NOMADS
Camels wander the desert searching for edible plants.

Living deserts

Every desert is a difficult habitat for the plants and animals living there. They have to cope with months without rain, extremes of temperature, sandstorms, and occasional flash floods. The animals must also find food, which is usually scarce. Most of the plants and animals living in the deserts of the world have similar ways of surviving, although some are unique.

Patagonian Desert
South America

Area 260,000 sq miles (670,000 sq km)
Annual rainfall 4–10 in (100–250 mm)
Average highest temperature 55°F (13°C)
Average lowest temperature 32°F (0°C)

The cold, dry highlands on the eastern flanks of the southern Andes are the home of tough desert shrubs and grasses. These provide food for ostrichlike rheas, pygmy armadillos, and llamalike guanacos. They are preyed on by foxes, pumas, and eagles.

Atacama Desert
South America

Area 40,600 sq miles (105,200 sq km)
Annual rainfall Less than 0.6 in (15 mm)
Average highest temperature 95°F (35°C)
Average lowest temperature -25°F (4°C)

Although it lies on the shores of the Pacific, this is the world's driest hot desert. A few cacti and other plants soak up the moisture carried in from the ocean by fog. Specialized brine shrimps survive on salt flats that flood after rare rainstorms.

Sahara Desert
North Africa

Area 3.5 million sq miles (9 million sq km)
Annual rainfall 0.8–4 in (20–100 mm)
Average highest temperature 100°F (38°C)
Average lowest temperature 32°F (0°C)

The world's largest hot desert stretches across 14 North African countries. It has a variety of landscapes, ranging from sand dunes to large areas of bare rock where tough spiny shrubs grow. Watery oases (small areas of fertile land) are fringed by date palms. Animals include mice, foxes, snakes, and scorpions.

▼ DESERT WANDERER
Long-legged ostriches roam widely over the desert fringes. They can go without water for several days.

Arabian Desert
Arabian Peninsula

Area 900,000 sq miles (2.3 million sq km)
Annual rainfall 1–2 in (25–50 mm)
Average highest temperature 120°F (49°C)
Average lowest temperature 32°F (0°C)

The hot deserts of the Arabian Peninsula contain the vast Empty Quarter—an area of dunes the size of France. Less arid parts support sparse scrub and small mammals such as jerboas, which are hunted by deadly vipers. The rare Arabian oryx is among the desert's larger animals.

▲ SEA OF SAND
Vast dunes fringe the Empty Quarter— the world's largest sand desert.

Sonoran Desert
Southwestern United States

Area 108,000 sq miles (275,000 sq km)
Annual rainfall 3–10 in (75–250 mm)
Average highest temperature 119°F (48°C)
Average lowest temperature 32°F (0°C)

This is one of several neighboring deserts in the southwestern United States and Mexico. It is famous for cacti such as the giant saguaro cactus, although the most common plant is the strong-smelling creosote bush. Desert tortoises, pocket mice, kit foxes, bighorn sheep, and elf owls are among the wildlife.

Namib Desert
Southwest Africa

Area 81,000 sq miles (31,000 sq km)
Annual rainfall 0.2–3 in (5–75 mm)
Average highest temperature 113°F (45°C)
Average lowest temperature 32°F (0°C)

This narrow strip of desert gets most of its moisture from fog rolling in from the Atlantic Ocean. Moisture is gathered by long-leaved welwitschia plants, and by beetles that allow the fog to condense onto their cool bodies at night. This web-footed gecko is another Namib inhabitant.

Kalahari Desert
Southern Africa

Area 275,000 sq miles (712,250 sq km)
Annual rainfall 6–10 in (150–250 mm)
Average highest temperature 115°F (46°C)
Average lowest temperature 32°F (0°C)

Although parts of the Kalahari are true desert, many areas are dry savanna with thorn scrub and acacia trees. This is the home of the meerkat, plus larger animals such as wildebeests and flocks of flamingos that gather on floodwaters after rain.

Gobi Desert
Mongolia and northern China

Area 500,000 sq miles (1.3 million sq km)
Annual rainfall 0.4–10 in (10–250 mm)
Average highest temperature 113°F (45°C)
Average lowest temperature -40°F (-40°C)

The continental climate of the Gobi Desert creates temperature extremes that make life very difficult. Despite this, grasses and scattered low shrubs support animals such as desert hamsters, wild asses, gazelles, and wild two-humped Bactrian camels.

Great Victoria Desert
Southern Australia

Area 150,000 sq miles (338,500 sq km)
Annual rainfall 6–10 in (150–250 mm)
Average highest temperature 104°F (40°C)
Average lowest temperature 64°F (18°C)

Much of the interior of Australia is desert, with vast expanses of red sand and bare rock, dotted with scrub and tussock grass. The Great Victoria Desert is known for its many reptiles, including the ant-eating thorny devil lizard, the powerful sand goanna, and a variety of venomous snakes.

▶ DESERT PEA
Sturt's desert pea is a plant famous for its striking blood-red, black-centered flowers.

DESERT IN BLOOM
Even deserts get occasional rainstorms, with magical results. Seeds that have survived for years in the dry ground suddenly sprout, producing short-lived plants that all burst into flower at once. Here, the Sonoran Desert in Arizona is transformed as drifts of Coulter's lupine bloom between cacti and desert shrubs.

Life in the mountains

The higher you climb, the colder it gets, especially at night, which makes mountains harsh places to live. They are dangerous, too, because of steep cliffs and crags. Mountains are also often surrounded by lowlands where people live, so animals cannot move from peak to peak to find breeding partners.

SNOWY PEAKS

Temperature drops with elevation, at a rate of about 3.56°F per 1,000 ft (6.5°C for each 1,000 m). As a result, mountains can be divided into distinct zones, each supporting very different plant and animal life. Only the hardiest species survive year-round in the harsh habitat above the tree line (the elevation at which it becomes too cold for trees to grow).

▲ SNOW LEOPARD
Thick fur keeps this stealthy hunter warm, even in the deep snow above the tree line of the Himalayas.

ALPINE HEATH

Different altitudes favor different types of plants. Mount Kenya lies on the equator, and its lower slopes are covered in tropical grassland. Higher up, this gives way to forest, then bamboo scrub. Above this lies alpine heath, where plants like this tree groundsel are adapted to cope with hot days and freezing nights.

FAST FACTS

■ The tropical mountain climate has been described as summer every day, and winter every night.
■ Some mountain birds, such as the Andean condor, live on the carcasses of animals that have fallen to their deaths.
■ The highest parts of mountains are almost completely barren except for a few lichens, insects, and spiders.
■ Some high-mountain insects are so specialized for low temperatures that they die if they warm up.

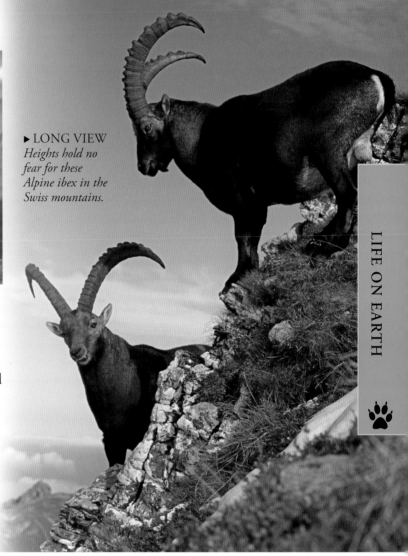

▶ LONG VIEW
Heights hold no fear for these Alpine ibex in the Swiss mountains.

BEATING THE CHILL

Many mountain animals have thick woolly coats to keep out the cold wind. They include this Andean llama, the angora, the mountain goat, and the squirrel-like chinchilla. Angora and llama wool is famously warm, and is often used to make winter clothing.

PEAK CONDITION

Rugged peaks and crags are dangerous places, and one wrong step can be fatal. Over time, this has ensured that only the most sure-footed animals survive long enough to breed. This harsh form of natural selection has resulted in the evolution of such amazingly agile creatures as the European chamois and ibex, and the American mountain goat.

FRAGILE BEAUTY

Despite the cold nights, several insect species thrive in the mountains. This Apollo butterfly lives in the flower meadows of high European mountains. Each butterfly group stays on its own mountain without interbreeding, and this has led to the evolution of many local subspecies.

ISOLATION

Some mountains are surrounded by farms that keep animals from traveling in search of breeding partners. This can lead to dangerous inbreeding—one reason why the giant panda has become so rare in the mountains of China. Animals' mountain habitats are also being destroyed by rising global temperatures.

Arctic tundra

The cold, almost treeless tundra is the zone of the Arctic lying between the northern forests and the polar ice. The landscape is frozen in winter because there is virtually no sunlight, but it thaws at the surface in the short summer, allowing plants to grow and insects to hatch. These attract animals from farther south, which leave again in winter.

FACT!

The thick white winter coat of the Arctic fox is so efficient that the fox only starts shivering if the temperature falls below -94°F (-70°C).

FROZEN SWAMPS

Over most of the tundra, the ground is permanently frozen below the surface. This layer of "permafrost" is waterproof, so although the ground surface thaws in summer, the meltwater cannot drain away. This creates vast areas of waterlogged peat dotted with bog pools, which form some of the largest swamps in the world. These freeze solid again when the temperature drops in winter.

▼ BLEAK LANDSCAPE
Trees are scarce on tundra because of the harsh climate and the way the ground keeps thawing and flooding.

SPRING THAW

When the Sun reappears in spring, it warms the ground, thawing the top layer of frozen earth. This gives the tundra plants their chance to grow, flower, and disperse their seeds in the patches of land that are not waterlogged. They are mostly very low-growing types that can resist strong, freezing winds often loaded with ice crystals. They include cotton grass (left), whose fluffy heads insulate the seeds against the cold, and miniature trees such as dwarf willow and dwarf birch.

184

SUMMER VISITORS

The summer flush of vegetation attracts herds of caribou, which migrate north to feed on the plants and breed. The plant and insect life also attracts flocks of birds, especially shorebirds and waterfowl like these snow geese. They fly north to the tundra to nest and raise their young, then fly south again when the temperature drops and the snow starts to fall.

BLOODSUCKING SWARMS

Tundra bog pools make ideal nurseries for the aquatic young of mosquitoes and blackflies. Later in the summer, the adults emerge in swarms that attack any animals they can find, driving caribou to higher ground to escape them.

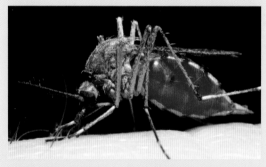

▲ BLOOD MEAL
Female mosquitoes like this one must drink blood to make their eggs. The males feed on flower nectar.

UNDER THE SNOW

At the end of summer, most birds and many of the big animals move south. Small mammals, such as voles and lemmings, stay on. Living in the grass beneath the snow protects them from the bitter winter chill. They are hunted by predators like this snowy owl, which can hear them moving under the snow.

SNOW SURVIVORS

Larger animals such as Arctic hares that spend the winter on the tundra shelter from the worst of the weather in snow burrows. But they feed in the open, where they risk being caught and eaten by wolves and Arctic foxes. The wolves also prey on the musk oxen (right) that stay on the tundra all year round. They are protected from the freezing winds by layers of fat and their long hairy coats.

185

Icy oceans

The open Arctic Ocean and the Southern Ocean around Antarctica freeze over in winter, then melt again in summer. The winter ice can seem almost lifeless but, as it melts, the midnight Sun of the polar summers encourages the growth of drifting, plantlike phytoplankton. These provide food for tiny creatures that multiply fast in the cold, oxygen-rich water, creating a feast for other animals.

LIVING WATERS

In winter, the phytoplankton lie dormant beneath the thick sea ice. As the Sun appears in spring, it thins the ice, so light gets through and the phytoplankton start multiplying. By midsummer, greenish blooms of phytoplankton spread across the oceans. Then, as winter approaches, the Sun sinks from sight and the sea freezes over again.

◄ SATELLITE VIEW
Swirling blooms of summer phytoplankton fill the Barents Sea in the Arctic.

DRIFTING SWARMS

Tiny creatures called zooplankton live under the winter ice alongside the phytoplankton. In spring, the zooplankton start eating the phytoplankton in vast quantities, and are soon breeding. Around Antarctica, small shrimplike krill swarm across huge areas of the Southern Ocean.

► TEEMING KRILL
Swarming Antarctic krill swim near the surface, where their massed bodies can make the ocean water appear red.

ANTIFREEZE

Plankton feed fish such as these Arctic cod, and are eaten by all kinds of marine animals, including bottom-living shellfish. Antifreezes in their blood allow these fish and shellfish to survive temperatures that can sink below freezing. Freshwater freezes at 32°F (0°C), but salt makes the freezing point of seawater lower, at about 28°F (-2°C).

FILTER-FEEDING GIANTS

Huge baleen whales use sievelike bristles lining their mouths to strain plankton from the cold water. Humpback whales have a special tactic, surging upward to engulf whole shoals of fish as well as plankton. In the seas around Antarctica, crabeater seals sift the water through their teeth to gather the swarming krill.

▼ AIRBORNE
A humpback whale launches itself out of the water in a spectacular demonstration of its size and power.

STREAMLINED HUNTERS

In the Southern Ocean, penguins, which look so clumsy on land, are transformed into sleek, streamlined hunters as they chase fish underwater. Other fish hunters include the southern elephant seal and the ringed seals of the Arctic. Small toothed whales, such as the narwhal and beluga, also take their share.

TOP PREDATORS

The final links in the food chain are the most powerful polar hunters—killer whales and polar bears. Killer whales roam the world's oceans, but polar bears hunt the Arctic sea ice. Their main prey are the ringed seals that breed on the ice floes. A polar bear can smell a seal from more than 20 miles (32 km) away, and kill it with a single blow of its paw.

WINTER CHILL

Most penguins nest on land, but emperors breed on the floating sea ice close to Antarctica. The penguins incubate their eggs through the bitter winter, huddling together for warmth. This ensures that the chicks hatch in spring, just as the weather improves. Here, a colony of adults and semigrown chicks battles the elements.

Life beneath the waves

The world's oceans average 12,470 ft (3,800 m) deep, but most oceanic animals live in the top 660 ft (200 m) or so—the sunlit zone. This is because the marine ecosystem is based on the microscopic phytoplankton that use the Sun's energy to make food. The phytoplankton are eaten by drifting zooplankton, which are targeted by fish. These are hunted by some of the most powerful predators on the planet.

Drifting phytoplankton are the oceanic equivalents of plants. They are tiny food factories that turn water and carbon dioxide into sugar, and use mineral nutrients to make proteins. If the water of the sunlit zone does not contain many nutrients, as in warm tropical oceans, there are very few phytoplankton. This is why tropical seas are so clear, but support fewer animals.

▲ MICROLIFE
Glassy diatoms and other phytoplankton soak up the energy of sunlight and use it to make the food that supports all oceanic life.

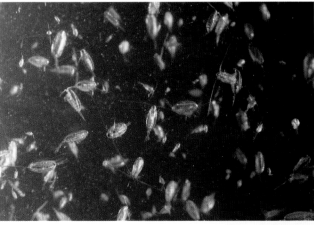

FREE DRIFTERS

The phytoplankton feed the tiny creatures known as zooplankton. These include adult animals, such as copepods, but also baby fish and the young stages of bottom-living creatures like crabs, barnacles, and clams. By drifting in ocean currents, these animals spread far and wide before settling in one place as adults.

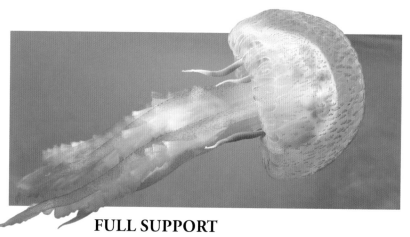

FULL SUPPORT

The salty seawater provides most of the nutrients that marine animals need. It also supports their bodies, so most do not need strong skeletons. This allows simple, soft-bodied, drifting creatures, such as this jellyfish, to flourish. On land, they would collapse, dry out, and die—as happens to jellyfish and even whales if they are washed ashore and stranded on beaches.

HUNGRY SHOALS

Small zooplankton provide food for fish such as anchovies and herring, which filter them from water flowing through their gills. Shoals of fish attract hunters such as tuna, marlin, and sharks. This blacktip reef shark has terrified its prey into forming a tight, swirling bait ball as they all try to hide behind each other.

FLOOR FEEDERS

Shallow seafloors are home to bottom-feeding fish such as cod and flatfish, various mollusks and anemones, spiny-skinned starfish and sea urchins, and crustaceans such as heavily armored crabs and lobsters. They feed on plankton, organic debris, and one another.

GENTLE GIANTS

The zooplankton are also targeted by huge filter-feeding whales and giant fish such as the whale shark, the basking shark, and the manta ray (below). These animals devour immense quantities of tiny sea creatures every day. They grow this large partly because of the way that the water supports their bodies.

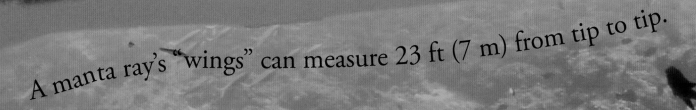

A manta ray's "wings" can measure 23 ft (7 m) from tip to tip.

Deep ocean

In open oceans, the water below about 660 ft (200 m) is too dark for plankton to make food using the energy of sunlight. Animals that live there must either visit the surface to feed, prey on each other, or eat debris sinking down from above. Most ocean-floor animals are scavengers or hunters. The only exceptions are the creatures that live around deep-sea volcanic vents.

UP AND DOWN

Swarms of zooplankton such as these tiny copepods swim up from the twilight zone at night to feed on plantlike phytoplankton near the ocean surface. They are trailed by hunters such as hatchetfish, which have upward-pointing eyes so they can see their prey against the faint starlight filtering down from above.

GLOWING IN THE DARK

Many deep-ocean creatures glow blue or green in the dark—a feature called bioluminescence. Some use this to attract mates, or to confuse enemies. A few hunters use red "spotlights" to target their prey, which cannot see red light. Some twilight-zone animals use blue light as camouflage, because it exactly matches the faint blue glow from the ocean surface.

▶ GLITTER BALL
This jellyfish uses a chemical reaction to emit an eerie blue light.

DEEP DIVERS

The mighty sperm whale dives deep into the twilight zone to prey on squid—including giant squid that can grow up to 46 ft (14 m) long. The air-breathing whale has special adaptations that enable it to stay underwater for up to 90 minutes before it has to come back to the surface to breathe.

NIGHTMARE HUNTERS

Many deepwater fish are predators with huge mouths, long needlelike teeth, super-acute senses, and enormous stretchable stomachs. Some even have spotlights to locate their targets, or luminous lures to tempt them within range. They need these extreme adaptations because prey is so hard to find. Once a hunter has found a victim, it must make sure it doesn't get away.

▲ DEATH TRAP
Meals are scarce in the deep. This ferocious viperfish plunges its long teeth deep into its victims so they cannot escape.

DEEP OCEAN FLOOR

Far below the surface lies the dark, cold world of the deep ocean floor. Most of the animals that live here feed on dead animals and plankton drifting down from above. They include debris-feeders like this sea cucumber, scavengers such as the slimy hagfish, and hunters such as rat-tail fish and chimeras. There are also anemones and worms that spend their lives attached to rocks or burrowing in soft mud.

CHEMICAL ENERGY

Volcanically active parts of the ocean floor are dotted with black smokers—rocky vents that gush hot, chemically rich water. Special microbes use the chemical energy to make food. Communities of crabs, clams, and giant tube worms crowd around the vents. They are among the few living things on the planet that do not rely on the energy of sunlight.

RED PLUMES ▶
This view from a deep-ocean research vehicle shows a cluster of giant tube worms, with plumes of red gills extending from their white tubes.

Coral reef

Tropical coral reefs are among the richest and most colorful wildlife habitats on Earth. They are built up by simple animals—corals—living in partnership with microbes that use the energy of sunlight to make food. This allows corals to live in clear tropical waters that contain few of the plankton that support life in cooler oceans. They provide a home for an amazing variety of fish and other sea creatures.

CORAL COLONIES

A coral is a creature resembling a sea anemone, with a crown of tentacles that it uses to catch small animals. Reef corals live in colonies where all the corals are linked to one another. Their transparent skin contains microscopic algae called zooxanthellae, which use solar energy to turn water and carbon dioxide into sugar.

◄ CORAL CROWN
A close-up view of a coral shows the tentacles that trap tiny drifting animals.

ROCKY REEFS

Reef-building corals absorb lime from the water, and use it to build skeletons of limestone. When old corals die, new corals grow on their rocky remains. Over the centuries, the rock builds up to form a reef. Many reefs are quite small, but others are enormous—the Great Barrier Reef (below) off the coast of Australia is 1,430 miles (2,300 km) long.

FACT!

The food-making microbes that live in the tissues of reef corals are so small that there may be more than 2 million of them in a fragment of coral the size of your fingernail.

CORAL ATOLLS

The tropical Pacific is dotted with extinct volcanic islands that are sinking into the ocean floor. The islands are fringed with coral reefs that grow upward as the islands sink. Gradually, fringing reefs turn into barrier reefs around the dwindling central islands. Eventually, the islands vanish, leaving coral atolls around shallow lagoons.

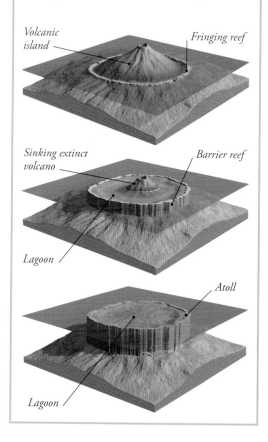

Volcanic island
Fringing reef

Sinking extinct volcano
Barrier reef

Lagoon

Atoll

Lagoon

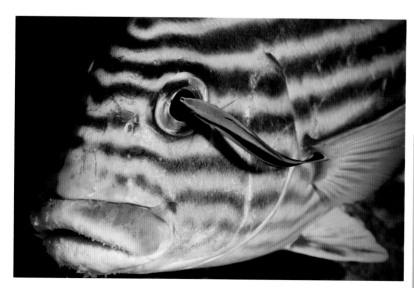

DAZZLING DIVERSITY

Coral reefs support an amazing diversity of sea life. This is because food is quite scarce, so reef animals have had to evolve unusual ways to survive, creating many species. One of the most intriguing is the bluestreak cleaner wrasse, which feeds on parasites that it picks off the skin of larger fish. It is so popular with its clients that they line up for treatment.

▲ VALET SERVICE
A cleaner wrasse wipes the eyes of an oriental sweetlips.

STARFISH PLAGUES

Coral reefs in the Indian and Pacific Oceans are often attacked by coral-eating crown-of-thorns starfish. These envelop the living coral and digest it, leaving just the stony reef skeletons. A big swarm of these spiny starfish can completely wreck a reef, but then the starfish run out of food and die off, allowing the reef to recover.

CORAL ISLANDS

The circular reefs known as atolls enclose shallow, sheltered lagoons, and are often topped by islands of white coral sand. The islands, and the trees that grow on them, are breeding sites for sea turtles and ocean birds such as these frigate birds.

▶ CORAL KILLER
The crown-of-thorns has sharp, venomous spines.

VITAL LIGHT

Tropical coral reefs are fueled by sunlight shining down through the clear, shallow water. The light gives algae the energy they need to turn water and carbon dioxide into sugar, creating the food that supports all the corals, reef fish, clams, shrimps, and other animals in one of the richest ecosystems on the planet.

On the shore

Many sea creatures live on tidal shores because they can find a lot to eat there. But seashores are dangerous places. They are exposed to waves that toss rocks around, crushing any animals that are in the way. Tidal zones also dry out at low tide—something that would kill most marine life. Few species are equipped to survive, but these few often flourish in vast numbers.

STRONG SHELLS

On rocky shores, many animals such as these limpets and barnacles have strong shells to resist the crash of the waves. The barnacles open up to gather food when they are submerged at high tide, while the larger limpets creep around, grazing on algae. But they all clamp shut or squeeze down tight when the falling tide leaves them exposed.

SLIPPERY SEAWEED

Like the attached animals of rocky shores, many coastal seaweeds can survive drying out as the tide falls twice a day. They grow in distinct zones, with a few very tough species growing high on the shore, and a much greater variety growing low down in the zone that is usually underwater.

◄ SHOREWEED
Rocks on the lower shore are often thick with layers of seaweed that flourish in the shallow, sunlit water.

CLAMS AND WORMS

Sandy shores are colonized by millions of burrowing animals. They include various types of clams, such as cockles, and marine worms like the lugworms that pushed up these worm casts. Most either feed on edible debris in the sand, or draw plankton-rich water into their bodies when they are submerged at high tide.

HUNGRY SHOREBIRDS

All the worms, clams, and other burrowing animals that live beneath beaches and mudflats attract flocks of hungry shorebirds. Many of these birds are specially adapted with long legs and long bills for wading in the shallows and probing into deep sand. Others forage on rocky shores, and use their shorter, stouter bills to flip over rocks and seize small animals as they try to escape.

▲ PROBING BILLS
The long bills of these curlew sandpipers have sensitive tips that allow them to feel for worms and other animals buried in the sand.

FAST FACTS

■ On some Australian beaches, up to 10,000 sea turtles come ashore every night to lay their eggs during the breeding season.
■ A sandy beach may conceal more than 2,000 buried shellfish such as cockles in every square yard (or meter) of sand.
■ On rocky shores, many sea creatures survive the hours of low tide in pools of seawater among the rocks.

MANGROVE SWAMPS

Sheltered tropical shores become overgrown by mangrove trees, which are able to grow in salt water and waterlogged, airless mud. They form swamp forests that flood with seawater at high tide. Many animals live among their roots, including the mudskipper—an extraordinary fish that can survive out of water, and even climb the low branches of mangrove trees.

BEACH SCAVENGERS

Crabs are sea creatures that cannot breathe air, but some carry supplies of oxygen-rich water that allow them to survive on the beach at low tide. They include the shore crab and the tropical ghost crab, which feed mainly on dead animals washed up by the waves. Tropical fiddler crabs also live out of the water, and feed by extracting edible particles from beach sand.

▼ TIME OUT
A ghost crab pauses on a South African beach before scuttling off in search of a meal.

THE HUMAN WORLD

The first modern humans were born just 200,000 years ago. In that tiny fraction of Earth's history, we have changed the face of the planet.

Population

For thousands of years before the invention of farming, the total human population was probably 15 million at most. Once people began to grow food about 9,000 years ago, the population began to increase, and by 1800 CE there were almost a billion people on Earth. With better technology and health care, the population has reached a staggering seven billion today.

THE HUMAN WORLD

LIVING OFF THE LAND

Until about 9,000 years ago, everyone lived by hunting animals and gathering wild food. Some tribal peoples around the world still do. Wild food is often seasonal and limited, which restricts how many people can live on the same area of land. This is one reason why the prehistoric population remained so small.

▶ HUNTER-GATHERERS
The San or bushmen in Namibia, southwest Africa, search for wild game, roots, and berries using methods unchanged for thousands of years.

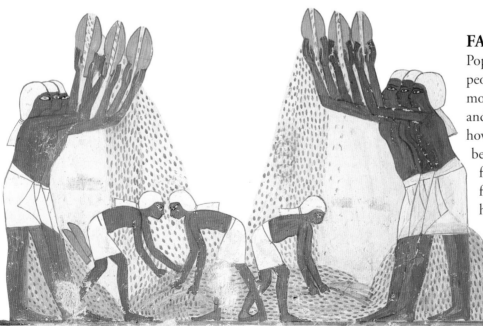

FARMING REVOLUTION

Populations began to rise when people figured out how to produce more food by domesticating animals and planting crops. They also learned how to dry and store crops that could be eaten in seasons when other foods were scarce. Storing extra food also meant that not everyone had to work on the land all year round—some people could do other work. By 3000 BCE, farmers such as these in Egypt were supporting a large and complex society.

ENERGY AND POPULATION

In Europe before about 1800, many people lived on the land and in poverty. Soon, however, coal was fueling the new steam-powered technologies in factories. As industries grew, so did workforces and the cities they lived in. By 1900, technology for refining oil (in refineries such as this one, above) created a new source of energy that fueled modern economies and rapidly expanding populations.

POPULATION GROWTH

In 1800, there were about 1 billion people living on the planet. This increased to roughly 2.5 billion by 1950, 3 billion by 1960, 6 billion by 2000, and 7 billion today. Experts believe that the global population will reach 8 billion by 2030, and could even grow to a colossal 9 billion by 2050.

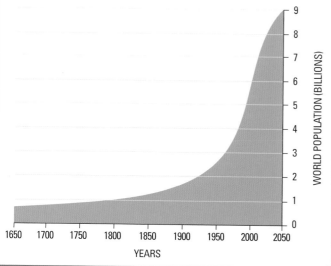

WORLD POPULATION (BILLIONS)

YEARS

▶ TEEMING CROWDS
One of the busiest crosswalks in the world is in Tokyo, Japan. The city is home to about 8.9 million people.

FIGHTING DISEASE

Throughout history, plagues have killed millions of people. The Black Death of 1346–1353, for example, spread across Asia and Europe and killed up to 200 million people. Thanks to medical advances, people now survive diseases that were once fatal, and vaccines protect against infection—by 1979, vaccinations had eradicated the deadly disease smallpox. These advances have allowed populations to grow quickly.

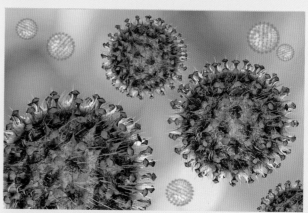

▲ KILLER VIRUS
A magnified image shows the influenza virus. A worldwide flu epidemic in 1918–1920 killed up to 50 million people.

IS THERE A LIMIT?

If the world's population rises to nine billion by 2050, we will have to produce 70 percent more food to ensure that everyone has enough to eat. Some scientists warn that our increasing use of natural resources threatens the future of the world's ecosystem—the global community of living things and their environments. As we rely on this for our survival, we may be close to reaching the limit of human population.

Farming

Since prehistoric times, people have been turning forests, wild grasslands, and even some deserts into farmland. For most of that time, the cropland has been fertilized by grazing livestock. As the world's population has grown, however, farmers have needed to produce more food by developing more intensive, mechanized methods that rely on chemical fertilizers and pesticides.

HERDING AND RANCHING

The first farmers were probably animal herders. Instead of hunting animals, they caught them and kept them for their milk, meat, and skins. The earliest herders may have followed animals as they roamed. Ranchers still herd animals today, driving them from pasture to pasture on open ranges for grazing.

SLASH AND BURN

The most primitive way of growing food is to clear an area of forest, burn the tree stumps, and plant crops on the soil fertilized by the ash. People in the Amazon rainforest have always farmed like this, but it only works on a small scale. The soil soon loses its nutrients and then more forest has to be cleared.

▼ OPEN RANGE
This rancher herds cattle across a vast open range in Idaho.

MIXED FARMING

If cattle or sheep are kept on an enclosed field, they eat the grass and drop manure that fertilizes the ground. The farmer can then plow the field and use the fertilized soil to grow crops, while the animals graze another field. After the crops are harvested, the animals can be brought back while the second field is sown with crops. Organic farming is still based on this method, which does not use farm chemicals.

INDUSTRIAL FARMING

Many farmers use artificial fertilizers instead of grazing animals on the land. This allows them to specialize in growing profitable crops, such as wheat, in large fields that can be harvested by large machines. But planting just a few crops can increase the risk of pests, diseases, and weeds, so these industrialized farms use a lot of chemical pesticides and weed killers. Over time, the soil can also become less healthy, and in serious cases it may turn to dust and blow away.

▲ WHEAT PRAIRIE
A huge combine harvester reaps a vast field of wheat in the American Midwest.

SELECTIVE BREEDING

Only the most basic farming uses species of animals and plants that are the same as those found in the wild. Most farm animals and crops are created by selecting the best examples and breeding them to ensure useful features such as better milk yield in cows, or size and flavor in fruits and vegetables. Selective breeding is also used to make crops more resistant to frost or disease, and has hugely boosted productivity.

◀ GREENHOUSE
If they are grown under glass, crops such as tomatoes can be produced all year round, even in cool or dry climates.

FARMING UNDER COVER

Some animals and many crops can be raised under cover. This allows more food to be produced in a smaller area, and also enables farmers to grow tender plants that would not survive outside. However, many people think that the intensive rearing of animals such as pigs and chickens is cruel. They also worry about the level of harmful pesticides that may be used on fruits and vegetables grown under glass.

▲ BRED FOR BEEF
The muscular Charolais cattle have been selectively bred for their high-quality beef.

TRANSFORMED LANDSCAPE

More and more of the natural wilderness is being
turned into farmland each year. These rice terraces in
Sapa, Vietnam, make use of steep hillsides to grow
food. In other parts of the world, huge areas of prairie
grassland have been turned into fields for growing
wheat and corn, and tropical forest is being replaced
by banana, soybean, and palm oil plantations.

Mining

People have been digging useful minerals from the ground for thousands of years. The earliest miners looked for pieces of flint to use as tools, and pure glittering metals such as silver and gold. Later miners extracted tin and copper from rock to make bronze, iron ore to make iron and steel, and other valuable materials such as building stone and precious gems. The coal, oil, and gas we use as fuel are also mined from the ground.

ANCIENT TECHNIQUES

Prehistoric miners dug shafts down into the ground to reach a seam (layer) of flint and then tunneled sideways along the seam to dig it out. Miners still use shafts and tunnels to dig for coal today. Other ancient mining techniques were less dangerous. They included panning for gold—a heavy metal that can be separated from river sand by rinsing it with water (below).

QUARRYING

Building stone must be cut out in blocks. In the past, quarrymen split the rock with wedges and hammers, or even explosives. But today many types of stone are sliced out with machine-operated saws studded with extra-hard minerals such as industrial diamonds.

OPEN-PIT MINES

Some of the largest mines are open holes in the ground, dug by colossal mechanical excavators. Huge trucks drive down access roads to the bottom of the mine to be loaded up. Open-pit mines are used for coal close to the surface, but the deepest pits are mines for metals such as copper and the radioactive uranium used as fuel in nuclear power plants.

OPEN PIT ▶
A truck rolls up the terraces of an open-pit mine, carrying 250 tons of rock. When the mine is exhausted, it will become a waste landfill.

DEEP SHAFTS

The most expensive and dangerous form of mining involves tunneling deep below ground. Horizontal galleries are linked to vertical shafts, which have lifts that carry miners down to seams. Deep-shaft mines have to be constantly drained of water and cooled, and miners such as these men in South Africa risk rockfalls and gas explosions.

FAST FACTS

■ The deepest mine is the TauTona gold mine in South Africa, which extends 2.4 miles (3.9 km) below the surface.

■ The deepest open-pit mine is the Bingham Canyon copper mine in Utah—0.75 miles (1.2 km) deep, it is the biggest artificial hole on Earth.

■ In 2009, an offshore oil well in the Gulf of Mexico was drilled to a depth of 6.6 miles (10.7 km).

DRILLING FOR OIL

By drilling boreholes down through rock, miners can reach reserves of liquid oil and natural gas. Deep beneath the ground, these fluids are often under pressure that squeezes them up the borehole to the surface. Offshore drilling platforms tap reserves beneath the seabed. This rig is drilling off the coast of California but some are towed out to far deeper waters.

Industry

People have always made and traded goods, but the late 18th century marked the beginning of the Industrial Revolution, when small workshops were replaced by large, machine-filled factories. Heavy industries such as steelmaking and shipbuilding employed whole towns of workers. Today, industry more often uses new technology and a small but skilled workforce to offer goods and services to customers near and far.

POWER

Early factories used waterwheels or large steam engines to provide the power for their machinery. Electric power is more convenient, because it can be used anywhere that can be connected to an electric cable. A constant, reliable supply of electricity is vital for modern industries, which depend more and more on computers and other electronic devices.

COTTAGE INDUSTRY

Despite the rise of modern manufacturing, many goods are still made by hand. Skilled workers like these potters make a living by producing things that local people need. They often make and sell their wares in areas of town that become known for certain types of products, such as leather bags and shoes on one street, and jewelry and metalwork on another.

FACTORIES

Large, mechanized factories were established from the 1750s onward, particularly in Britain, where the cotton industry used spinning machines and power looms. Later, industrialists such as American car manufacturer Henry Ford introduced assembly lines to speed up production. Today, these lines are often partly automated with robots controlled by computers.

▶ AUTOMATION
These welding robots in a car factory are fast and precise, and do not tire of doing the same task over and over again.

HEAVY INDUSTRY

The wealth of many of today's developed countries came originally from heavy industries such as steel production, oil refining, vehicle manufacturing, railroads, and shipbuilding (right). All of these enterprises require a huge investment in buildings and equipment, and use a lot of raw materials and fuel. They also need large, skilled workforces.

LIGHT INDUSTRY

With a reliable supply of electricity, small workshops can be set up almost anywhere. Many use traditional crafts such as woodworking or dressmaking, but others use new technology. Large or small, these companies are often at the cutting edge of research, making key breakthroughs in electronics, medicine, and new materials.

SERVICE INDUSTRY

Many modern industries do not produce any goods that you can touch. Instead, they provide services such as banking and finance, legal advice, or insurance. The London Stock Exchange (right) provides a service for investors worldwide, but your local hospital, restaurant, and movie theater provide services too.

▲ SKILLED WORK
Many light industries rely on the hands-on skills of their workers. These American technicians are assembling the main circuit boards of computers.

Transportation

The products of industry are used worldwide, thanks to efficient transportation networks that allow international trade. These networks also enable people to travel anywhere on the globe. Along with communications networks, power supplies, and water and drainage systems, transportation is part of the infrastructure of modern civilization.

SHIPPING

Shipping routes are among the oldest of all trade routes. The first sea traders stayed close to the coast so they knew where they were, but by 1000 BCE Phoenician traders were criss-crossing the Mediterranean Sea. Ships are still the best means of transporting heavy goods, and powerful engines and satellite navigation have greatly reduced the risks of long sea voyages.

▲ OCEAN TRADER
Stacked high with containers, each as large as a truck, this ship can carry a huge cargo between continents.

FACT!

Air travel has become so popular that, at any time of day or night, there are now half a million people flying through the world's skies.

INLAND WATERWAYS

Canal networks link many major cities. They were vital to the growth of industry, carrying coal and raw materials. Barges such as this one in Germany still carry heavy freights efficiently. They are slow, but this doesn't matter if a fleet of barges can deliver a continuous stream of cargo to its destination.

AIR TRAVEL

Air travel was once a luxury that few could afford, but in the 1970s cheaper air fares and the introduction of wide-body aircraft made long-distance travel possible for millions of people. Airlines carry a lot of lightweight cargo too, especially mail and perishable goods such as fruit and flowers. Smaller aircraft also provide regional transportation, which can be vital in large, sparsely populated countries such as Australia and Canada.

▶ TIME MACHINES
Jet aircraft have slashed the time it takes to travel vast distances, making the world seem smaller.

ROAD NETWORKS

Before the internal combustion engine was invented, road transportation moved at the speed of a horse. Now multilane highways link major cities and are connected to local roads that give access to even the smallest, most remote settlements. Road networks are vital for local travel, but also for the delivery of food, fuel, and other supplies.

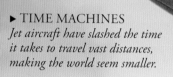

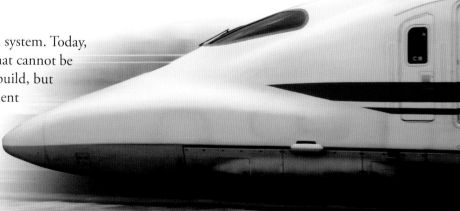

URBAN TRANSPORTATION

The major cities of the world could barely function without rapid transit systems that allow millions of people to move around quickly and efficiently—on buses, streetcars, local trains, and subway networks such as this one in Chengdu, China.

HIGH-SPEED RAIL

Railroads were the first high-speed transportation system. Today, modern electrified rail networks achieve speeds that cannot be matched on the road. Railroads are expensive to build, but once they are up and running they are more efficient than any other form of land transportation.

▶ BULLET TRAIN
The Shinkansen train can streak through the Japanese landscape at 186 mph (300 km/h).

Cities

The first cities were built about 7,000 years ago, amid fertile farmlands. Over time, many cities became rich through trade. Their wealth attracted raiding armies, so high walls were built around the cities to protect them from attack. Some of these ancient settlements are still thriving cities today. Modern cities, however, look very different, with geometric street plans and high-rise buildings of steel and glass.

THE FIRST CITIES

About 7,000 years ago, farming in Mesopotamia (present-day Iraq) produced enough wealth to support the first cities. These are now ruined, but similar cities of narrow alleys and mud-brick houses survive in countries such as Morocco, North Africa (left).

CITY-STATES

Cities often become centers of culture and civilization. This was the case in the city-states of Ancient Greece, which were ruled like small countries. Athens (above) was the greatest of these, but modern examples such as Monaco and Singapore also flourish.

TRADING WEALTH

Cities need food and other goods, which are supplied by traders. All the buying and selling in their busy marketplaces generates profits and wealth, which encourages more trade and more wealth. Many cities lying on major trade routes grew rich in this way, and their wealth paid for spectacular buildings designed to impress.

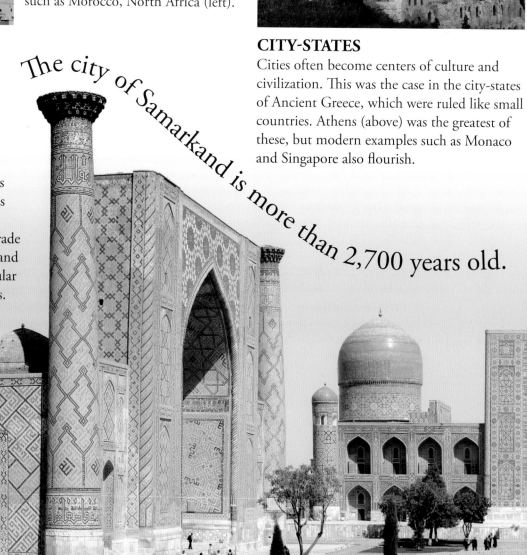

The city of Samarkand is more than 2,700 years old.

CITY WALLS

In the past, wealthy cities were a target for bandits and armies. Many were defended by walls and towers, plus ditches and secondary walls. This image of Carcassonne in medieval France shows how the walls surrounded the entire city, including its castle, church, and all the houses.

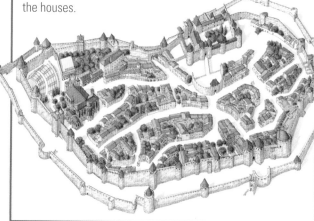

MASTER PLANS

Most ancient cities grew over time without any real planning, and many of their winding streets were once country roads. But some cities were built according to an organized plan— this aerial view of Amsterdam in the Netherlands shows its 17th-century web of semicircular canals. Modern cities are usually laid out on a grid plan of rectangular blocks.

HIGH-RISE

Many old cities have been transformed by modern architecture, and some newer cities are almost entirely composed of high-rise towers. Supported by frames of steel girders and clad in glass, they allow huge numbers of people to live and work within a small area.

▲ HONG KONG SKYSCRAPERS
Perched between hills and sea on China's south coast, Hong Kong is home to 7 million people.

▼ GATEWAY TO THE EAST
Wealthy Samarkand in Central Asia lay on the Silk Road—the medieval trade route between China and the Mediterranean. It is now the second largest city in Uzbekistan.

Modern cities

Today, more than half of the world's population lives in cities, drawn by the opportunities for work and wealth. As a result, many cities are now very large. Not all of this growth has been planned, however, and cities in developing countries are sometimes fringed by sprawling shantytowns with poor housing and no proper services.

New York
United States of America

Area 303 sq miles (786 sq km)
Population 8.4 million
Founding date 1609

Originally a Dutch colony known as New Amsterdam, New York's name changed when it was surrendered to the English in 1664. Its huge natural harbor on the Atlantic coast made it an important trading port, and it became the main point of entry for European immigrants to the United States. New York is now the largest and most prosperous city in North America, and is famous worldwide as a financial, commercial, and cultural center.

▼ THE BIG APPLE
The high-rise skyline of New York City is an emblem of American wealth and aspiration.

Rio de Janeiro
Brazil

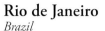

Area 462 sq miles (1,198 sq km)
Population 6.3 million
Founding date 1565

Rio is the second largest city in Brazil, and the most spectacular. It lies along the shores of Guanabara Bay on the Atlantic coast, famous for its dramatic granite landscapes and beautiful beaches. Rio Carnival is the largest festival of its kind in the world, and attracts millions of tourists every year.

Cairo
Egypt

Area 175 sq miles (453 sq km)
Population 7.2 million
Founding date 969 CE

Although it is near several ancient Egyptian sites, including the pyramids of Giza, Cairo itself was founded on the Nile River by the Islamic Fatimid dynasty in the 10th century. The "city of a thousand minarets" is famous for its Islamic architecture, but it is also a vibrant modern city—the political and cultural capital of Egypt.

Rome
Italy

Area 505 sq miles (1,308 sq km)
Population 2.8 million
Founding date 753 BCE

The capital of Italy, Rome was once the capital of the Roman Empire, which controlled Europe for more than 500 years until 476 CE. Today, its rich heritage of ancient Roman, medieval, and Renaissance architecture attracts visitors from all over the world.

Paris
France

Area 41 sq miles (105 sq km)
Population 2.2 million
Founding date Before 52 BCE

Famous as one of the most romantic cities in the world, Paris is the capital and cultural center of France. The city lies at the heart of one of the largest urban areas in Europe, home to 12 million people, and the whole region is responsible for more than a quarter of France's national wealth.

Moscow
Russian Federation

Area 969 sq miles (2,510 sq km)
Population 11.5 million
Founding date Before 1147

Moscow lies farther north than any of the world's other great cities, and is noted for its very long, cold winters. Despite this, it is Russia's largest city and the sixth-largest in the world. At its center lies the medieval fortress of the Kremlin, which is still the center of government today.

Beijing
China

Area 6,336 sq miles (16,410 sq km)
Population 19.6 million
Founding date 1045 BCE

Beijing has been the capital of China for most of its 3,000-year history. The imperial palace, known as the Forbidden City, is a spectacular complex of 980 medieval buildings hidden behind huge stone walls. The surrounding city is one of the largest in the world, and the political and cultural hub of the nation.

London
United Kingdom

Area 607 sq miles (1,570 sq km)
Population 8.3 million
Founding date 43 CE

Founded by the Romans soon after their invasion of Britain, London was sited near the mouth of the Thames River. It was a major port for many centuries, and is still one of the world's leading financial, cultural, and educational centers. The capital is home to about 12 percent of the UK population, with more than 300 languages spoken there.

CITY LIGHTS

This image of the world at night
shows cities and towns spread over
Earth's surface. Taken from satellite
data, it shows the high population
density of regions such as the United
States and Europe. The bright
concentrations of light are major
urban areas, including some on the
coasts of South America and Africa.

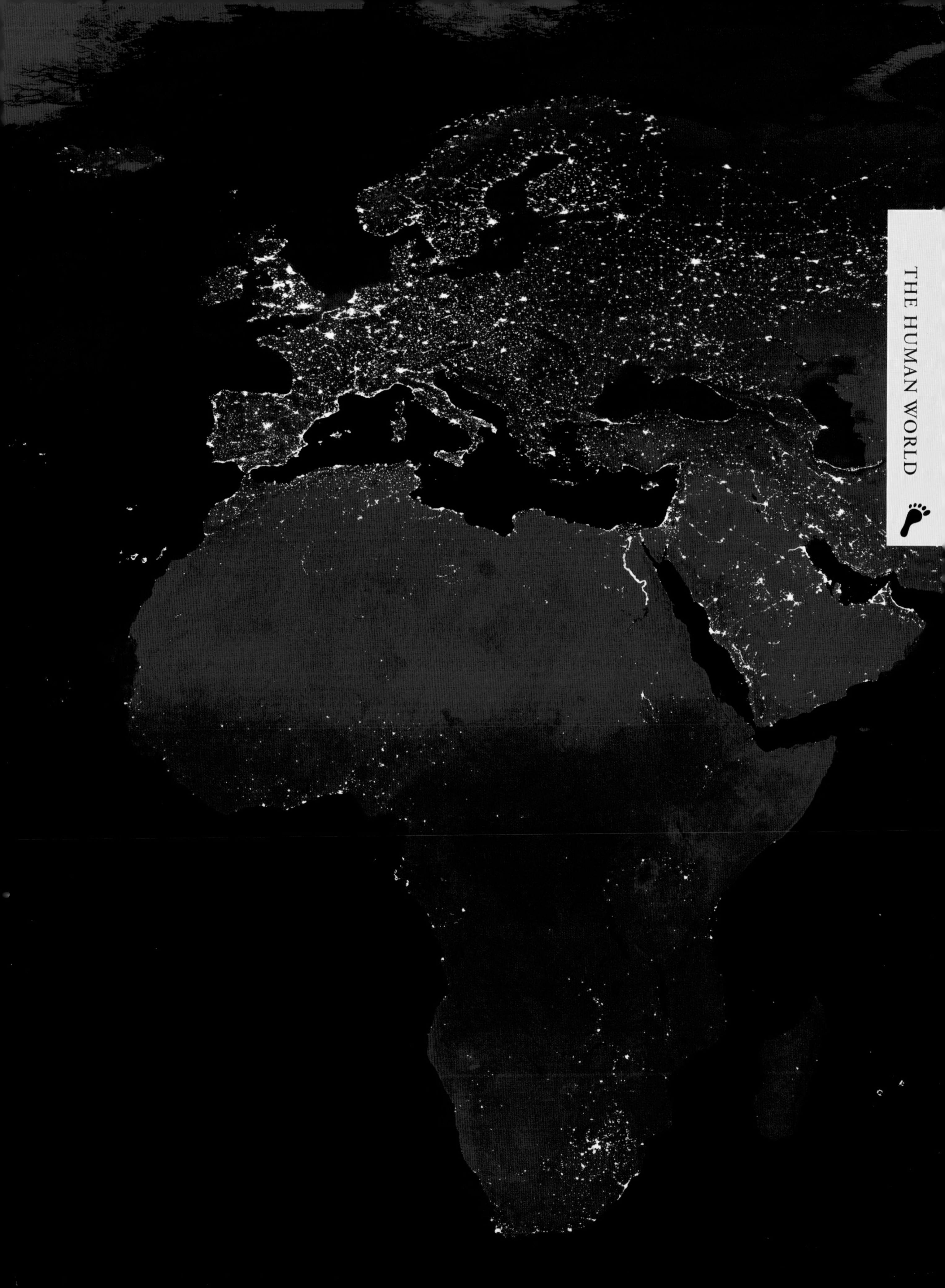

Pollution

The growing human population is producing more and more waste, ranging from sewage to spent radioactive fuel. Dealing with all this waste is a huge problem. Much of it is just dumped, buried, pumped into the atmosphere, or poured into rivers and oceans. The resulting pollution is inflicting terrible damage on nature—and on our health.

GARBAGE
Until the mid-20th century, most of the waste we produced was buried and slowly decayed. But most modern plastics are almost indestructible by any natural process, so they pile up in great multicolored heaps of garbage. Much of it ends up in the oceans, where it kills wildlife.

▼ BLIGHTED BEACH
Goats, cats, and birds scavenge for edible scraps among the plastic garbage swept onto this North African beach by the waves.

DEADLY FILTH
Over much of the world, untreated sewage from badly drained towns pours into rivers and seas, causing water pollution that spreads disease. It also upsets the balance of nature by making the water too rich in plant nutrients. This can encourage the explosive growth of toxic algae that kill other organisms such as these fish.

TOXIC WASTE
Industries such as mining, papermaking, and chemical manufacturing produce poisonous wastes. These are often released into rivers, killing everything farther downstream. The wildlife may recover from one accidental spill, but industries that routinely release toxic waste can poison entire river systems.

SMOG AND ACID RAIN

Factories, power plants, road vehicles, aircraft, and even cooking fires release masses of soot and waste gas into the atmosphere every day. The soot and gases can cause dangerous clouds of thick, choking smog, especially in cities. Some gases may also combine with water vapor in the air to form acid rain, which kills trees and fish.

OIL SPILLS

Although shipwrecks are less common today thanks to advances in navigation technology, oil tankers still occasionally hit rocks and spill their cargoes into the sea. The oil is deadly to marine wildlife, and if it comes ashore it causes terrible coastal pollution.

▼ SMOG CITY
On a warm day, a thick layer of pollution from traffic fumes and industrial emissions settles over Jakarta, Indonesia.

FACT!

In December 1952, a four-day smog in London killed more than 4,000 people. The thick, dirty fog was caused by smoke from coal fires, which are now banned in the city.

ACIDIFIED OCEANS

Vehicles and factories release vast amounts of carbon dioxide into the atmosphere each day. Much of the gas is absorbed by the oceans and turns into carbonic acid, which is making the oceans less alkaline. This is disastrous for animals such as corals that cannot survive without alkaline minerals. This coral reef in the Philippines is dying.

Climate change

The world is warming up. Records show a steady increase in average global air temperature, which is melting polar ice and altering the pattern of the world's weather. The temperature rise is caused by a change in the nature of the atmosphere that makes it retain more heat. This change has been brought about by more than 200 years of air pollution, caused by burning coal, oil, and other fossil fuels.

WARMING WORLD

Since the 1880s, the world has warmed by an average of almost 1.8°F (1°C). It doesn't sound like much, but altogether the world has warmed by only 7°F (4°C) over the past 12,000 years, so the rate of warming is speeding up. The evidence is plain to see in the Arctic, where the area of ocean covered by ice in the late summer of 2012 was 18 percent smaller than any other September on record.

GREENHOUSE EFFECT

Certain atmospheric gases such as carbon dioxide, methane, and water vapor act like the glass of a greenhouse. They let sunshine through to heat Earth's surface but stop the heat from escaping into space. This keeps us warm—indeed, without it the planet would be too cold for life to exist. But more "greenhouse gases" in the atmosphere are boosting the greenhouse effect and raising global temperatures.

Some heat escapes, but gases trap the rest

Sun's rays penetrate the atmosphere

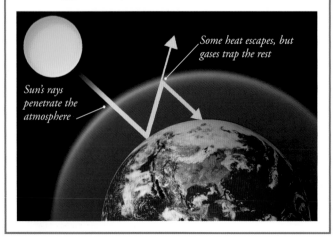

▲ BLEAK FUTURE
Polar bears live on the Arctic sea ice. As it melts away, they have nowhere to hunt, and could become extinct.

FAST FACTS

■ In 2003, a heatwave in Europe killed up to 50,000 people.
■ Rising ocean temperatures trigger more storms, which then cause chaos on nearby continents.
■ Since 1990, 163,000 sq miles (423,000 sq km) of forest—an area the size of California—have been felled in Brazil.
■ If climate change melts the Antarctic and Greenland ice sheets, sea levels could rise by up to 82 ft (25 m).

FOSSIL FUELS

Atmospheric levels of carbon dioxide, the main greenhouse gas, have increased by 30 percent since 1900. Scientists agree that this has been caused by burning coal, oil, and gas—the remains of life that was fossilized millions of years ago. The carbon they contain is released as carbon dioxide when the fuel is burned.

RISING SEA LEVELS

The fringes of continental ice sheets are breaking up, dumping continental ice into the oceans as icebergs. This is steadily raising global sea levels, and is already causing flooding on low-lying coral islands in the south Pacific. Ultimately, rising sea levels could permanently flood coastal cities such as Shanghai and New York. Frozen ground in the Arctic is also thawing out, releasing methane that is an even more potent greenhouse gas than carbon dioxide.

BURNING FORESTS

In many parts of the world, vast areas of forest are being cut down and burned. Trees absorb carbon dioxide when they are growing, and use the carbon to make their timber. But if a forest is felled and burned, all the carbon in the timber is turned into carbon dioxide again, and released into the air to add to the greenhouse effect.

NEW TECHNOLOGY

These solar panels generate electricity by absorbing the energy of the Sun. They don't use fossil fuels, so they don't add to the greenhouse effect that is causing climate change. If we could generate all our energy using this kind of technology, we could fix the problem. But meanwhile we can all help by using as little energy as possible.

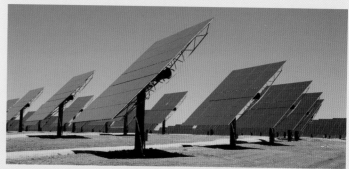

▶ CRUMBLING ICE
As more glacier ice tumbles into the sea, it adds to the volume of ocean water.

Conservation

The future of the world depends on maintaining a healthy biosphere—the web of life that produces our food and makes the air fit to breathe. We can help keep it healthy by protecting threatened species and the wild places where they live. In the process, we also help maintain the beauty of the natural world.

PROTECTED SPECIES

The simplest form of conservation is to protect certain species by making it illegal to kill them. Such bans have to be global in order to work, and international treaties have helped in the case of animals such as elephants and whales. As long as these laws are enforced, they can help endangered species recover from near extinction.

▲ THREATENED CAT
Rare animals such as tigers are protected by laws that make hunting them a criminal offense.

ILLEGAL TRADE

There are laws banning the trade in endangered species and goods such as ivory, rhino horns, and tiger skins. But demand for illegal goods remains, encouraging poachers to break the laws. Wildlife rangers often have to cope with armed poachers and carry out raids to confiscate illegal materials.

◀ BLACK-MARKET IVORY
Conservation officers inspect a huge haul of illegal elephant tusks recovered from a rogue trader.

UMBRELLA SPECIES

Many people are eager to protect certain rare animals such as the giant panda, but are not so concerned about the fate of less famous species. However, pandas cannot survive unless the ecosystem that supports them survives too. By working to protect panda habitats, we may also ensure the survival of other animals and plants.

▲ PROTECTING THE PANDA
Giving the giant panda a future in the wild has helped conserve other species that share its forest habitat.

WILDLIFE RESERVES

Protecting endangered species often involves turning areas of land into wildlife reserves like this one on the African savanna. Other reserves protect wildernesses such as peat bogs, rainforests, or even coral reefs. Such places can pay for their cost of operation by earning money as tourist attractions.

CONSERVING HABITATS

Wildlife reserves are important, but they cover only small areas of the world—often far too small to secure the future of the wildlife that lives in them. This means that conservation efforts need to be coordinated over much wider areas, such as all forests, all wild grasslands, and all the oceans.

◀ FRAGILE BEAUTY
This woodland in northern England supports diverse wildlife, from tiny mosses and insects to lofty conifers. Such habitats are easily destroyed but almost impossible to replace.

MAPPING THE WORLD

Thanks to the latest satellite technology and powerful computers, maps can now show us the whole world with more accuracy and detail than ever before.

The physical world

Just under 30 percent of Earth's surface is land, mostly contained in giant continental landmasses. Around the seven continents, tens of thousands of islands are scattered across the world's seas and oceans. People have been exploring and mapping the globe for thousands of years, to chart its wealth of natural features and mark their place in the world.

Horizontal lines of latitude show how many degrees north or south places are from the equator.

ANDES MOUNTAINS

Running through seven countries on the west coast of South America, the Andes form the longest mountain range in the world. More than 4,500 miles (7,000 km) long and up to 199 miles (320 km) wide, the Andes are rich in metals and also contain most of South America's volcanoes.

VICTORIA FALLS

Around 39.5 million gallons (180 million liters) of water flows over Victoria Falls every minute. Located on the Zambezi River in southern Africa, the waterfall is 5,500 ft (1.68 km) wide and 355 ft (108 m) high.

FRASER ISLAND

Sand carried by the ocean can form
mounds, which over time become islands.
Fraser Island, off the coast of Queensland,
Australia, is the world's biggest sand island.
It measures 76 miles (123 km) long and
14 miles (22 km) across at its widest point.
Its surface is heavily forested and contains
more than 100 freshwater lakes.

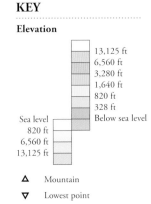

KEY

Elevation

	13,125 ft
	6,560 ft
	3,280 ft
	1,640 ft
	820 ft
	328 ft
Sea level	Below sea level
820 ft	
6,560 ft	
13,125 ft	

△ Mountain

▽ Lowest point

Sandy desert

Marsh

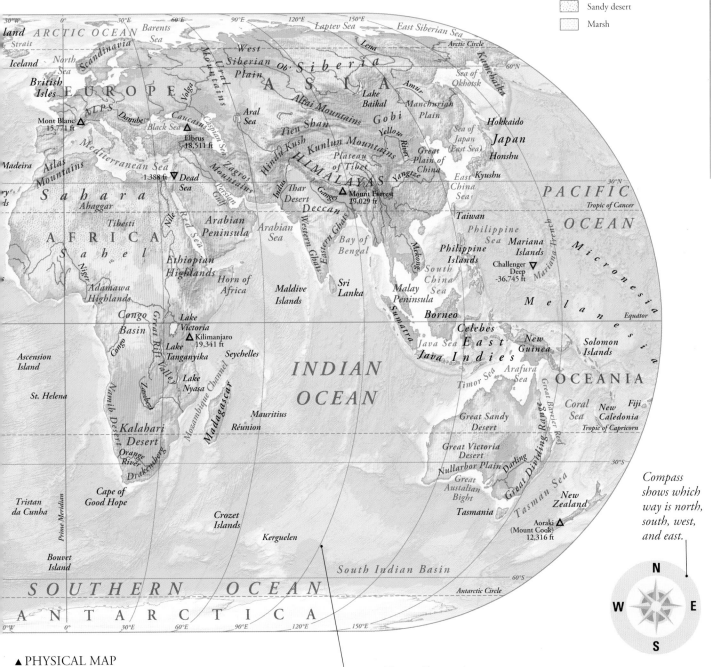

*Compass
shows which
way is north,
south, west,
and east.*

▲ PHYSICAL MAP

*This map shows Earth's physical geography at a glance.
It uses different colors for different landscapes and their
height above sea level, which you can check against the key.
The scale bar shows you how distance on the map compares
to miles and kilometers on the ground.*

*Vertical lines of longitude
show how many degrees
east or west places are
from the line called the
prime meridian at 0°.*

Scale 1:103,000,000

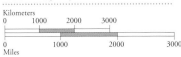

Kilometers

Miles

The political world

Almost all of the world's land is claimed by countries or nations. The largest nation by area is the Russian Federation, with almost twice the land area of the second-largest, Canada. Some countries have a single neighbor while others have many more. China shares land borders with 16 different countries. A fifth of the world's countries are landlocked, with no direct outlet to Earth's seas or oceans.

Some territories belong to other countries (in this case, to France).

VATICAN CITY

Surrounded by the Italian capital city of Rome, Vatican City is the world's smallest independent state. The center of the Roman Catholic religion, the state has a total land area of just 0.17 square miles (0.44 sq km). That's two-thirds the size of the Disneyland theme park in California.

NEW COUNTRIES

In 2011, South Sudan became independent from Sudan to form the newest country in Africa. New nations can be formed by splitting one country or by joining together separate states. In 1990, East and West Germany reunified to form one country.

ARCTIC OCEAN

Arctic Circle

Alaska (to US)

60°N

Aleutian Islands (to US)

CANADA

Baffin Bay

Great Lakes

PACIFIC OCEAN

UNITED STATES OF AMERICA

St. Pierre & Miquelon (to France)

ATLANTIC OCEAN

30°N

Midway Islands (to US)

Tropic of Cancer

Bermuda (to UK)

Hawaii (to US)

MEXICO

Gulf of Mexico

BAHAMAS

CUBA

DOMINICAN REPUBLIC

HAITI

BELIZE   JAMAICA

GUATEMALA   HONDURAS

EL SALVADOR   NICARAGUA

COSTA RICA

PANAMA

Caribbean Sea

BARBADOS

TRINIDAD & TOBAGO

VENEZUELA

GUYANA

French (to France)

SURINAM

COLOMBIA

Equator

Wallis & Futuna (to France)

KIRIBATI

Galapagos Islands (to Ecuador)

ECUADOR

PERU

BRAZIL

Tokelau (to NZ)

Cook Islands (to NZ)

PACIFIC OCEAN

SAMOA

American Samoa (to US)

TONGA   Niue (to NZ)

French Polynesia (to France)

BOLIVIA

Tropic of Capricorn

PARAGUAY

Pitcairn Islands (to UK)

CHILE

30°S

ARGENTINA

URUGUAY

Falkland Islands (to UK)

60°S

Antarctic Circle

SOUTHERN OCEAN

150°W   120°W   90°W

INTERNATIONAL BORDERS

Borders are dividing boundaries between nations. The border between the United States and Mexico is 1,970 miles (3,169 km) long and one of the busiest in the world, with 20 million crossings each year. The U.S. also shares the world's longest border with a single nation, Canada, stretching 5,525 miles (8,891 km).

▼ POLITICAL MAP
This political map shows the borders between countries. By the end of 2012, there were 194 independent, internationally recognized countries in the world.

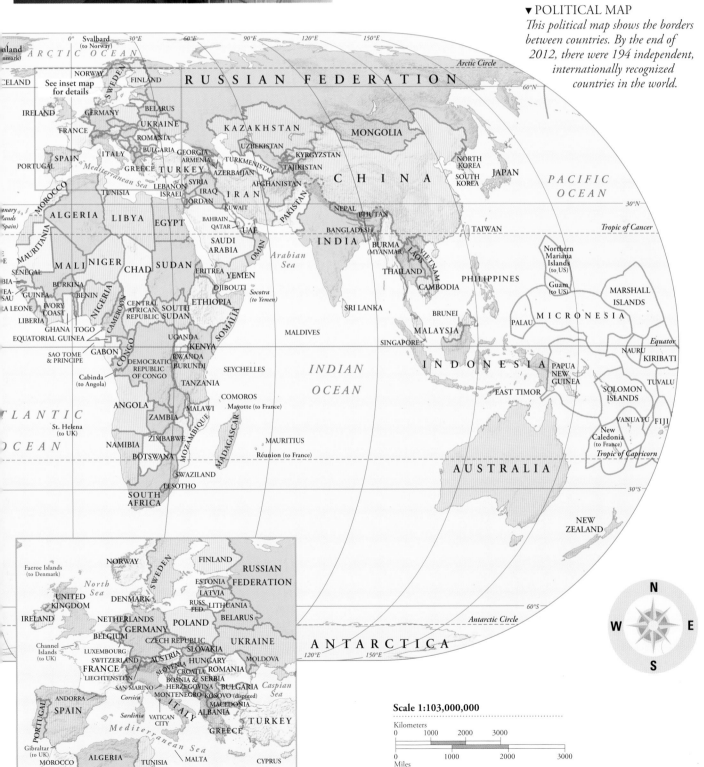

Scale 1:103,000,000

Kilometers
0   1000   2000   3000

0   1000   2000   3000
Miles

231

Population density

In 2011, the human population passed seven billion for the first time. Sixty percent of the world's peoples are found in Asia, with China (1.35 billion) and India (1.21 billion) far and away the world's most populous nations. However, people are not spread evenly around the planet, so similar-sized countries can have very different numbers of inhabitants.

LOW DENSITY

The large Asian nation of Mongolia has a population of just 2.67 million, yet it is more than four times the size of the United Kingdom, which has more than 60 million inhabitants. Mongolia's population density is just 4.4 people per sq mile (1.7 people per sq km), with most people living in urban areas.

POPULATION BOOM

Between 1990 and 2010, India's population grew by 40 percent and it now has a sixth of the world's population. There are 200 million more people in India than in the whole of Africa, and experts predict that India may overtake China as the world's most populous country by 2030.

Toronto 5.7m
New York 8.4m
Mexico 20.1m
Lima 8.5m
São Paolo 11.2m
Buenes Aires 13m

Arctic Circle
60°N
30°N
Tropic of Cancer
Equator
Tropic of Capricorn
30°S
60°S
Antarctic Circle
150°W   120°W   90°W

232

HIGH DENSITY

The tiny European principality of Monaco is just 0.76 sq miles (1.98 sq km). Although only around 35,000 people live there, Monaco has the highest population density of any country in Europe at more than 43,250 people per sq mile (17,000 people per sq km).

KEY

Population density
(people per square mile)

	more than 520
	260 to 520
	130 to 260
	26 to 130
	2.6 to 26
	less than 2.6

● cities and their populations (in millions)

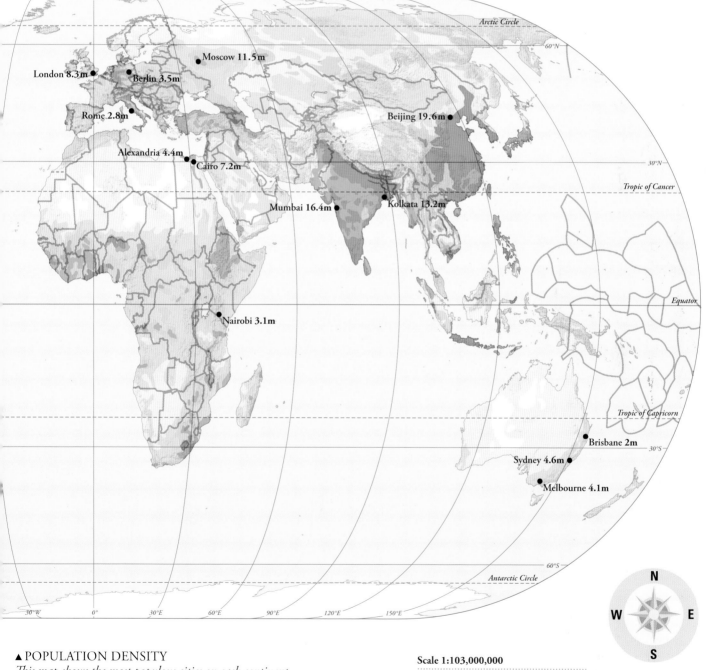

London 8.3m
Berlin 3.5m
Moscow 11.5m
Rome 2.8m
Beijing 19.6m
Alexandria 4.4m
Cairo 7.2m
Mumbai 16.4m
Kolkata 13.2m
Nairobi 3.1m
Brisbane 2m
Sydney 4.6m
Melbourne 4.1m

Arctic Circle
60°N
30°N
Tropic of Cancer
Equator
Tropic of Capricorn
30°S
60°S
Antarctic Circle

30°W 0° 30°E 60°E 90°E 120°E 150°E

▲ POPULATION DENSITY

This map shows the most populous cities on each continent. Some also include sprawling urban areas that spread out around the cities themselves. Beijing, China, tops the list with just under 20 million.

Scale 1:103,000,000

Kilometers
0   1000   2000   3000

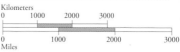

0   1000   2000   3000
Miles

233

North America

The third-largest of the seven continents, North America lies entirely in the Northern Hemisphere and has a population of more than 528 million people. Dominated by Canada and the United States, its land area of more than 9.3 million sq miles (24 million sq km) stretches from frozen tundra in the Arctic down through spectacular mountain ranges, prairies, and desert scrub to the tropical rainforests of Central America.

CANADIAN PRAIRIES

These vast swaths of grassland possess fertile soil suitable for farming. They are part of the Great Plains that stretch for 1.2 million sq miles (3 million sq km) from the Mississippi River to southern Canada, and they make up four-fifths of Canada's farmland. Canada is a leading exporter of wheat, rapeseed, and soybeans, among other products.

▶ GREENLAND
Greenland is the world's largest island. Although physically part of the North American continent, it is officially part of the Kingdom of Denmark, in Europe.

234

The scale shows that this map is 38 million times smaller than the continent.

Scale 1:38,000,000

Kilometers 0 300 600 900
Miles 0 300 600 900

KEY

Elevation

13,125 ft
6,560 ft
3,280 ft
1,640 ft
820 ft
328 ft
Sea level
Below sea level

Sea level
820 ft
6,560 ft
13,125 ft

△ Mountain
▽ Lowest point

Settlements

■ Capital city
● over 1 million
◎ 500,000 to 1 million
◉ 100,000 to 500,000
○ below 100,000

ATLANTIC OCEAN

UNITED STATES OF AMERICA

Coast Ranges
Great Basin
Great Plains
Appalachian Mountains

Boston
Hartford
Albany
New York
Philadelphia
Baltimore
WASHINGTON, D.C.
Richmond
Raleigh
Columbia
Jacksonville
Toronto
Detroit
Cleveland
Chicago
Columbus
Indianapolis
Nashville
Atlanta
Montgomery
Memphis
Jackson
Saint Louis
Little Rock
Oklahoma City
Kansas City
Des Moines
Lincoln
Saint Paul
Denver
Albuquerque
El Paso
Phoenix
Salt Lake City
Boise
Reno
Sacramento
San Francisco
Oakland
San Jose
Los Angeles
San Diego
Las Vegas
Death Valley -282 ft▽
Tijuana
Mexicali
Hermosillo
Ciudad Juárez
Chihuahua
Monterrey
Dallas
Austin
San Antonio
Houston
Baton Rouge
New Orleans
Tampa
Miami
Nassau

Lake Superior
Lake Huron
Lake Ontario
Lake Erie
Lake Michigan
Great Salt Lake
Columbia
Colorado
Missouri
Ohio
Mississippi
Arkansas
Rio Grande
Mississippi Delta

MEXICO
Sierra Madre Occidental
Sierra Madre Oriental
Guadalajara
León
Querétaro
MEXICO CITY
Puebla
Volcán Pico de Orizaba 18,701 ft △
Acapulco
Mérida
Yucatán Peninsula
Gulf of California
Lower California
Gulf of Mexico

BAHAMAS
NASSAU
Turks & Caicos Islands (to UK)
CUBA
HAVANA
Guantanamo Bay (to US)
Cayman Islands (to UK)
HAITI
PORT-AU-PRINCE
DOMINICAN REPUBLIC
SANTO DOMINGO
JAMAICA
KINGSTON
Greater Antilles
Caribbean Sea
Lesser Antilles
West Indies
British Virgin Islands (to UK)
Virgin Islands (to US)
Puerto Rico (to US)
SAN JUAN
Anguilla (to UK)
ANTIGUA & BARBUDA
ST. KITTS & NEVIS
Montserrat (to UK)
Guadeloupe (to France)
DOMINICA
Martinique (to France)
ST. LUCIA
BARBADOS
ST. VINCENT & THE GRENADINES
GRENADA
Aruba (to Neth.)
Curaçao (to Neth.)
Bonaire (to Neth.)
TRINIDAD & TOBAGO
PORT-OF-SPAIN

GUATEMALA
GUATEMALA CITY
BELIZE
BELMOPAN
HONDURAS
TEGUCIGALPA
EL SALVADOR
SAN SALVADOR
NICARAGUA
MANAGUA
Lake Nicaragua
COSTA RICA
SAN JOSÉ
PANAMA
PANAMA CITY
Panama

SOUTH AMERICA

LAS VEGAS

In 1910, a year before it officially became a city, Las Vegas, Nevada, had a population of just 800 people and was surrounded by desert. Today, its population of more than 580,000 residents is continuously swelled by millions of visitors to its famous casinos, hotels, and entertainment.

MONUMENT VALLEY

A famous landmark on the Colorado Plateau in the southwestern United States, Monument Valley contains a number of distinctive steep-sided, isolated hills called buttes. These sandstone monuments reach up to 1,000 ft (300 m) and were formed when the surrounding terrain was eroded.

South America

South America is the fourth-largest continent, with a land area of just over 6.9 million sq miles (17.8 million sq km). Running almost the entire western length of the continent, the Andes mountain range contains the highest peak in the Americas, Mount Aconcagua. East of the Andes lies the giant Amazon River basin, with an area of 2.7 million sq miles (7 million sq km) mostly covered in tropical rainforest.

SÃO PAULO, BRAZIL

The largest country in South America, Brazil has a population of more than 197 million. It is the fifth-largest nation in the world, by population and area. The largest city in Brazil and the Southern Hemisphere is São Paulo, which is home to 11.2 million people.

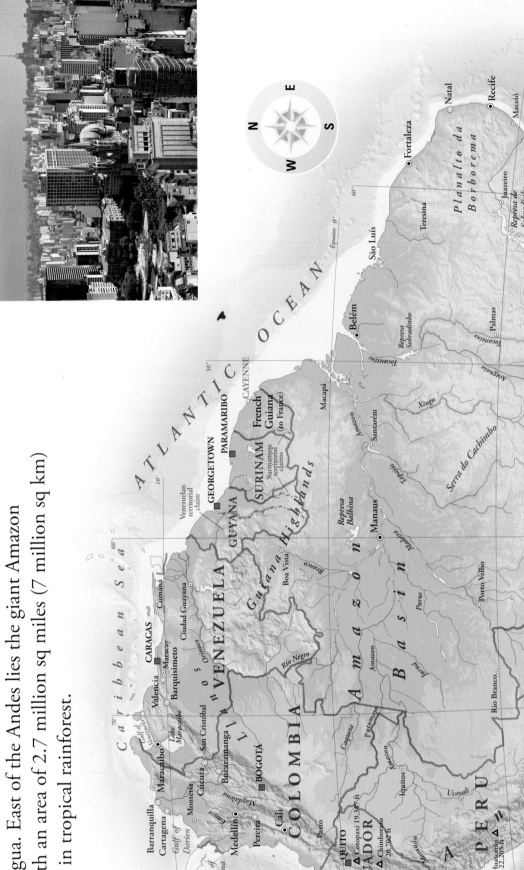

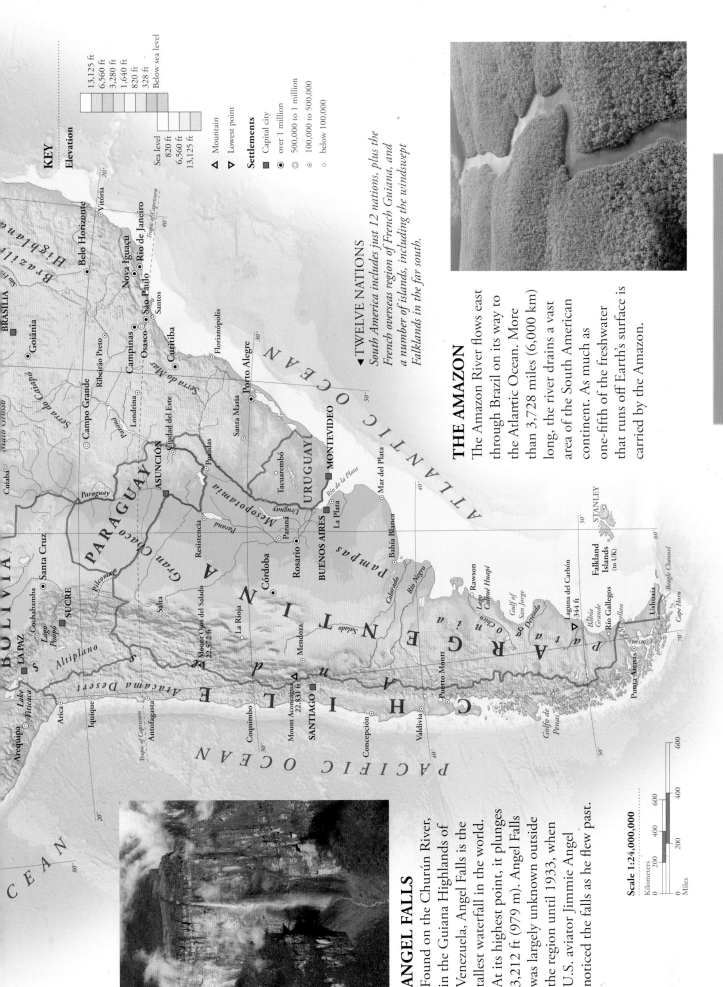

KEY

Elevation

- 13,125 ft
- 6,560 ft
- 3,280 ft
- 1,640 ft
- 820 ft
- 328 ft
- Below sea level

- Sea level
- 820 ft
- 6,560 ft
- 13,125 ft

△ Mountain
▽ Lowest point

Settlements

- ■ Capital city
- ◉ over 1 million
- ◎ 500,000 to 1 million
- ⊙ 100,000 to 500,000
- ○ below 100,000

▼ TWELVE NATIONS
South America includes just 12 nations, plus the French overseas region of French Guiana, and a number of islands, including the windswept Falklands in the far south.

THE AMAZON

The Amazon River flows east through Brazil on its way to the Atlantic Ocean. More than 3,728 miles (6,000 km) long, the river drains a vast area of the South American continent. As much as one-fifth of the freshwater that runs off Earth's surface is carried by the Amazon.

ANGEL FALLS

Found on the Churún River, in the Guiana Highlands of Venezuela, Angel Falls is the tallest waterfall in the world. At its highest point, it plunges 3,212 ft (979 m). Angel Falls was largely unknown outside the region until 1933, when U.S. aviator Jimmie Angel noticed the falls as he flew past.

Scale 1:24,000,000

Kilometers 0 200 400 600
Miles 0 200 400 600

Map labels:

Brazilian Highlands · Vitória · Belo Horizonte · BRASÍLIA · Goiânia · Nova Iguaçu · Rio de Janeiro · São Paulo · Osasco · Santos · Campinas · Ribeirão Preto · Londrina · Curitiba · Florianópolis · Porto Alegre · Santa Maria · Serra do Mar · Campo Grande · Ciudad del Este · Posadas · Tacuarembó · MONTEVIDEO · URUGUAY · Mar del Plata · Rio de la Plata · La Plata · BUENOS AIRES · Rosario · Paraná · Mesopotamia · Uruguay · ASUNCIÓN · PARAGUAY · Paraguay · Resistencia · Gran Chaco · Pilcomayo · Bahía Blanca · PAMPAS · Córdoba · Salado · Mount Ojos del Salado 22,572 ft · La Rioja · Salta · Mendoza · ARGENTINA · Colorado · Rio Negro · Rawson · Lago Colhué Huapi · Gulf of San Jorge · Río Chico · Patagonia · Laguna del Carbón -344 ft · Bahía Grande · Río Gallegos · STANLEY · Falkland Islands (to UK) · Ushuaia · Beagle Channel · Cape Horn · St. of Magellan · Punta Arenas · Golfo de Penas · Puerto Montt · Valdivia · Concepción · SANTIAGO · Mount Aconcagua 22,831 ft · CHILE · Coquimbo · Atacama Desert · Antofagasta · Iquique · Tropic of Capricorn · Arica · Arequipa · Lake Titicaca · Altiplano · Lago Poopó · LA PAZ · Cochabamba · SUCRE · Santa Cruz · BOLIVIA · Cuiabá · Mato Grosso · Serra do Caiapó

ATLANTIC OCEAN · PACIFIC OCEAN

Europe

The sixth-largest continent, Europe is home to more than 740 million people. It is located on the single landmass that also includes Asia, and the combined area is known as Eurasia. Europe has three coastal borders, with the Arctic Ocean to the north, the Atlantic Ocean to the west, and the Mediterranean Sea to the south. To the east, it is separated from Asia by the Ural and Caucasus mountains. These mountain ranges are located in Russia, a vast country that is part of both Europe and Asia.

EUROPEAN LANDSCAPES

Europe has a wide range of dramatic geographical features, from glacial landscapes to mountain ranges, and from rolling plains to dry, warm islands in the Mediterranean. About 270 mammal species are found on the continent, including this red deer in the Scottish Highlands.

Scale 1:19,000,000

Kilometers
0   200   400   600

0   200   400   600
Miles

NORWEGIAN FJORD

This long, narrow inlet surrounded by steep land on three sides is called a fjord. Formed through the erosion of land by glaciers, fjords form much of the western coast of Norway. The longest fjord in Norway, Sognefjord, runs for 126 miles (203 km).

◄ RUSSIA
Russia is the largest country in the world. Its area of more than 6.5 million sq miles (17 million sq km) is more than one-eighth of Earth's inhabited land area.

KEY

Elevation

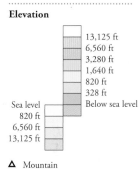

13,125 ft	
6,560 ft	
3,280 ft	
1,640 ft	
820 ft	
328 ft	
Sea level	Below sea level
820 ft	
6,560 ft	
13,125 ft	

△ Mountain
▽ Lowest point

Settlements
- ■ Capital city
- ◉ over 1 million
- ◎ 500,000 to 1 million
- ⊙ 100,000 to 500,000
- ○ below 100,000

GROWING GRAPES

Wine has been produced in Europe for many thousands of years. Grapevines flourish in the warm and relatively dry Mediterranean climate of southern Europe. Together, Spain, France, and Italy produced 2.8 million gallons (12.5 billion liters) of wine in 2011, which was more than 40 percent of the world's total.

Map labels

Novaya Zemlya
Kara Sea
Vorkuta
Arctic Circle
Ural Mountains
Barents Sea
RUSSIAN
Murmansk
Kola Peninsula
White Sea
FINLAND
Archangel
Northern Dvina
FEDERATION
Gulf of Bothnia
Lake Onega
Lake Ladoga
Perm'
Turku
HELSINKI
Kirov
St. Petersburg
Vologda
Ufa
STOCKHOLM
TALLINN
ESTONIA
Yaroslavl'
Kazan'
LATVIA
RIGA
Nizhniy Novgorod
LITHUANIA
Ul'yanovsk
Tol'yatti
Orenburg
MOSCOW
Samara
RUSS. FED.
(Kaliningrad)
Kaliningrad
VILNIUS
Vitsyebsk
Central Russian Upland
MINSK
Tula
BELARUS
Saratov
WARSAW
Homyel'
Voronezh
POLAND
Brest
Western Dvina
Kharkiv
Volgograd
Krakow
KIEV
Volga
UKRAINE
Astrakhan'
Caspian Sea
L'viv
-92 ft
Carpathian Mountains
Dnipropetrovs'k
Dniester
Donets'k
Rostov-na-Donu
SLOVAKIA
Chernivtsi
Dnieper
BUDAPEST
MOLDOVA
Sea of Azov
Stavropol'
Cluj-Napoca
CHISINAU
Groznyy
ROMANIA
Odesa
Novorossiysk
Brasov
Simferopol'
Caucasus
BELGRADE
BUCHAREST
Elbrus 18,511 ft
SERBIA
Danube
Ruse
Constanta
KOSOVO
(disputed)
SOFIA
Black Sea
PRISHTINË
Burgas
SKOPJE
MACEDONIA
Istanbul
ALBANIA
Salonica
Turkey
Larisa
Aegean Sea
GREECE
ATHENS
Irákleio
Crete

Africa

The second-largest continent, Africa is home to more than a billion people, with more than 3,000 different ethnic groups scattered across 54 countries. The north of the continent is dominated by the world's largest hot desert, the Sahara, with large belts of grassy highlands and rich rainforest farther south. A number of large river systems drain the continent, including the Nile, Niger, Congo, and Zambezi.

THE NILE

About 4,132 miles (6,650 km) long, the Nile is the longest river in the world. It provides a vital water source for nearby farmlands and settlements. Fed by several sources, the Nile flows northward through 10 countries, including Sudan and Egypt, before flowing into the Mediterranean Sea.

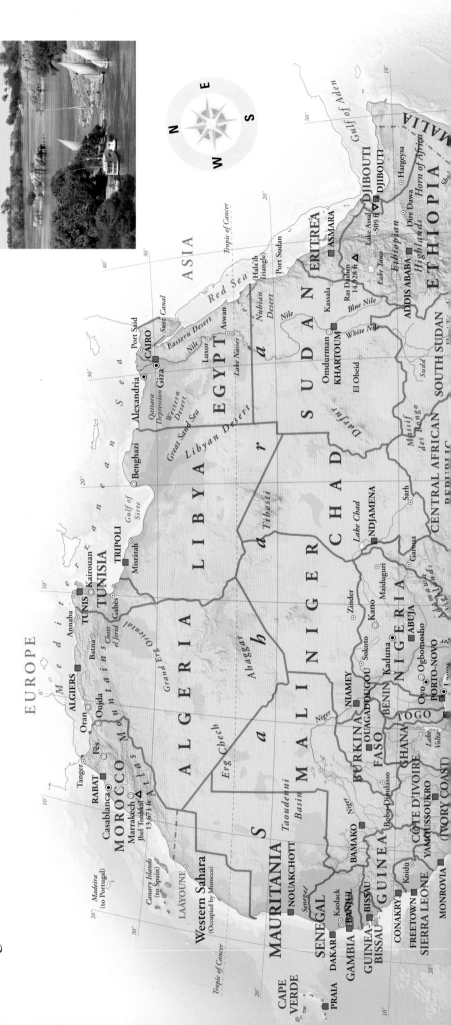

KEY

Elevation

13,125 ft
6,560 ft
3,280 ft
1,640 ft
820 ft
328 ft
Below sea level

Sea level
820 ft
6,560 ft
13,125 ft

▲ Mountain
▽ Lowest point

Settlements

■ Capital city
◉ over 1 million
◎ 500,000 to 1 million
◌ 100,000 to 500,000
○ below 100,000

Scale 1:33,000,000

Kilometers 0   300   600   900
Miles 0   300   600   900

THE EQUATOR ▶

The equator passes through seven countries in Africa. Temperatures are generally very high all year round near the equator, but snow and ice are found at the summit of Africa's highest mountain, Mount Kilimanjaro in Tanzania.

CONGO BASIN

Stretching across parts of six countries, the Congo Basin is rich in dense rainforest and swamps that provide homes for more than 400 species of mammals, including chimpanzees (left) and gorillas. Around a third of the basin's 10,000 plant species are found only in this region.

MAASAI MARA

Located in Kenya, the Maasai Mara nature reserve is home to more than 90 species of mammals, including lions and cheetahs, as well as more than 500 bird species. Each year, more than two million wildebeests, zebras, and gazelles migrate to the area in search of suitable grazing.

Kismaayo
VICTORIA ■
SEYCHELLES
Mombasa
Kirinyaga
17,060 ft ▲
Kilimanjaro 19,341 ft ▲
NAIROBI
DODOMA
Zanzibar
Dar es Salaam
TANZANIA
COMOROS
MORONI
Mayotte (to France)
Mahajanga
MADAGASCAR
ANTANANARIVO
Toamasina
Fianarantsoa
MAURITIUS
PORT LOUIS
Réunion (to France)
Tropic of Capricorn

INDIAN OCEAN

Bukavu
RWANDA
KIGALI
BURUNDI
BUJUMBURA
Kalemie
Lake Tanganyika
Lake Victoria
Lake Nyasa
MALAWI
LILONGWE
Blantyre
Nacala
Beira
MOZAMBIQUE
Mozambique Channel

Lulaba
Lubumbashi
Kitwe
ZAMBIA
LUSAKA
Zambezi
HARARE
ZIMBABWE
Bulawayo
Mbuji-Mayi
Ilebo
DEM. REP. CONGO
KINSHASA
Mbandaka Basin
CON
BRAZZAVILLE
GABON
Port-Gentil
ANGOLA (Cabinda)
LUANDA
Namibe
ANGOLA
Bié Plateau
Lubango
Okavango Delta
NAMIBIA
WINDHOEK
Namib Desert
Walvis Bay
Lüderitz
Kalahari Desert
BOTSWANA
GABORONE
Mahalapye
Limpopo
PRETORIA/TSHWANE
MAPUTO
MBABANE SWAZILAND
Johannesburg
Welkom
MASERU
LESOTHO
Pietermaritzburg
Drakensberg
Kimberley
BLOEMFONTEIN
Orange River
SOUTH AFRICA
CAPE TOWN
Cape of Good Hope
East London
Port Elizabeth

ATLANTIC OCEAN

Tropic of Capricorn

Asia

The largest continent, Asia is also home to the world's largest city: Beijing, China. It is a continent of physical extremes, containing both the lowest point on Earth (the Dead Sea, in Jordan) and the highest point on Earth (Mount Everest, in the Himalayas) as well as vast deserts, Arctic tundra, tropical rainforests, and large river deltas.

TRANS-SIBERIAN RAILWAY

Spanning 5,717 miles (9,200 km), the Trans-Siberian Railway is one of the longest in the world. It runs eastward from Moscow, in western Russia (see page 239), through Siberia, and on to Vladivostok, close to Russia's border with China and North Korea. The line carries more than 200,000 cargo containers a year.

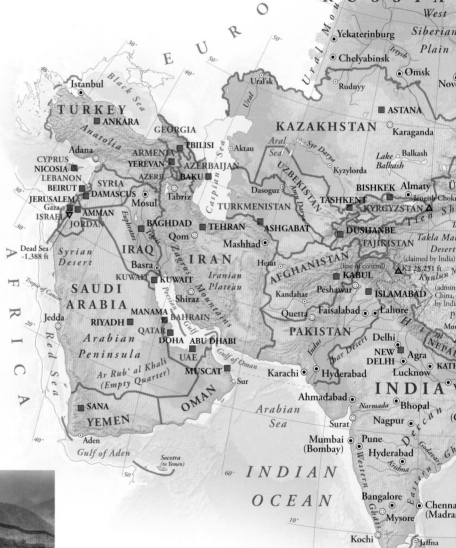

GREAT WALL OF CHINA

Begun in the third century BCE, the Great Wall is a series of fortified walls, towers, and ditches built and rebuilt over many centuries. Stretching about 13,000 miles (21,000 km) from North Korea to northwestern China, it was designed to repel foreign invaders from the north.

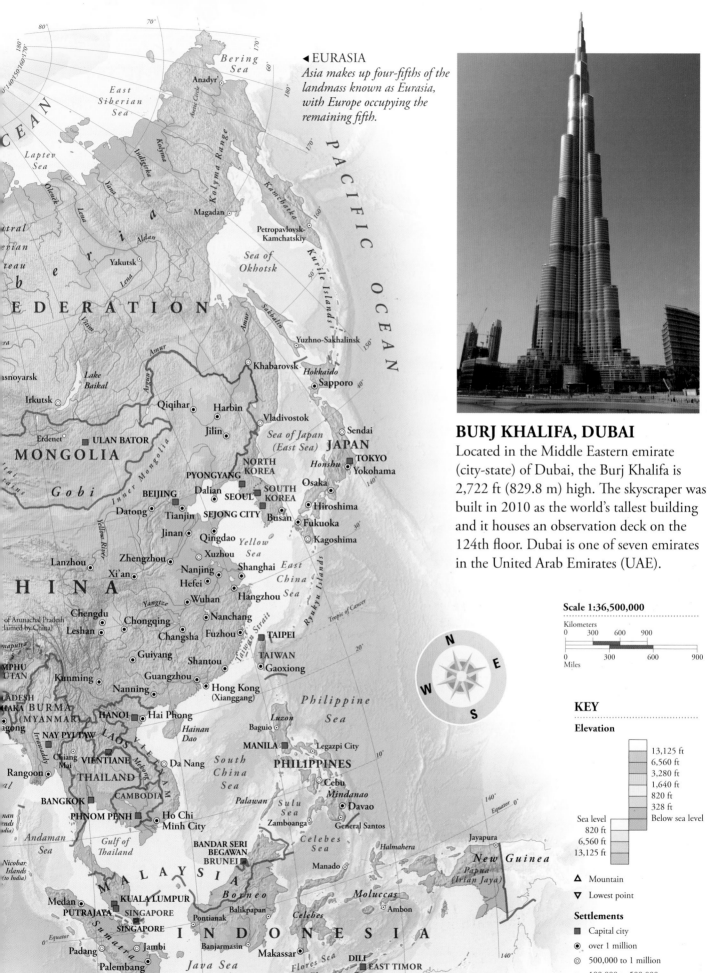

◄ EURASIA

Asia makes up four-fifths of the landmass known as Eurasia, with Europe occupying the remaining fifth.

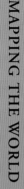

BURJ KHALIFA, DUBAI

Located in the Middle Eastern emirate (city-state) of Dubai, the Burj Khalifa is 2,722 ft (829.8 m) high. The skyscraper was built in 2010 as the world's tallest building and it houses an observation deck on the 124th floor. Dubai is one of seven emirates in the United Arab Emirates (UAE).

Scale 1:36,500,000

Kilometers
0   300   600   900

0   300   600   900
Miles

KEY

Elevation

	13,125 ft
	6,560 ft
	3,280 ft
	1,640 ft
	820 ft
	328 ft
Sea level	Below sea level
820 ft	
6,560 ft	
13,125 ft	

△ Mountain

▽ Lowest point

Settlements

■ Capital city

◉ over 1 million

◎ 500,000 to 1 million

⊙ 100,000 to 500,000

○ below 100,000

243

Oceania

The smallest continent by land area, Oceania is also the least populated. There are fewer than 40 million people living in its sprawling range of islands dotted across 19.3 million sq miles (50 million sq km) of the Pacific Ocean. Australia, Papua New Guinea, and New Zealand are the biggest landmasses in the region, which mostly consists of coral atolls and volcanic islands. Sometimes called the world's largest island and smallest continent, Australia dominates the region in size, population, and economic strength, partly due to its rich natural resources.

SYDNEY HARBOUR

Situated on Australia's eastern coast, Sydney is the largest city in Oceania. The city is home to about 4.6 million people. Sydney Harbour is the deepest natural harbor in the world.

Scale 1:40,000,000

Kilometers
0   300   600   900

0   300   600   900
Miles

▲ AUSTRALASIA
Australia and New Zealand are often jointly known as Australasia. Papua New Guinea is also sometimes included in this grouping.

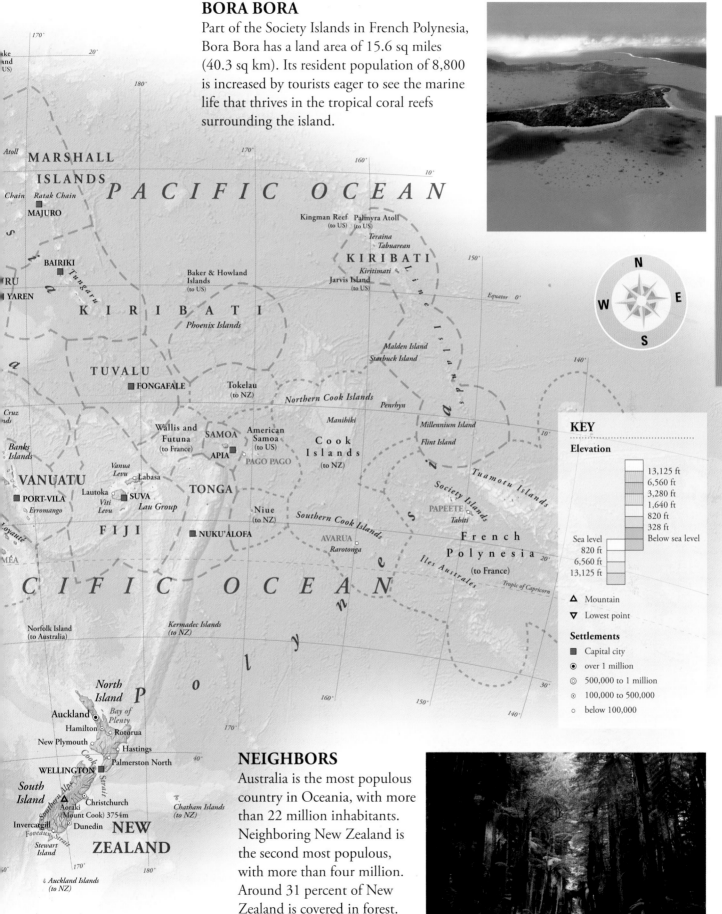

BORA BORA

Part of the Society Islands in French Polynesia, Bora Bora has a land area of 15.6 sq miles (40.3 sq km). Its resident population of 8,800 is increased by tourists eager to see the marine life that thrives in the tropical coral reefs surrounding the island.

MARSHALL ISLANDS

Chain Ratak Chain
■ MAJURO

PACIFIC OCEAN

Kingman Reef (to US) Palmyra Atoll (to US)

Teraina
Tabuarean

KIRIBATI

Atoll

■ BAIRIKI

Tungaru

Baker & Howland Islands (to US)

Kiritimati
Jarvis Island (to US)

Equator 0°

■ YAREN

K I R I B A T I

Phoenix Islands

Malden Island
Starbuck Island

Line Islands

TUVALU

■ FONGAFALE

Tokelau (to NZ)

Northern Cook Islands

Penrhyn

Cruz ands

Banks Islands

Wallis and Futuna (to France) SAMOA
■ APIA

American Samoa (to US)
□ PAGO PAGO

Manihiki

C o o k
I s l a n d s
(to NZ)

Millennium Island

Flint Island

Tuamotu Islands

VANUATU

Vanua Levu Labasa

TONGA

■ PORT-VILA
Erromango

Lautoka ◎ SUVA
Viti Levu *Lau Group*

Niue (to NZ)

Southern Cook Islands

Society Islands
◎ PAPEETE
Tahiti

Loyauté

F I J I

■ NUKU'ALOFA

AVARUA
Rarotonga

F r e n c h
P o l y n e s i a
(to France)

Îles Australes

Tropic of Capricorn

MÉA

C I F I C   O C E A N

Norfolk Island (to Australia)

Kermadec Islands (to NZ)

North Island *Bay of Plenty*

Auckland ◎
Hamilton ◎ Rotorua
New Plymouth
Hastings
Palmerston North
Cook Strait

■ WELLINGTON

South Island *Southern Alps*
△ Aoraki
(Mount Cook) 3754m Christchurch

Invercargill Dunedin
Foveaux Strait

NEW ZEALAND

Stewart Island

Auckland Islands (to NZ)

Chatham Islands (to NZ)

KEY

Elevation

	13,125 ft
	6,560 ft
	3,280 ft
	1,640 ft
	820 ft
	328 ft
Sea level	Below sea level
820 ft	
6,560 ft	
13,125 ft	

△ Mountain

▽ Lowest point

Settlements

■ Capital city

◉ over 1 million

◎ 500,000 to 1 million

◉ 100,000 to 500,000

○ below 100,000

NEIGHBORS

Australia is the most populous country in Oceania, with more than 22 million inhabitants. Neighboring New Zealand is the second most populous, with more than four million. Around 31 percent of New Zealand is covered in forest.

Antarctica

With an area of 5.4 million sq miles (14 million sq km), Antarctica is the fifth-largest continent, and the coldest. Almost all of its land is covered in an ice sheet that is 15,400 ft (4,700 m) thick in places. It is the southernmost continent, with the South Pole at its center. With rainfall of only 8 in (20 cm) per year, Antarctica is also classified as a desert.

RESEARCH BASES

Antarctica belongs to no single nation and has no permanent human residents. But up to 4,000 people (mostly scientists) live there at research bases during the summer months, when there is sunlight for 24 hours a day and ships can get through the sea ice.

SURVIVING THE COLD

Various species of penguins and seals live on Antarctica, feeding on fish and other marine life from the surrounding ocean. These creatures are thickly insulated with a layer of fat in order to survive in the icy waters.

▲ ANTARCTIC ICE SHEET
Antarctica's gigantic ice sheet shrinks in summer but expands in winter (marked by a small dotted line above) as temperatures fall. The parts of an ice sheet that stretch out over the sea are known as ice shelves.

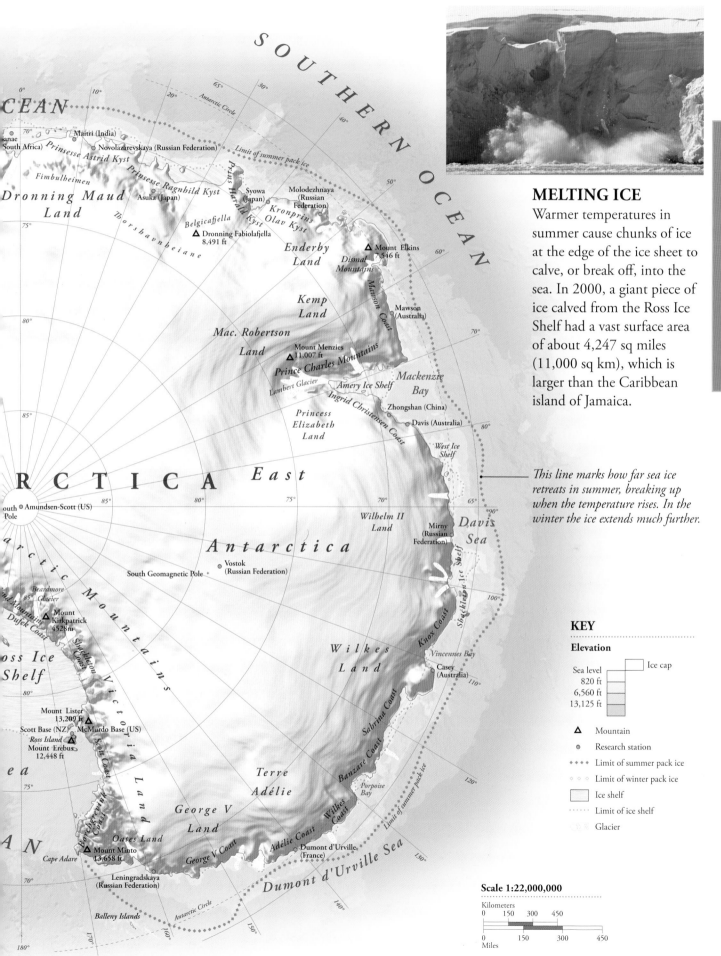

SOUTHERN OCEAN

OCEAN

70°
anae
South Africa
Maitri (India)
Novolazarevskaya (Russian Federation)
Prinsesse Astrid Kyst
Fimbulheimen
Dronning Maud Land
Thorshavnheiane
Prinsesse Ragnhild Kyst
Prins Harald Kyst
Syowa (Japan)
Asuka (Japan)
Belgicafjella
△ Dronning Fabiolafjella 8,491 ft
Molodezhnaya (Russian Federation)
Kronprins Olav Kyst
Enderby Land
△ Mount Elkins 7,546 ft
Dismal Mountains
Mawson Coast
Kemp Land
Mawson (Australia)
Mac. Robertson Land
Mount Menzies △ 11,007 ft
Prince Charles Mountains
Lambert Glacier
Amery Ice Shelf
Ingrid Christensen Coast
Mackenzie Bay
Zhongshan (China)
Davis (Australia)
Princess Elizabeth Land
West Ice Shelf
East
Antarctica

RCTICA

South Pole
Amundsen-Scott (US)
South Pole

South Geomagnetic Pole +
Vostok (Russian Federation)

Wilhelm II Land
Mirny (Russian Federation)
Davis Sea
Shackleton Ice Shelf
Knox Coast

Beardmore Glacier
nd Mountains
Dufek Coast
△ Mount Kirkpatrick 4528m
Shackleton Coast
Ross Ice Shelf
Victoria Land
Mount Lister 13,209 ft △
Scott Base (NZ)
McMurdo Base (US)
Ross Island
Mount Erebus 12,448 ft
Scott Coast

ea

Wilkes Land
Vincennes Bay
Casey (Australia)
Sabrina Coast

Terre Adélie
Banzare Coast
Porpoise Bay

George V Land
Oates Land
Bory greiim Coast
△ Mount Minto 13,658 ft
Cape Adare
George V Coast
Adélie Coast
Wilkes Coast
Adélie Coast
Dumont d'Urville (France)

Leningradskaya (Russian Federation)
Balleny Islands
Antarctic Circle
Dumont d'Urville Sea

Limit of summer pack ice

0° 10° 20° 65° 30° 40° 50° 60° 70° 80° 90° 100° 110° 120° 130° 140° 150° 160° 170° 180°
Antarctic Circle
70° 75° 80° 85° 85° 80° 75° 70°

MELTING ICE

Warmer temperatures in summer cause chunks of ice at the edge of the ice sheet to calve, or break off, into the sea. In 2000, a giant piece of ice calved from the Ross Ice Shelf had a vast surface area of about 4,247 sq miles (11,000 sq km), which is larger than the Caribbean island of Jamaica.

This line marks how far sea ice retreats in summer, breaking up when the temperature rises. In the winter the ice extends much further.

KEY

Elevation

Sea level	Ice cap
820 ft	
6,560 ft	
13,125 ft	

△ Mountain

● Research station

✦✦✦ Limit of summer pack ice

◇◇◇ Limit of winter pack ice

▭ Ice shelf

.... Limit of ice shelf

Glacier

Scale 1:22,000,000

Kilometers
0   150   300   450

0   150   300   450
Miles

COUNTRY FACTFILE

A country is a place that has its own government and a permament population, and that is widely recognized by other countries. Today, there are 194 countries—more than ever before.

North America

The third-largest continent is dominated by the United States and Canada—two of the world's largest countries. It is bordered on the east by the Atlantic Ocean, and by the Pacific Ocean on the west. At its northern tip, in the freezing waters of the Arctic Ocean, are the ice sheets of Greenland. In the southernmost part of the continent lie the seven countries of Central America and the Caribbean islands, where the climate is warm all year round.

▼ SONORAN DESERT
Stretching across the southwestern United States and northwestern Mexico is the hot, dry, and windy Sonoran Desert. It is the exclusive home of the saguaro cactus. Covered in spines, and white flowers in late spring, this huge, tree-sized cactus lives for about 200 years.

United States of America

Area 3,716,654 sq miles
(9,626,091 sq km)
Population 313 million
Capital Washington, D.C.
Currency US dollar
Official language English
Life expectancy 78 years

The United States of America (USA) was founded in 1776 on principles of individual freedom and a government voted for by the people. It is now the most powerful country in the world and the third most populated. The main landmass is made up of 48 of the country's 50 states. The other two are Alaska, on the northwest tip of the North American continent, and Hawaii, an island chain in the Pacific Ocean. The country's Hispanic community makes up 13 percent of the population, and is growing rapidly. The first African-American president, Barack Obama, was elected in 2008.

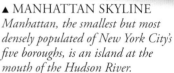

▲ MANHATTAN SKYLINE
Manhattan, the smallest but most densely populated of New York City's five boroughs, is an island at the mouth of the Hudson River.

Canada

Area 3,855,103 sq miles
(9,984,670 sq km)
Population 34.3 million
Capital Ottawa
Currency Canadian dollar
Official languages English and French
Life expectancy 80 years

Canada is the world's second-largest country in terms of land area. It spans six time zones, from Newfoundland in the east to British Columbia in the west. To its north lies the Arctic Ocean. Most Canadians are descendants of immigrants from Britain, France, Ireland, and other European countries. Canada also has an indigenous population of about one million people, who are known as the First Nations. Canada is ranked by the United Nations (UN) as one of the best countries to live in, with the cities of Vancouver, Toronto, and Calgary featuring in the world's top ten cities according to living conditions.

▶ BROWN BEAR
One of the largest land animals, the brown bear lives in the mountainous regions of Canada. Activities such as logging have affected its habitat and reduced its numbers.

Guatemala

Area 42,043 sq miles
(108,890 sq km)
Population 14.8 million
Capital Guatemala City
Currency Quetzal
Official language Spanish
Life expectancy 70 years

Once home to the ancient Mayan civilization, Guatemala is mostly made up of highlands. More than half of Guatemalans are descendants of the original Mayas, who mostly live in the highlands as farmers. Agriculture contributes to nearly a quarter of Guatemala's export earnings.

Belize

Area 8,867 sq miles
(22,966 sq km)
Population 300,000
Capital Belmopan
Currency Belizean dollar
Official language English
Life expectancy 72 years

Formerly known as British Honduras, Belize was the last Central American country to gain independence, in 1981. On its east coast, in the waters of the Caribbean Sea, lies the world's second largest coral reef system. Belize has the lowest population of Central America, and almost half of its land area is still covered in forests.

El Salvador

Area 8,124 sq miles
(21,040 sq km)
Population 6.2 million
Capital San Salvador
Currency Salvadorean colón
Official language Spanish
Life expectancy 72 years

Located on the Pacific coast, El Salvador is the smallest and most densely populated nation in Central America. Within its borders lie the boundaries of three tectonic plates, which means there are frequent earthquakes and volcanic eruptions. The volcanic activity provides a source of relatively cheap geothermal energy.

Costa Rica

Area 19,730 sq miles
(51,100 sq km)
Population 4.7 million
Capital San José
Currency Costa Rican colón
Official language Spanish
Life expectancy 79 years

◀ RED-EYED TREE FROG
Known for its bulging red eyes, the colorful red-eyed tree frog can be found near ponds, streams, and rivers along Costa Rica's Caribbean coast. This tree frog eats insects that it catches with its long, sticky tongue. Suction cups on its toes allow it to climb trees.

The Republic of Costa Rica is a small country in Central America located near the southern tip of the North American continent. To its east is the Caribbean Sea and to its west is the Pacific Ocean. Costa Rica was ruled by Spain until 1821, gaining full independence in 1838. The population is mostly *mestizo*, of partly Spanish origins, with only about 35,000 indigenous Amerindians. The main language is Spanish, but English Creole is also spoken. Coffee, technology, and tourism are the country's main industries. More than 90 percent of Costa Rica's electricity comes from renewable sources.

Mexico

Area 761,606 sq miles
(1,972,550 sq km)
Population 115 million
Capital Mexico City
Currency Mexican peso
Official language Spanish
Life expectancy 74 years

The most populated Spanish-speaking country in the world, Mexico separates the United States from the rest of Latin America (the countries whose main language is Spanish or Portuguese). Mexico was ruled by the Aztecs until the 16th century, when it became part of the Spanish Empire for nearly 300 years. Greater Mexico City, which

includes the capital and 18 connected districts, is one of the largest metropolitan areas in the world. Mexican national identity is formed of *mestizaje*—a combination of European and indigenous cultures. In addition to Spanish, indigenous languages such as Nahuatl, Mayan, and Tzeltal are also spoken. Despite Mexico being a global oil producer, its exports have dropped in recent years and it now faces great wealth inequality. More than 44 percent of the population live below the national poverty line. Indigenous communities living in the country's rural areas are the most disadvantaged groups.

▼ CHACMOOL, MEXICO CITY
A chacmool is a sculpture of a reclining male figure holding a bowl. Chacmools were made by Native Americans and have been excavated from sites across central Mexico.

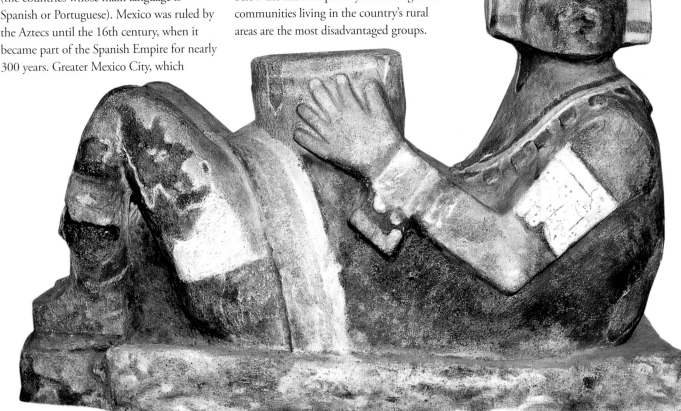

Honduras

Area 43,278 sq miles (112,090 sq km)
Population 7.8 million
Capital Tegucigalpa
Currency Lempira
Official language Spanish
Life expectancy 70 years

Honduras is a mountainous country lying between Guatemala and Nicaragua. It has a small southern coastline facing the Pacific Ocean and a much longer shoreline on the north facing the Caribbean Sea. It is the second-poorest country in Central America, with about 60 percent of the population living below the national poverty line.

Nicaragua

Area 49,998 sq miles (129,494 sq km)
Population 5.9 million
Capital Managua
Currency Nicaraguan córdoba
Official language Spanish
Life expectancy 72 years

Nicaragua lies in the heart of Central America. The country is divided into three geographical zones: Pacific lowlands; cooler, wet central highlands; and Caribbean lowlands. About a third of the population lives in the capital, Managua. Indigenous Miskito tribes and descendants of African slaves live mainly along the Caribbean coast.

Panama

Area 30,193 sq miles (78,200 sq km)
Population 3.6 million
Capital Panama City
Currency Balboa and US dollar
Official language Spanish
Life expectancy 75 years

Panama is the southernmost of the seven Central American countries. Deforestation threatens Panama's rainforests, which cover about 40 percent of the land. Since 1999, Panama has had full control of the Panama Canal, which connects the Pacific and Atlantic Oceans and is a major international shipping route.

COUNTRY FACTFILE

Cuba

Area 42,803 sq miles (110,860 sq km)
Population 11.3 million
Capital Havana
Currency Cuban peso
Official language Spanish
Life expectancy 78 years

The Republic of Cuba is the largest island in the Caribbean Sea. Cuba has three mountainous regions—the Sierra Maestra, the Sierra de los Órganos, and the Sierra de Trinidad. Fertile lowlands are used for farming sugarcane and rice. Cuba has been a one-party Communist nation led by Fidel Castro since 1959. In 2008, his younger brother Raúl Castro took over the reins. Living standards in Cuba fell dramatically in the early 1990s, when Communist Eastern Europe—previously Cuba's main trading partner—collapsed. Since then, the number of people trying to leave has risen markedly.

▶ CLASSIC CARS IN HAVANA
Cars dating back to the 1950s dot the streets of Cuba's capital, Havana. Taxi services offer tours in these classic cars, which are well maintained and in excellent condition.

Bahamas

Area 5,382 sq miles (13,940 sq km)
Population 300,000
Capital Nassau
Currency Bahamian dollar
Official language English
Life expectancy 73 years

The Commonwealth of the Bahamas is an archipelago (a stretch of water containing many islands) of 700 islands and islets. It sits to the northeast of Cuba in the western Atlantic. Two-thirds of the population live in the capital city of Nassau, on New Providence island. The Bahamas is a popular destination for vacationers.

▲ DASHEEN
A root vegetable, dasheen is a staple crop cultivated in Jamaica. Its leaves are often used to make a popular breakfast dish called callaloo, *which is enjoyed throughout the Caribbean.*

Jamaica

Area 4,243 sq miles (10,990 sq km)
Population 2.8 million
Capital Kingston
Currency Jamaican dollar
Official language English
Life expectancy 71 years

Jamaica is an island in the Caribbean Sea, located 90 miles (145 km) south of Cuba. Most Jamaicans are of African descent, with small Indian, Chinese, and European minorities. Jamaican music is famous the world over. The musical styles of ska, ragga, and reggae originated in the poverty-stricken districts of Jamaica's capital, Kingston.

Dominican Republic

Area 18,680 sq miles
(48,380 sq km)
Population 10.1 million
Capital Santo Domingo
Currency Dominican peso
Official language Spanish
Life expectancy 72 years

The Dominican Republic, the Caribbean's most popular tourist spot, occupies two-thirds of the island of Hispaniola. It is home to the Caribbean's highest point, Pico Duarte, as well as its lowest, Lake Enriquillo.

▲ COCOA POD
The Dominican Republic is one of the chief producers of cocoa beans, which are dried, roasted, and ground to make chocolate.

Haiti

Area 10,714 sq miles
(27,750 sq km)
Population 10.1 million
Capital Port-au-Prince
Currency Haitian gourde
Official languages French and French Creole
Life expectancy 60 years

Haiti lies on the west of Hispaniola. In 1804, it was the first ethnically black nation to gain independence. Already the poorest country in the Americas, Haiti was set back even further by a devastating earthquake in 2010.

St. Kitts and Nevis

Area 101 sq miles
(261 sq km)
Population 50,000
Capital Basseterre
Currency East Caribbean dollar
Official language English
Life expectancy 71 years

The Federation of Saint Kitts and Nevis is a tiny two-island country. St. Kitts, a volcanic island, is separated from the more lush island of Nevis by a channel 2 miles (3 km) wide called the Narrows. It is the smallest country in North America by land size and population. The islands' greatest environmental threat is from hurricanes.

Dominica

Area 291 sq miles
(754 sq km)
Population 73,000
Capital Roseau
Currency East Caribbean dollar
Official language English
Life expectancy 74 years

Dominica became independent from the UK in 1978. It is known as the "Nature Island of the Caribbean" because of its spectacular and lush flora and fauna, which are protected in large national parks. Dominica's volcanic origin has given it very fertile soils and the second-largest boiling lake in the world.

St. Lucia

Area 239 sq miles
(620 sq km)
Population 162,000
Capital Castries
Currency East Caribbean dollar
Official language English
Life expectancy 74 years

The island of St. Lucia has many beaches and a rich variety of wildlife in its rainforests. The twin Pitons (cone-shaped volcanic plugs) on its southern coast have been given World Heritage status. The country's population is mostly of African and African-European descent. The economy relies on income from tourism and banana production.

Barbados

Area 166 sq miles
(430 sq km)
Population 300,000
Capital Bridgetown
Currency Barbados dollar
Official language English
Life expectancy 77 years

Located to the northeast of Trinidad, Barbados was originally inhabited by the indigenous Arawak peoples. Today, most Barbadians are descended from Africans brought to the island between the 16th and 19th centuries. In the 1990s, tourism overtook sugar as the main source of the nation's income.

St. Vincent and the Grenadines

Area 150 sq miles
(389 sq km)
Population 103,500
Capital Kingstown
Currency East Caribbean dollar
Official language English
Life expectancy 71 years

St. Vincent and the Grenadines is a group of islands in the Caribbean Sea. St. Vincent is a volcanic island, made up of volcanic mountains that are partly underwater. The Grenadines is a chain of smaller coral islands surrounded by coral reefs. The country is the world's largest producer of arrowroot, a starchy vegetable.

▲ HIBISCUS
The St. Vincent Botanical Gardens in Kingstown are home to many tropical plants, including the colorful and fragrant hibiscus.

Grenada

Area 131 sq miles (340 sq km)
Population 109,000
Capital St. George's
Currency East Caribbean dollar
Official language English
Life expectancy 68 years

Grenada is a group of islands north of Trinidad and Tobago. A former British colony, Grenada became independent in 1974. It was the world's second-largest producer of nutmeg until Hurricane Ivan devastated crops in 2004.

Trinidad and Tobago

Area 1,980 sq miles (5,128 sq km)
Population 1.3 million
Capital Port-of-Spain
Currency Trinidad and Tobago dollar
Official language English
Life expectancy 70 years

The islands of Trinidad and Tobago are located just 9 miles (15 km) from the South American mainland. The mountains and swamps of the islands are rich in tropical flora and fauna. Trinidad has the largest south Asian community in the Caribbean.

▲ SCARLET IBIS
The national bird of Trinidad, the scarlet ibis, is native to the Caribbean islands and parts of South America.

Antigua and Barbuda

Area 171 sq miles (442 sq km)
Population 89,000
Capital St. John's
Currency East Caribbean dollar
Official language English
Life expectancy 75 years

Antigua and Barbuda lies between the Caribbean Sea and the Atlantic Ocean. In addition to the two major islands, Antigua and Barbuda, there are also several smaller islands, some of which are uninhabited.

The country was colonized by the British in 1632, and gained its independence in 1981. British cultural influence remains strong, and Antiguans have a passion for the popular British sport of cricket. Most of the population of Antigua and Barbuda is descended from the Africans brought to the islands between the 16th and 19th centuries to work as slaves. There are also small European and south Asian communities. In recent years, many Spanish-speaking immigrants from the Dominican Republic have moved to Antigua and Barbuda.

Luxury tourism is a major industy here. However, sewage from tourist hotels has caused serious environmental problems: Uncontrolled and untreated waste from the hotels pollute the sea, killing valuable fish stocks in the large mangrove swamps.

▼ VACATION DESTINATION
Antigua has 365 beaches. The clear Caribbean waters off these sandy beaches are ideal for snorkeling and attract many vacationers.

South America

South America is the fourth-largest continent in the world. Its terrain is a mix of mountains and highlands, river basins, and coastal plains. Along its western coast lie the Andes mountains, the world's longest mountain range. South America also has the world's largest river (by volume of water), the Amazon, and the world's driest hot desert, the Atacama. The continent is home to incredibly rich and diverse animal and plant life unlike anything else on Earth.

▼ SALAR DE UYUNI
The Salar de Uyuni is a salt flat (a stretch of solid salt crust) in Bolivia. It has formed over hundreds of years on a prehistoric lake, is a few yards thick, and stretches over 4,086 sq miles (10,582 sq km).

Surinam

Area 63,039 sq miles
(163,270 sq km)
Population 500,000
Capital Paramaribo
Currency Surinamese dollar
Official language Dutch
Life expectancy 70 years

The smallest independent country in South America, Surinam is located on the north coast of the continent. Rainforested highlands take up most of the inland areas. About 90 percent of the population live along the Atlantic coast.

Guyana

Area 83,000 sq miles
(214,970 sq km)
Population 800,000
Capital Georgetown
Currency Guyanese dollar
Official language English
Life expectancy 66 years

Guyana, on South America's northern edge, became a republic in 1966 after achieving independence from the UK. People of Indian and African origin make up about 63 percent of the population. Dense rainforests cover much of the country.

▲ HOATZIN
Guyana's national bird, the hoatzin, is also called the stinkbird because of its foul smell. Its chicks are born with claws on their wing tips.

Brazil

Area 3,286,488 sq miles
(8,511,965 sq km)
Population 197 million
Capital Brasília
Currency Brazilian real
Official language Portuguese
Life expectancy 72 years

Brazil is the largest country in South America and the fifth-largest nation in the world. Its varied landscape includes mountains, wetlands, grasslands, deserts, and a long coastline. One-third of Brazil's land area is covered by the tropical rainforests, which grow around the massive Amazon River. Brazil's biggest and most populated cities are São Paulo and Rio de Janeiro. The iconic statue of *Cristo Redentor*, "Christ the Redeemer," overlooks the city of Rio de Janeiro and is considered one of the seven new wonders of the world. Brazil has a very diverse population and, as a result, enjoys a rich religious and cultural heritage. The seventh-largest economy in the world, Brazil is the leading producer of coffee and sugarcane ethanol, which is used as an alternative to gasoline. It also has rich reserves of gold, diamonds, oil, iron ore, and uranium.

▶ CARNIVAL IN RIO
Rio de Janeiro's Carnival is one of the largest festivals in the world. Celebrated 40 days before Easter, the Carnival is a massive street party with costumes, music, dance, and feasts.

Ecuador

Area 109,483 sq miles (283,590 sq km)
Population 14.7 million
Capital Quito
Currency US dollar
Official language Spanish
Life expectancy 75 years

Located on the continent's west coast, Ecuador is one of the smallest countries in South America. The volcanic Galápagos Islands in the Pacific Ocean are also a part of Ecuador. Most Ecuadorians live either in the lowland coastal region called Costa or in the Andean Sierra highlands. Many of the world's bananas are grown in the Costa region, making Ecuador the biggest exporter of bananas. Another main source of income is from oil drilling around the Amazon Basin. This, however, has had a negative effect on the environment and on the indigenous tribes living in the area.

▶ GALÁPAGOS WILDLIFE
The great frigate bird, native to the Galápagos Islands, puffs out its inflatable throat pouch to attract mates during the breeding season.

Bolivia

Area 424,164 sq miles (1,098,580 sq km)
Population 10.1 million
Capital Sucre and La Paz
Currency Boliviano
Official languages Spanish, Quechua, and Aymara
Life expectancy 65 years

A landlocked nation, Bolivia lies in the central part of South America. It has two capitals—Sucre is the judicial capital, while La Paz is the administrative capital. La Paz, at 11,975 ft (3,650 m) above sea level, is the highest capital city in the world. Bolivia is home to the world's highest golf course, ski run, and soccer stadium.

Colombia

Area 430,736 sq miles (1,138,910 sq km)
Population 46.9 million
Capital Bogotá
Currency Colombian peso
Official language Spanish
Life expectancy 73 years

Colombia is in northwest South America, where the continent connects with Central and North America. A land of extremes, Colombia has snow-covered mountains, tropical beaches, deserts, and grasslands called Los Llanos. Colombia sits on the Pacific Ring of Fire, and has many volcanoes and frequent earthquakes.

Venezuela

Area 352,144 sq miles (912,050 sq km)
Population 29.4 million
Capital Caracas
Currency Bolívar fuerte
Official language Spanish
Life expectancy 74 years

With a long Caribbean coastline, the Bolivarian Republic of Venezuela is part of northern South America. Venezuela has some of the largest known oil deposits outside the Middle East. Though it is one of the most urbanized societies in South America, extreme poverty still exists in the *barrios,* or shantytowns, on the hillsides.

Peru

Area 496,218 sq miles (1,285,200 sq km)
Population 29.4 million
Capital Lima
Currency Nuevo sol
Official languages Spanish and Quechua
Life expectancy 71 years

Lying just south of the equator, on the Pacific coast of South America, is the Republic of Peru. It is the third largest South American country, after Brazil and Argentina. Most Peruvians are of mixed cultures, including Amerindian, European, African, and Asian. Peru's varied landscape can be divided into three regions—the coast, the mountains, and the rainforests. The arid Pacific coast is where all the major cities, including the capital city of Lima, are located. This area is home to about half of Peru's population. From the coastal plains rise the Andes mountains, dominated in the south by volcanoes. The east of the country contains Amazon rainforests. These dense forests are home to many unique species of plants and animals. Peru is rich in natural resources—gold, silver, copper, zinc, lead, and iron are found across the country. However, Peru remains one of the poorest nations in the world, with about 40 percent of the population living below the poverty line.

▲ MACHU PICCHU
A UNESCO World Heritage site, the historic city of Machu Picchu is nestled on a hilltop in the Andes mountains. It was built by the Inca people around 600 years ago.

Argentina

Area 1,068,302 sq miles
(2,766,890 sq km)
Population 40.8 million
Capital Buenos Aires
Currency Argentine peso
Official language Spanish
Life expectancy 75 years

Argentina is the second largest country in South America and covers most of the southern portion of the continent. Its capital, Buenos Aires, is one of the continent's largest cities. Nearly 40 percent of Argentina's population live here.

Paraguay

Area 157,047 sq miles
(406,750 sq km)
Population 6.6 million
Capital Asunción
Currency Guaraní
Official languages Spanish and Guaraní
Life expectancy 72 years

Paraguay is a landlocked country bordered by Argentina, Brazil, and Bolivia. Most Paraguayans are of combined Spanish and native Guaraní origin. Although the majority of people are bilingual, Guaraní is largely spoken outside of the big cities.

Uruguay

Area 68,039 sq miles
(176,220 sq km)
Population 3.4 million
Capital Montevideo
Currency Uruguayan peso
Official language Spanish
Life expectancy 76 years

Sandwiched between its larger neighbors, Brazil and Argentina, Uruguay lies in the southeast part of South America. Much of Uruguay is farmland, mainly used for the rearing of livestock, especially cattle and sheep. It is a leading exporter of wool.

Chile

Area 292,260 sq miles
(756,950 sq km)
Population 17.3 million
Capital Santiago
Currency Chilean peso
Official language Spanish
Life expectancy 78 years

Chile extends in a narrow ribbon 2,700 miles (4,350 km) down the Pacific coast of South America. Its unique shape means that its landscape ranges from the deserts of the High Andes in the north to fertile valleys in the center. In the south are the fjords (sea inlets with steep cliffs) and lakes of the Southern Andes. Chile also includes a part of Tierra del Fuego, an archipelago that it shares with Argentina, and the remote Easter Island in the south Pacific Ocean. Chile has many natural resources, including gold, coal, oil, and natural gas. It is the largest producer of copper, which is a major contributor to Chile's export earnings. However, large-scale logging and gold mining in the Andes have raised concerns about environmental damage.

▼ EASTER ISLAND
These giant statues are called moai. *Carved by the early Rapa Nui people of Easter Island, they date back to 400–1600* CE.

Europe

Europe is made up of 46 independent nations, each with its own distinct identity and culture – and often its own language, too. More than half of Europe's countries are members of the European Union (EU), a unified group that acts as one economic and political unit.

▼ BRUGES
The city of Bruges in Belgium is a historic center based on a network of canals and known for its medieval architecture. The bell tower shown here is a popular tourist attraction.

Iceland

Area 39,768 sq miles
(103,000 sq km)
Population 300,000
Capital Reykjavík
Currency Icelandic krona
Official language Icelandic
Life expectancy 81 years

Lying just south of the Arctic Circle in the North Atlantic Ocean, Iceland is a former Danish possession that became fully independent in 1944. It is a small volcanic island, with many glaciers, volcanoes, and geysers. The country produces cheap geothermal power, which meets almost all of its electricity and domestic heating needs. Icelanders are of Scandinavian descent and more than half the population lives in or near the capital city of Reykjavík. In July, the warmest month of the year, temperatures average around 50–55 °F (10–13 °C).

Norway

Area 125,182 sq miles
(324,220 sq km)
Population 4.9 million
Capital Oslo
Currency Norwegian krone
Official language Norwegian
Life expectancy 80 years

The Kingdom of Norway occupies the western part of Scandinavia, between Sweden to its east and the Norwegian Sea to its west. Norway is a constitutional monarchy, which means it has a monarch as the head of state and an elected parliament. Norwegian society has social and economic equality, but living here is costly—Oslo, its capital, is one of the world's most expensive cities. Norway was one of the first countries to grant women the vote, in 1913, and Gro Harlem Brundtland was Norway's first woman prime minister in 1990.

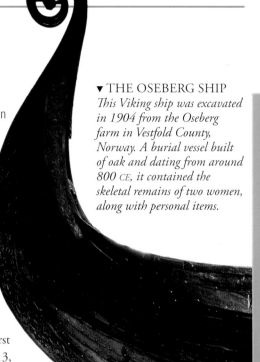

▼ THE OSEBERG SHIP
This Viking ship was excavated in 1904 from the Oseberg farm in Vestfold County, Norway. A burial vessel built of oak and dating from around 800 CE, it contained the skeletal remains of two women, along with personal items.

Sweden

Area 173,732 sq miles
(449,964 sq km)
Population 9.4 million
Capital Stockholm
Currency Swedish krona
Official language Swedish
Life expectancy 81 years

Situated in the east of the Scandinavian peninsula, Sweden is a densely forested country with many lakes. A constitutional monarchy, Sweden has a monarch and an elected parliament that is led by a prime minister. It has one of the largest welfare systems in the world, with all Swedes having access to publicly funded childcare, health care, schooling, and care for the elderly.

▶ NORTHERN LIGHTS
The Aurora borealis, *or Northern Lights, is a natural light display that can be seen in northern Sweden, as well as other Arctic regions. The bright green or red lights are caused by the collision of charged particles high in Earth's atmosphere.*

Finland

Area 130,128 sq miles (337,030 sq km)
Population 5.4 million
Capital Helsinki
Currency Euro
Official languages Finnish and Swedish
Life expectancy 79 years

A country of forests and 187,888 lakes, Finland is bordered on the north and west by Norway and Sweden. To its east lies Russia, which ruled Finland from 1809 until 1917, when Finland became a republic. It joined the EU in 1995 and adopted the Euro (the official currency of the EU) in 2002. Finnish women have long been involved in the running of the country. They were the first in Europe, in 1906, to get the right to vote and the first in the world to be able to run for parliament. Finland has a large high-tech sector, which includes the mobile phone company Nokia.

▶ REINDEER IN LAPLAND
In Lapland, in northern Finland, reindeer are herded by the Sami people, who use the animal's meat for food and its hide for clothing and shelter.

Estonia

Area 17,462 sq miles (45,226 sq km)
Population 1.3 million
Capital Tallinn
Currency Euro
Official language Estonian
Life expectancy 73 years

After decades of Soviet rule, Estonia gained its independence in 1991. Its terrain is flat, boggy, and partly wooded, and includes more than 1,500 islands. Estonia's chief energy resource is oil shale, a rock from which oil is extracted. However, industrial pollution from power plants burning oil shale has now become a growing concern.

Latvia

Area 24,938 sq miles (64,589 sq km)
Population 2.2 million
Capital Riga
Currency Latvian lats
Official language Latvian
Life expectancy 71 years

Latvia is one of the three Baltic countries (along with Estonia and Lithuania) that gained independence from the Communist Soviet Union in 1991. The Latvian economy is dominated by the service sector, though agriculture continues to play an important role. More than 25 percent of the population is ethnically Russian.

Lithuania

Area 25,174 sq miles (65,200 sq km)
Population 3.3 million
Capital Vilnius
Currency Lithuanian litas
Official language Lithuanian
Life expectancy 71 years

Lying on the eastern coast of the Baltic Sea, Lithuania is the largest of the three Baltic countries. It was the last European country to formally embrace Christianity, around 1400 CE. Its terrain is mostly flat, with many lakes, moors, and bogs. A member of the EU since 2004, Lithuania intends to adopt the Euro in 2013.

Denmark

Area 16,639 sq miles (43,094 sq km)
Population 5.6 million
Capital Copenhagen
Currency Danish krone
Official language Danish
Life expectancy 78 years

With one of the flattest terrains in the world, Denmark is the southernmost country in Scandinavia. It occupies most of the Jutland (Jylland) peninsula and includes the islands of Sjælland, Fyn, Lolland, and Falster, and more than 400 smaller islands. Two self-governing nations lying in the North Atlantic, the Faeroe Islands and Greenland, fall under the sovereignty of Denmark. The population is largely of Danish ethnicity with small minorities of Turks and Inuit, Greenland's indigenous inhabitants. Denmark's income distribution is the most even among Western countries, with most Danes able to live comfortably. Denmark is also a strong supporter of developing countries, especially in Africa.

▶ THE LITTLE MERMAID
This iconic statue of a mermaid in Copenhagen is based on the fairy tale The Little Mermaid *by the Danish author Hans Christian Andersen.*

Ireland

Area 27,135 sq miles
(70,280 sq km)
Population 4.5 million
Capital Dublin
Currency Euro
Official languages Irish
and English
Life expectancy 79 years

After centuries of struggle against British rule, the Irish Republic became a sovereign state in 1937. It covers about 85 percent of the island of Ireland (the rest remains part of the UK). The population is almost entirely ethnically Irish.

Belgium

Area 11,780 sq miles
(30,510 sq km)
Population 10.8 million
Capital Brussels
Currency Euro
Official languages Dutch,
French, and German
Life expectancy 79 years

Belgium is located between Germany, France, and the Netherlands. The south includes the forested Ardennes region. Belgium has two main communities—the majority Dutch-speaking Flemings and the French-speaking Walloons.

▲ BELGIAN CHOCOLATES
Belgian chocolates are considered to be some of the best chocolates in the world. They come in a variety of flavors, and are sold all over the world.

United Kingdom

Area 94,525 sq miles
(244,820 sq km)
Population 62.4 million
Capital London
Currency Pound sterling
Official languages English
and Welsh (in Wales)
Life expectancy 79 years

The United Kingdom (UK) occupies a major portion of the British Isles. It includes the countries of England, Scotland, Wales, Northern Ireland, and several outlying islands. The UK is a democracy with a monarch as the ceremonial head of state. Queen Elizabeth II, who celebrated 60 years on the throne with her Diamond Jubilee in 2012, is the second-longest reigning queen in British history, after Queen Victoria (1837–1901). The UK heads the Commonwealth—an organization of 54 independent member states—is a world leader in financial services, and is home to many major multinational companies.

▼ RED MAILBOX
A traditional red Royal Mail box is mounted in front of a drystone wall in the Lake District, England.

Netherlands

Area 16,033 sq miles
(41,526 sq km)
Population 16.7 million
Capital Amsterdam
Currency Euro
Official language Dutch
Life expectancy 80 years

The Netherlands lies at the meeting point of four major rivers in northern Europe. The country's few hills, in the east and south, descend to a flat coastal area bordered by the North Sea to the north and the west. This is protected by dunes, dykes, and canals, since 27 percent of the coast is below sea level. The country became independent from Spain in 1648 and is a constitutional monarchy. Although the Netherlands' capital is Amsterdam, its government functions from the Hague. The country is a major trading hub, with Europe's biggest port, Rotterdam, located here. The Netherlands has a highly skilled and educated workforce and a tradition of high-tech innovation, including the development of the music cassette and CD. Multinational companies such as Philips and Shell are headquartered here.

◄ AMSTERDAM
The capital and the biggest city of the Netherlands, Amsterdam has a large canal system running through it. It is one of the most bicycle-friendly cities in the world.

Luxembourg

Area 998 sq miles
(2,586 sq km)
Population 500,000
Capital Luxembourg-Ville
Currency Euro
Official languages French, German, and Luxembourgish
Life expectancy 79 years

Luxembourg shares borders with Germany, France, and Belgium. It has the highest per capita income in the EU. It is also known as a banking center and is the headquarters of key EU institutions, such as the European Court of Justice.

Liechtenstein

Area 62 sq miles
(160 sq km)
Population 36,700
Capital Vaduz
Currency Swiss franc
Official language German
Life expectancy 80 years

This small, politically stable country is nestled in the Alps. Many overseas banks and investment companies operate here, and a third of its residents are foreign nationals. It has close ties with Switzerland, which handles its foreign relations and defense.

▲ MALBUN, LIECHTENSTEIN
The only ski resort in Liechtenstein, Malbun is a small mountain village located 5,200 ft (1,600 m) high in the Alps.

▲ WOLFGANG AMADEUS MOZART
The musical genius Mozart (1756–1791) was born in Salzburg, Austria. He remains one of the most influential classical music composers.

Austria

Area 32,378 sq miles
(83,858 sq km)
Population 8.4 million
Capital Vienna
Currency Euro
Official language German
Life expectancy 80 years

Austria is dominated by the Alps in the west, while fertile plains form the east and north. Its economy is based on income from high-tech sectors, tourism, and agriculture. Austria's main trading partner is its northern neighbor, Germany.

Slovenia

Area 7,820 sq miles
(20,253 sq km)
Population 2 million
Capital Ljubljana
Currency Euro
Official language Slovenian
Life expectancy 78 years

A small country located at the northeastern end of the Adriatic Sea, Slovenia controls some of Europe's major transit routes. It is a former Yugoslav republic that became independent in 1991. Slovenes are of the same ethnicity as the neighboring Croats.

Monaco

Area 0.75 sq miles
(1.95 sq km)
Population 30,510
Capital Monaco-Ville
Currency Euro
Official language French
Life expectancy 80 years

The Principality of Monaco is a city-state located on the Côte d'Azur, the Mediterranean coastline of southeastern France. Monaco is a lucrative banking center. It is also a popular tourist spot, especially since the opening of the Monte Carlo casino by Prince Charles III in 1863.

Switzerland

Area 15,942 sq miles
(41,290 sq km)
Population 7.7 million
Capital Bern
Currency Swiss franc
Official languages French, German, Italian, and Romansch
Life expectancy 82 years

Switzerland, one of the most prosperous countries in the world, lies at the center of western Europe. Its foreign policy has remained largely neutral, without favoring any country in most of the European conflicts since 1815. Switzerland has so far not joined the EU.

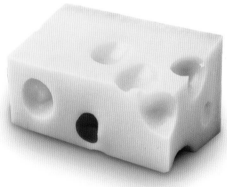

▲ SWISS CHEESE
Cheese making has been a Swiss tradition for hundreds of years. Swiss cheese typically has a mild flavor and characteristic holes.

Germany

Area 137,846 sq miles
(357,021 sq km)
Population 82.2 million
Capital Berlin
Currency Euro
Official languages German
Life expectancy 79 years

Germany is bordered by nine countries, with coastlines on both the Baltic and North seas. Germany is Europe's foremost industrial power, and the world's second-biggest exporter. In 1945, after the defeat of Adolf Hitler's Nazi regime at the end of World War II, Germany was divided into East Germany and West Germany. The country was reunited in 1990 with the collapse of

the Communist East German government. However, the east remains economically poorer, with many people choosing to migrate to the west for better opportunities. The German government is led by an elected chancellor. In 2005, Angela Merkel became the first female chancellor. By and large, women play a bigger role in German politics than in most other European countries. Germany was one of the original 12 nations to adopt the Euro in 2002.

▶ BAVARIA, GERMANY
With traditional German architecture and first-rate museums, Bavaria is said to be one of the most scenic travel destinations in Germany.

▲ OLIVE OIL
Olives are grown across the Mediterranean. They are pressed to produce olive oil, an essential part of Italian cuisine.

Italy

Area 116,305 sq miles (301,230 sq km)
Population 60.8 million
Capital Rome
Currency Euro
Official language Italian
Life expectancy 81 years

Italy is a boot-shaped peninsula that stretches southward into the Mediterranean Sea. It is bordered by the Alps to the north. Italy includes Sicily, Sardinia, and other smaller islands. The two famous volcanoes, Vesuvius and Etna, are located in southern Italy. A world leader in industrial and product design and textiles, Italy is also home to many prestigious fashion houses.

San Marino

Area 23.6 sq miles (61 sq km)
Population 32,000
Capital San Marino
Currency Euro
Official language Italian
Life expectancy 82 years

A small nation lying within Italy, San Marino is perched around the slopes of Monte Titano in the Appennine Mountains. San Marino is the world's oldest republic. It is entirely dependent on Italy, which controls most of its affairs. The people of San Marino are called the Sammarinese. About one-third of them live in the northern town of Serravalle.

France

Area 211,209 sq miles (547,030 sq km)
Population 63.1 million
Capital Paris
Currency Euro
Official language French
Life expectancy 81 years

France straddles western Europe from the English Channel to the Mediterranean Sea. It borders Germany and Belgium in the north, and Spain in the south. France was Europe's first modern republic, and once had a colonial empire second only to the British Empire. Today, it is one of the world's major industrial powers, as well as Europe's leading agricultural producer.

With a large immigrant population, France is one of the most ethnically diverse countries in Europe. It is a secular (nonreligious) state. Throughout history, French culture, art, philosophy, literature, and fashion have influenced the rest of the world. It is also the most visited country in the world and its capital, Paris, is considered to be one of the world's most beautiful cities. Many influential artists, writers, and filmmakers of the modern era have lived there.

▼ FRENCH CHATEAU
Chateau de La Brède in Gironde, France, is a castle dating from the early 14th century. Built on a small islet surrounded by water-filled moats, it was the birthplace and residence of the writer and philosopher Montesquieu (1689–1755).

Vatican City

Area 0.17 sq miles (0.44 sq km)
Population 800
Capital Vatican City
Currency Euro
Official languages Italian and Latin
Life expectancy 80 years

Vatican City is the smallest independent nation in the world. It lies within a walled enclave in the heart of Italy's capital, Rome. It is the headquarters of the Roman Catholic Church, led by the Pope. As spiritual leader of the Roman Catholics, he has supreme powers and usually holds office until he dies. (In 2013, however, Pope Benedict XVI announced his retirement at the age of 85.)

▲ THE PIETÀ
Housed in St. Peter's Basilica in Vatican City, the Pietà by Michelangelo shows the Virgin Mary with Jesus's body after the Crucifixion.

Andorra

Area 181 sq miles (468 sq km)
Population 85,100
Capital Andorra la Vella
Currency Euro
Official language Catalan
Life expectancy 84 years

Andorra is a tiny, landlocked country between France and Spain, lying high in the Pyrenees Mountains. It is known as a principality because the state is headed by two coprinces—the Bishop of Urgell and the President of France. Andorra's spectacular scenery and mountain climate have made tourism—especially skiing—its main source of income.

Spain

Area 194,896 sq miles (504,782 sq km)
Population 46.5 million
Capital Madrid
Currency Euro
Official languages Spanish, Galician, Basque, and Catalan
Life expectancy 81 years

Occupying a major part of the Iberian Peninsula of southwestern Europe, Spain has an Atlantic as well as a Mediterranean coast. Spain was ruled by the military dictator General Franco from 1939 until his death in 1975. His successor, King Juan Carlos I, peacefully led the nation toward democracy, and the first free elections were held in 1977. Although the economy saw rapid growth in the 1980s, a financial slump in 2008 led to severe unemployment. However, tourism has been a key strength of the Spanish economy; the country's vibrant culture, dance, music, and food attract many visitors.

▶ CASA BATLLÓ, BARCELONA
This remarkable landmark in Barcelona, Spain, was built by Antoni Gaudí, the celebrated Spanish architect. Among its unique features is its arched roof, which is shaped like a dragon's back, with ceramic tiles for scales.

Portugal

Area 35,672 sq miles (92,391 sq km)
Population 10.7 million
Capital Lisbon
Currency Euro
Official language Portuguese
Life expectancy 78 years

Portugal lies on the western side of the Iberian Peninsula. Its long-standing dictatorship ended with a bloodless military coup (takeover) in 1974. Portugal has been a multiparty democracy since then. The economic slowdown in 2008 pushed the Portuguese economy into severe debt.

Malta

Area 122 sq miles (316 sq km)
Population 400,000
Capital Valletta
Currency Euro
Official languages Maltese and English
Life expectancy 79 years

Malta is a group of tiny islands that lie between Europe and North Africa. Only the islands Kemmuna, Gozo, and Malta are inhabited. After being ruled by successive colonial powers, Malta gained its independence from the UK in 1964. Tourism is Malta's chief source of income.

Cyprus

Area 3,571 sq miles (9,250 sq km)
Population 1.1 million
Capital Nicosia
Currency Euro
Official languages Greek and Turkish
Life expectancy 79 years

The island of Cyprus lies south of Turkey in the eastern Mediterranean. The island was partitioned in 1974, with the north inhabited by Turkish Cypriots and the south by Greek Cypriots. However, Northern Cyprus is officially recognized as an independent state only by Turkey.

Greece

Area 50,942 sq miles (131,940 sq km)
Population 11.4 million
Capital Athens
Currency Euro
Official language Greek
Life expectancy 79 years

The Hellenic Republic, or Greece as it is popularly known, is surrounded by the Aegean, Ionian, and Mediterranean seas, and includes about 2,000 islands. Greece's idyllic beaches and historical sites are very popular with tourists. The country has had debt problems since 2009.

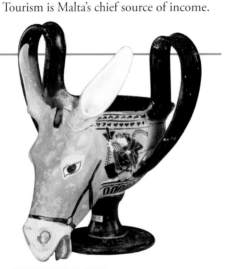

▲ DRINKING CUP
This Ancient Greek drinking cup with handles rising above the brim, called a kantharos, *has been styled in the shape of a donkey's head.*

Albania

Area 11,100 sq miles (28,748 sq km)
Population 3.2 million
Capital Tirana
Currency Albanian lek
Official language Albanian
Life expectancy 76 years

A mountainous country lying at the southeastern end of the Adriatic Sea, Albania is one of the poorest countries in Europe. Albania is home to a small minority of ethnic Greeks. Dominated by the Communist ruler Enver Hoxha for 40 years, it became a democracy in 1991.

Macedonia

Area 9,781 sq miles (25,333 sq km)
Population 2.1 million
Capital Skopje
Currency Macedonian denar
Official languages Albanian and Macedonian
Life expectancy 74 years

The Republic of Macedonia is a landlocked nation in southeastern Europe. Formerly part of Yugoslavia, which collapsed in 1992, it remains one of the poorest former Yugoslav countries, with more than 30 percent unemployment. Slav Macedonians make up the majority of the population, with ethnic Albanians forming the minority.

Bulgaria

Area 42,822 sq miles (110,910 sq km)
Population 7.4 million
Capital Sofia
Currency Lev
Official language Bulgarian
Life expectancy 73 years

Bulgaria extends south from the Danube River, with the Black Sea to its east. The country was under a Communist regime until 1989, after which it became a democracy. Bulgaria's thermal and nuclear power plants have made it a major producer and exporter of energy in southeast Europe.

Croatia

Area 21,831 sq miles (56,542 sq km)
Population 4.4 million
Capital Zagreb
Currency Kuna
Official language Croatian
Life expectancy 76 years

From medieval times, Croatia was controlled by Hungary. It was a part of the Yugoslav state for much of the 20th century, becoming a republic in 1991. Croatia has very few minerals, although it does have oil and gas fields. The Adriatic Sea's rich fishing grounds are a major natural resource.

Turkey

Area 301,384 sq miles (780,580 sq km)
Population 73.6 million
Capital Ankara
Currency Turkish lira
Official language Turkish
Life expectancy 71 years

Turkey's location, straddling both the European and the Asian continents, gives it great strategic influence over the Black Sea, the Mediterranean, and the Middle East. Most Turks are Sunni Muslim, though the Shi'a community is growing fast. Turkey is projected to have a larger population than any EU country by 2020.

Serbia

Area 29,905 sq miles (77,453 sq km)
Population 9.9 million
Capital Belgrade
Currency Serbian dinar
Official language Serbian
Life expectancy 73 years

Serbia became a sovereign republic after the union of Serbia and Montenegro ended in 2006. Ethnic conflicts in the 1990s greatly affected Serbian society. The mainly Albanian province of Kosovo, which rebelled against Serbian rule, declared independence in 2008.

Bosnia and Herzegovina

Area 19,741 sq miles (51,129 sq km)
Population 3.8 million
Capital Sarajevo
Currency Maraka
Official languages Bosnian, Serbian, and Croatian
Life expectancy 75 years

Following the collapse of Yugoslavia, Bosnia and Herzegovina suffered devastating internal conflicts in the 1990s. These were fought between the Muslim Bosniaks, Orthodox Christian Serbs, and Roman Catholic Croats. The country received aid from the EU and the United States to rebuild its economy.

▲ STUFFED VINE LEAVES
Dolma, a popular Turkish dish, consists of vegetables or meat wrapped in vine leaves. The dish is also common in the Balkans, the Middle East, and in Central and South Asia.

Montenegro

Area 5,333 sq miles (13,812 sq km)
Population 600,000
Capital Podgorica
Currency Euro
Official language Montenegrin
Life expectancy 74 years

The tiny republic of Montenegro, which literally means "Black Mountain," became independent in 2006 when it split from Serbia. It was formerly part of Yugoslavia. With its many scenic beaches, Montenegro's tourist industry is rapidly expanding. However, rural poverty is widespread.

▲ STARI MOST BRIDGE
Located over the Neretva River is the country's most recognizable landmark. The bridge was originally built by the Ottomans in 1566.

Hungary

Area 35,919 sq miles
(93,030 sq km)
Population 10 million
Capital Budapest
Currency Forint
Official language Hungarian
Life expectancy 74 years

Hungary, lying at the heart of central Europe, is a landlocked nation sharing borders with seven countries. The majority of the population is of Magyar ethnicity, with small minorities of Roma, Germans, Jews, Romanians, Serbs, Slovaks, and Croats. With many state-of-the-art factories, Hungary has high industrial production.

▲ HUNGARIAN PULI
The fun-loving and intelligent Puli dog originated in Hungary. Traditionally a herding dog, the Puli's corded coat gives it a distinctive appearance.

Romania

Area 91,699 sq miles
(237,500 sq km)
Population 21.4 million
Capital Bucharest
Currency New Romanian leu
Official language Romanian
Life expectancy 72 years

Romania lies on the Black Sea coast, with the Danube River forming its southern border. The Carpathian Mountains run across the center of the country. Romania has large oil reserves, and is currently trying to find natural oil and gas deposits in the Black Sea. It joined the EU in 2007, and plans to adopt the Euro in 2015.

Moldova

Area 13,067 sq miles
(33,843 sq km)
Population 3.5 million
Capital Chisinau
Currency Moldovan leu
Official language Moldovan
Life expectancy 71 years

Moldova was part of Romania until 1940, when it became part of the USSR (a Communist state that incorporated Russia and 14 other Soviet republics). Moldova is now Europe's poorest country and depends on Russia for raw materials and fuel. A high proportion of Moldovans are farmers.

Poland

Area 120,728 sq miles
(312,685 sq km)
Population 38.3 million
Capital Warsaw
Currency Polish zloty
Official language Polish
Life expectancy 75 years

Poland extends from the shores of the Baltic Sea on the north coast to the Tatra Mountains in the south. Since the collapse of Communism in Poland in 1989, the country has undergone massive social and political changes, and has experienced rapid economic growth.

▲ EUROPEAN BISON
The European bison is the largest living land animal in Europe. The Białowieża Forest in Poland is home to about 800 of these animals.

Czech Republic

Area 30,450 sq miles
(78,866 sq km)
Population 10.5 million
Capital Prague
Currency Czech koruna
Official language Czech
Life expectancy 77 years

Landlocked in central Europe, the Czech Republic consists of the territories of Bohemia and Moravia. Previously part of Czechoslovakia, it became an independent republic in 1993. Czechs make up 90 percent of the population, and Moravians make up the next largest group.

▲ LEAD CRYSTAL CHANDELIER
Glassmaking is an important industry in the Czech Republic, where glassmakers are famous for skilled craftsmanship and elaborate designs.

Slovakia

Area 18,859 sq miles
(48,845 sq km)
Population 5.5 million
Capital Bratislava
Currency Euro
Official language Slovak
Life expectancy 75 years

Slovakia was the less developed half of Czechoslovakia for much of the 20th century. It became an independent democracy in 1993 and joined the EU in 2004. The country has since experienced major economic growth, helped by its highly skilled, cheap labor force.

Belarus

Area 80,155 sq miles
(207,600 sq km)
Population 9.6 million
Capital Minsk
Currency Belarussian rouble
Official languages Russian
and Belarussian
Life expectancy 71 years

Belarus literally means "white Russia." White is a color associated in Slavic culture with freedom and the name may be a reference to the fact that the country was never conquered by the Mongols in the 13th century. Belarus was part of the USSR until 1991. Most people here speak Russian, and only 11 percent of the population are fluent in Belarussian, which is used mainly in rural areas. Plans to construct a nuclear power plant were postponed after the 1986 Chernobyl disaster, which occurred in nearby Ukraine, but are now underway again. Currently, the country is heavily dependent on Russia for fuel and energy supplies.

Ukraine

Area 233,090 sq miles
(603,700 sq km)
Population 45.2 million
Capital Kiev
Currency Hryvnya
Official language Ukrainian
Life expectancy 68 years

The word Ukraine translates as "on the border." It was long considered merely a fringe of the Russian Empire, but since the collapse of the USSR in 1991 it has been an independent state and is now the second-largest country in Europe after Russia. The country is divided between the Ukrainian-speaking west and a large ethnic Russian population in the east. Ukraine has vast natural resources, including natural gas, oil, and titanium. In 1986, the world's worst nuclear disaster occurred at the Ukraine's Chernobyl power plant. A massive plume of radioactive particles spread across Europe, polluting the environment and raising fears for the long-term health of thousands of people.

Russian Federation

Area 6,592,772 sq miles
(17,075,200 sq km)
Population 143 million
Capital Moscow
Currency Russian rouble
Official language Russian
Life expectancy 66 years

The Russian Federation was formed in 1991, after the USSR collapsed. Bounded by the Arctic and Pacific Oceans to the north and east, it is by far the world's largest country. Ethnic Russians make up four-fifths of the population. However, there are around 150 smaller ethnic groups, many with their own national territories within Russia's borders. Russia has some of the world's largest reserves of key resources such as gold, diamonds, and timber. It is a major producer of oil, natural gas, and electricity, and launched the world's first floating nuclear power station in 2010 to provide electricity to remote areas. Russia is one of the fastest-growing economies in the world.

▶ ST. BASIL'S CATHEDRAL
With its multicolored, domed towers, St. Basil's Cathedral in Red Square, Moscow, is one of Russia's biggest tourist attractions.

Africa

Covering almost 20 percent of Earth's total land area, Africa is the second-largest and the second most populous continent. It is also the hottest continent—the world's largest desert, the Sahara, is located here. Africa is home to the African elephant and the giraffe, the world's biggest and tallest animals, respectively. *Homo sapiens* (modern humans) are thought to have evolved in Africa and then spread out across the world.

▲ NAMIB DESERT
Visitors climb to the summit of a sand dune in the Namib Naukluff National Park, Namibia. The burnt orange dunes found here are the tallest sand dunes in the world.

Morocco

Area 172,317 sq miles
(446,300 sq km)
Population 32.3 million
Capital Rabat
Currency Moroccan dirham
Official languages Arabic
and Tamazight
Life expectancy 71 years

The Kingdom of Morocco, a former French colony, is located in North Africa. It is a constitutional monarchy—the prime minister heads the government while the king is the spiritual leader. About 99 percent of the population follow the Sunni Islam faith. Morocco's key economic sectors are tourism, textiles, mining, agriculture, and leather. In 2000, large oil and gas deposits were discovered in the Sahara Desert, which spans the southeastern part of Morocco. The country's rich culture is a blend of Arab, Berber, African, and European influences.

▲ BABOUCHES
A trademark of the city of Marrakesh in Morocco, babouches are handmade heel-less slippers made from leather. They are very popular with the tourists in Morocco.

Mauritania

Area 397,955 sq miles
(1,030,700 sq km)
Population 3.5 million
Capital Nouakchott
Currency Ouguiya
Official language Arabic
Life expectancy 64 years

The Islamic Republic of Mauritania lies in northwest Africa. Much of its territory is covered by the Sahara Desert. Mauritania has recently changed from being a country of nomads to a largely urban-dwelling one, though many people retain their traditions. The country is made up of the Maures, who are politically and economically dominant, and a black minority. The main mineral resources found here are iron (from the Cominor mine at Zouérat), gypsum, copper, gold, diamonds, oil, phosphate, and silver. Mauritania's offshore fishing is among the best in West Africa.

Cape Verde

Area 1,557 sq miles
(4,033 sq km)
Population 500,000
Capital Praia
Currency Escudo
Official language Portuguese
Life expectancy 71 years

Off the west coast of Africa is Cape Verde, an archipelago of 10 islands located in the Atlantic Ocean. Most of the islands are mountainous and volcanic. A Portuguese colony until 1975, Cape Verde has been one of the most stable democracies in Africa. Around 50 percent of the population lives on the island of Santiago. The majority of Cape Verde's population is a Portuguese-African mix, and the remainder is largely made up of Africans who are descended either from slaves or from more recent immigrants from the African mainland. Tourism and fishing are important sources of revenue in Cape Verde. The islands face severe droughts and water supply problems. Lack of agricultural land has led to a shortfall in food production, making it dependent on aid from other countries.

Senegal

Area 75,749 sq miles
(196,190 sq km)
Population 12.8 million
Capital Dakar
Currency CFA franc
Official language French
Life expectancy 63 years

Mostly low-lying, Senegal is made up of open savanna and semidesert in the north, and thicker savanna in the south. Senegal gained independence from France in 1960, after which it was ruled by President Léopold Senghor for nearly two decades. Although Senegal became a multiparty democracy in 1981, the ruling Socialist Party stayed in power until 2000. Senegal's economy is supported by fishing, the production and export of groundnuts, phosphate mining, and a relatively strong industrial sector. A large number of Senegalese live abroad, and this has helped spread global awareness about the country's culture, particularly its music. The money they send home is also an important source of revenue.

▶ SENEGAL PARROT
A shy bird that feeds on fruit, seeds, and blossoms, the Senegal parrot lives in the open woodlands in west Africa. However, it is considered a farm pest since it often feeds on corn or millet.

Gambia

Area 4,363 sq miles
(11,300 sq km)
Population 1.8 million
Capital Banjul
Currency Dalasi
Official language English
Life expectancy 59 years

A narrow country on the western coast of Africa, Gambia is one of the smallest nations on the continent. It became independent in 1965 and was a stable democracy until 1994, when an army coup brought military leader Yahya Jammeh to power. President Jammeh has been ruling Gambia ever since. About 90 percent of Gambians follow Islam, though there is no official state religion. Agriculture is Gambia's economic mainstay, particularly the export of groundnuts. Tourism is also an important source of revenue, with most travelers visiting the resorts on Gambia's Atlantic coast. However, the impact of tourism and overfishing in Gambian waters are major environmental concerns today.

◀ KORAS
A traditional harplike instrument, the kora is made from a large calabash gourd cut in half and partially covered with cow skin. These koras are in the process of being made—when finished, they will have long necks and strings.

Guinea

Area 94,926 sq miles
(245,857 sq km)
Population 10.2 million
Capital Conakry
Currency Guinea franc
Official language French
Life expectancy 56 years

Guinea lies on the western coast of Africa. Its central highlands are either densely forested or covered in savanna, while the north is semidesert. Guinea gained independence from France in 1958. Its main ethnic groups are the Peul and the Malinké. Guinea is rich in natural resources including bauxite, gold, and diamonds. However, the lack of a stable government has made Guinea one of the poorest countries in West Africa.

Guinea-Bissau

Area 13,946 sq miles
(36,120 sq km)
Population 1.5 million
Capital Bissau
Currency CFA franc
Official language Portuguese
Life expectancy 46 years

Guinea-Bissau is a former Portuguese territory that became independent in 1974. It became a multiparty democracy in 1990, but there has been a series of army rebellions and military coups, the latest in 2003. The largest ethnic group is the Balante, while mixed-race *mestiço* and European minorities make up 2 percent of the population. Many people live and work on small family farms grouped into self-contained villages.

▲ CASHEW NUTS AND FRUIT
Guinea-Bissau's second-largest crop, and most important export product, is cashews. Most of the cashews are grown on small farms.

Liberia

Area 43,000 sq miles
(111,370 sq km)
Population 4.1 million
Capital Monrovia
Currency Liberian dollar
Official language English
Life expectancy 45 years

Liberia lies in West Africa. It was founded in 1847 by freed American slaves. Liberia faced civil wars from the 1990s, until peace was declared in 2003. In 2006, Liberia's president, Ellen Johnson Sirleaf, became Africa's first female elected head of state.

Sierra Leone

Area 27,699 sq miles
(71,740 sq km)
Population 6 million
Capital Freetown
Currency Leone
Official language English
Life expectancy 42 years

The West African nation of Sierra Leone was set up by the British in 1787 for freed African slaves. In 2002, it emerged from a decade of civil wars, which displaced nearly two million people. Economic recovery, with the help of foreign aid, has been slow.

▲ DIAMONDS
Sierra Leone is rich in diamonds—a major revenue source for the country. However, much of its civil war was funded by the illegal trade of diamonds, known as "blood diamonds."

Ivory Coast

Area 124,502 sq miles
(322,460 sq km)
Population 20.2 million
Capital Yamoussoukro
Currency CFA franc
Official language French
Life expectancy 48 years

Ivory Coast—officially Côte d'Ivoire—was a French colony until 1960. Once a politically stable country, it slipped into internal chaos following an army coup in 1999. Civil erupted in 2002, and much of the north is still under the control of rebel groups. Ivory Coast is the world's biggest producer of cocoa.

▲ OUR LADY OF PEACE BASILICA
The Basilica of Our Lady of Peace in Yamoussoukro is one of the largest churches in the world. Construction was completed in 1989.

Mali

Area 478,766 sq miles
(1,240,000 sq km)
Population 15.8 million
Capital Bamako
Currency CFA franc
Official language French
Life expectancy 54 years

Mali is a landlocked country in the heart of West Africa. The Niger River flows through its central and southwestern regions. Mali became a multiparty democracy in 1992. However, a military coup overthrew the elected president in 2012, and nearly two-thirds of Mali's northern regions have been captured by Islamic extremists.

Algeria

Area 919,595 sq miles
(2,381,740 sq km)
Population 36 million
Capital Algiers
Currency Algerian dinar
Official language Arabic
Life expectancy 72 years

Extending from a densely populated Mediterranean coast to the uninhabited northern Sahara is Africa's largest country, Algeria. It won independence from France in 1962. Algerians are predominantly Arabs who follow the Sunni Islam faith. The indigenous Berbers, who still have their own language and culture, make up about 24 percent of the population. The Berber language, Tamazight, was recognized as a national language in 2002. Algeria's economic mainstay is its energy exports to Europe.

► BERBER MUSIC
Accompanied by rhythmic drumbeats, Berber songs are an important feature of religious ceremonies, marriages, and festivals.

Tunisia

Area 63,170 sq miles
(163,610 sq km)
Population 10.6 million
Capital Tunis
Currency Tunisian dinar
Official language Arabic
Life expectancy 74 years

North Africa's smallest country, Tunisia lies sandwiched between Libya and Algeria. Its population is almost entirely Muslim, of Arab and Berber descent, though there are Jewish and Christian minorities. Tourism is an important sector of Tunisia's economy.

Libya

Area 679,362 sq miles
(1,759,540 sq km)
Population 6.4 million
Capital Tripoli
Currency Libyan dinar
Official language Arabic
Life expectancy 74 years

Libya is located in North Africa, between Egypt and Algeria. In 2011, a civil war ended Colonel Muammar al-Gaddafi's 42 years of dictatorial rule. Libya is now headed by its newly elected parliament, the General National Congress.

Niger

Area 489,191 sq miles
(1,267,000 sq km)
Population 16.1 million
Capital Niamey
Currency CFA franc
Official language French
Life expectancy 56 years

Landlocked in the west of Africa, Niger is covered by the Sahara Desert in the north. It has large deposits of uranium, which is its main export. Niger is one of the poorest countries in Africa and faces regular food shortages. It is highly dependent on aid.

Egypt

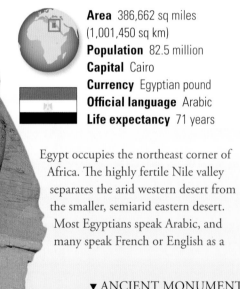

Area 386,662 sq miles
(1,001,450 sq km)
Population 82.5 million
Capital Cairo
Currency Egyptian pound
Official language Arabic
Life expectancy 71 years

Egypt occupies the northeast corner of Africa. The highly fertile Nile valley separates the arid western desert from the smaller, semiarid eastern desert. Most Egyptians speak Arabic, and many speak French or English as a second language. Egypt's capital, Cairo, is the second most populous city in Africa and its population is predicted to reach 100 million by 2025. In addition to oil and gas, Egypt's economy is also dependent on agriculture (especially cotton) and its well-developed tourist industry. Egyptian women have been among the most liberated in the Arab world, and enjoy more rights under the law than women in many other Arab nations. However, growing Islamic fundamentalism in the country is seen as a possible threat to their position, especially in the rural areas.

▼ ANCIENT MONUMENTS
The Great Sphinx—a human-headed lion—is set against the towering pyramid of Khafre in the desert region of Giza, Egypt.

Burkina Faso

Area 105,869 sq miles (274,200 sq km)
Population 17 million
Capital Ouagadougou
Currency CFA franc
Official language French
Life expectancy 52 years

◄ TRADITIONAL DRESS
Traditionally, women in Burkina wear long cotton skirts that are wrapped at the waist, along with matching tops. Shown here is a mother carrying her baby on her back.

Landlocked in West Africa, Burkina (officially called Burkina Faso) gained independence from France in 1960. Most of Burkina lies on the arid edge of the Sahara Desert known as the Sahel. Following independence, it was ruled by military dictators until 1991, when it became a multiparty democracy. However, it is now ruled by a former military dictator, Blaise Compaoré, who was elected president in 1991. It has large mineral deposits such as gold, antimony, marble, manganese, silver, and zinc. Despite this, Burkina's economy remains largely agricultural.

COUNTRY FACTFILE

Ghana

Area 92,100 sq miles (238,540 sq km)
Population 25 million
Capital Accra
Currency Cedi
Official language English
Life expectancy 60 years

Ghana was the first West African nation to gain independence from its colonial power, Britain, in 1957. It is Africa's second largest gold producer and is a major exporter of cocoa. Ghana has made good progress in reducing poverty, thanks to a growing economy—it has a well-developed industrial base and started producing oil in 2011.

Togo

Area 21,925 sq miles (56,785 sq km)
Population 6.2 million
Capital Lomé
Currency CFA franc
Official language French
Life expectancy 58 years

Togo is sandwiched between Ghana and Benin in West Africa. Its center is forested, surrounded by savanna lands in the north and south. The port of Lomé is an important center for West African trade. The "Nana Benz," the market women of Lomé, control the retail trade. However, political power is held only by the men.

Benin

Area 43,843 sq miles (112,620 sq km)
Population 9.1 million
Capital Porto-Novo
Currency CFA franc
Official language French
Life expectancy 56 years

Formerly the kingdom of Dahomey, Benin was under French rule until it gained independence in 1960. Ending 17 years of one-party Communist rule, Benin became a multiparty democracy in 1990. Benin has 42 different ethnic groups. About 50 percent of the population follow indigenous beliefs, including voodoo.

Nigeria

Area 356,669 sq miles (923,768 sq km)
Population 162 million
Capital Abuja
Currency Naira
Official language English
Life expectancy 47 years

Africa's most populous country, the Federal Republic of Nigeria gained its independence from the UK in 1960. Its terrain varies from tropical rainforest and swamps in the south to savanna in the north. After a series of military regimes, Nigeria now has an elected government. It has a strongly growing economy, boosted by the fact that Nigeria is one of the world's top oil producers. However, oil industry pollution in the Niger Delta—the origin of most of Nigeria's oil production—is a major concern. Natural gas, coal, tin, and iron are some of the other mineral resources found here. More than half the country is poor: Ethnic violence from 1999 to 2003 drove about 800,000 people out of their homes, adding to Nigeria's poverty levels.

► LAGOS, NIGERIA
Shown here is the skyline of Lagos, the most populous city and the financial heart of Nigeria. Lagos is one of the fastest-growing cities in Africa.

Chad

Area 495,755 sq miles
(1,284,000 sq km)
Population 11.5 million
Capital N'Djamena
Currency CFA franc
Official languages Arabic
and French
Life expectancy 51 years

This landlocked nation in north central
Africa is a largely semidesert country. It
gained independence from France in 1960.
Since then, Chad has had a chaotic history,
with civil wars and military coups. As a
result, the country has an underdeveloped
economy. Recently, large oil deposits were
discovered in the southern Doba region.

Cameroon

Area 183,553 sq miles
(475,400 sq km)
Population 20 million
Capital Yaoundé
Currency CFA franc
Official languages French
and English
Life expectancy 50 years

Cameroon is a forested country located
on the central west African coast. It was
formed in 1961 when two former British
and French colonies came together.
Ethnically diverse, Cameroon is home
to about 230 groups, the largest being
the Bamileke. Cameroon has one of the
highest literacy rates in Africa.

▲ CARVED WOODEN MASK
*Masks hold great significance in traditional
African culture. This one is from the
Cross River region of Cameroon.*

Equatorial Guinea

Area 10,830 sq miles
(28,051 sq km)
Population 700,000
Capital Malabo
Currency CFA franc
Official languages Spanish
and French
Life expectancy 51 years

Lying just north of the equator, Equatorial
Guinea is made up of five islands and the
territory of Río Muni on the west coast of
Africa. The republic gained independence
in 1968 after 190 years of Spanish rule.
Equatorial Guinea is the only Spanish-
speaking country in Africa.

Gabon

Area 103,347 sq miles
(267,667 sq km)
Population 1.5 million
Capital Libreville
Currency CFA franc
Official language French
Life expectancy 57 years

Gabon, located on the west coast of Africa,
has some of the world's most unspoiled
rainforests. It is also one of Africa's most
urbanized countries. Gabon's economy
is based on the production of oil, and the
wealth from oil exports has given rise to
an affluent middle class.

◀ GUINEA TURACO
*This green bird is found in the
forests of Central and West Africa.
Its call sounds like "g'way," which is why
it is often referred to as the go-away bird.*

São Tomé and Principé

Area 386 sq miles
(1,001 sq km)
Population 200,000
Capital São Tomé
Currency Dobra
Official language Portuguese
Life expectancy 65 years

Made up of two main islands and their
surrounding islets, São Tomé and Principé
was a Portuguese colony until 1975. It was
a single-party Marxist nation until 1990,
when multiparty democracy was adopted.
Its population is 90 percent black African
and 10 percent Portuguese and Creole.

▲ PARADISE ISLANDS
*São Tomé and Principé is a traveler's paradise,
with its palm-fringed beaches, crystal-clear
water, and barely explored jungles.*

Congo

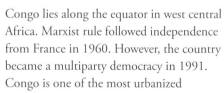

Area 132,047 sq miles
(342,000 sq km)
Population 4.1 million
Capital Brazzaville
Currency CFA franc
Official language French
Life expectancy 55 years

Congo lies along the equator in west central
Africa. Marxist rule followed independence
from France in 1960. However, the country
became a multiparty democracy in 1991.
Congo is one of the most urbanized
countries in the region, with most people
living in Brazzaville and Pointe-Noire.

Central African Republic

Area 240,535 sq miles
(622,984 sq km)
Population 4.5 million
Capital Bangui
Currency CFA franc
Official language French
Life expectancy 44 years

The Central African Republic (CAR) has been a politically unstable country since its independence from France in 1960. CAR's main ethnic groups are the Baya and Banda.

▶ FISHING IN THE UBANGI
The Ubangi River is a tributary of the Congo River. It flows through the Central African Republic's capital, Bangui.

Sudan

Area 718,722 sq miles
(1,861,481 sq km)
Population 34 million
Capital Khartoum
Currency Sudanese pound
Official language Arabic
Life expectancy 58 years

Sudan was the largest country in Africa until the southern part became a separate nation in 2011. The split came after decades of civil war between the Arab north and the African south. An ongoing conflict in Darfur in western Sudan has seen some of the worst ethnic violence in recent world history.

South Sudan

Area 248,777 sq miles
(644,329 sq km)
Population 8.3 million
Capital Juba
Currency South Sudan pound
Official language English
Life expectancy not available

A landlocked country in sub-Saharan Africa, South Sudan won recognition as an independent nation only in 2011. It has significant oil reserves, but lack of economic development prevents the country from exploiting them. South Sudan is highly diverse, both ethnically and linguistically.

▲ MOUNTAIN FOREST
South Sudan's evergreen mountain forests are home to a wide variety of flora and fauna.

Eritrea

Area 46,842 sq miles
(121,320 sq km)
Population 5.4 million
Capital Asmara
Currency Nakfa
Official languages Tigrinya,
English, and Arabic
Life expectancy 57 years

Lying along the shore of the Red Sea, Eritrea has a landscape of rugged mountains, bush, and desert. In 1993, Eritrea gained independence from Ethiopia after a long war. Tigrinya speakers, mainly Orthodox Christians, form the largest of Eritrea's nine main ethnic groups.

Ethiopia

Area 455,186 sq miles
(1,127,127 sq km)
Population 84.7 million
Capital Addis Ababa
Currency Birr
Official language Amharic
Life expectancy 52 years

Ethiopia is the only African country to have escaped colonization. It has 86 ethnic groups, and 286 languages. Ethiopia is drought prone and frequently faces food shortages. Its economy is highly dependent on aid, especially from the World Bank, the US, and the European Union.

Djibouti

Area 8,494 sq miles
(22,000 sq km)
Population 900,000
Capital Djibouti
Currency Djibouti franc
Official languages Arabic
and French
Life expectancy 54 years

Djibouti lies in northeast Africa on the strait linking the Red Sea and the Indian Ocean. Its capital city is the main port on the Red Sea, and the main shipping terminal for East Africa. Djibouti also depends on international aid, of which almost half is provided by France.

Somalia

Area 246,200 sq miles
(637,657 sq km)
Population 9.6 million
Capital Mogadishu
Currency Somali shilling
Official languages Somali
and Arabic
Life expectancy 48 years

The Federal Republic of Somalia was
formed when Italian and British territories
joined to form an independent nation in
1960. However, since then, Somalia's
development has been affected by civil
war. Somalia is semiarid and is prone to
droughts. As a result, it is heavily dependent
on international food aid.

Rwanda

Area 10,169 sq miles
(26,338 sq km)
Population 10.9 million
Capital Kigali
Currency Rwandan franc
Official languages French,
English, and Kinyarwanda
Life expectancy 46 years

Rwanda lies landlocked in east central
Africa. Since independence from France
in 1962, ethnic conflict between the Hutu
and Tutsi groups has dominated politics.
Rwanda is trying to rebuild its war-damaged
economy, mainly through tea and coffee
exports. It is still dependent on foreign aid.

Angola

Area 481,353 sq miles
(1,246,700 sq km)
Population 19.6 million
Capital Luanda
Currency Readjusted Kwanza
Official language Portuguese
Life expectancy 42 years

An oil- and diamond-rich country, Angola has
suffered almost continuous civil war since its
independence from Portugal in 1975. With
hostilities finally ending in 2002, Angola is
now on a path to economic recovery. The
predominant ethnic groups living here are
the Ovimbundu and the Kimbundu.

Kenya

Area 224,962 sq miles
(582,650 sq km)
Population 41.6 million
Capital Nairobi
Currency Kenyan shilling
Official languages Kiswahili
and English
Life expectancy 53 years

Kenya straddles the equator on Africa's east
coast. It gained independence from the UK
in 1963. Kenya's capital, Nairobi, is the
communications and financial hub for East
Africa. Culturally diverse, Kenya has about
70 different ethnic groups. The country's
scenic beauty and abundant wildlife have
made it a popular tourist destination.

Democratic Republic of Congo

Area 905,568 sq miles
(2,345,410 sq km)
Population 67.8 million
Capital Kinshasa
Currency Congolese franc
Official language French
Life expectancy 46 years

Located in east central Africa and formerly
known as Zaire, the Democratic Republic
of the Congo (DRC) is Africa's second
largest country, with vast areas covered
by rainforests. Although rich in mineral
wealth, it is one of the world's poorest
nations due to decades of internal conflicts.

Zambia

Area 290,586 sq miles
(752,614 sq km)
Population 13.5 million
Capital Lusaka
Currency Zambian kwacha
Official language English
Life expectancy 42 years

Zambia is a landlocked country in the
heart of southern Africa, bordered by the
Zambezi River to the south. Tourism is
growing, thanks to Zambia's many natural
features—including Victoria Falls, one of
the Seven Natural Wonders of the World—
and a wealth of wildlife.

Uganda

Area 91,133 sq miles
(236,040 sq km)
Population 34.5 million
Capital Kampala
Currency Ugandan shilling
Official language English
Life expectancy 51 years

Uganda, an east African country, gained
independence from the UK in 1962. It is
made up of 13 main ethnic groups, with the
largest being the Baganda. Uganda faced
many ethnic conflicts in the 1970s and
1980s. Since 1986, President Museveni has
ushered in democratic and economic
changes, and peace has mostly been restored.

▲ WESTERN LOWLAND GORILLA
*Found in the thick rainforests, the endangered
western lowland gorilla lives on a vegetarian
diet of roots, shoots, and fruit.*

Burundi

Area 10,745 sq miles
(27,830 sq km)
Population 8.6 million
Capital Bujumbura
Currency Burundian franc
Official languages French
and Kirundi
Life expectancy 49 years

Lying just south of the equator, Burundi is
a landlocked nation partly bordered by Lake
Tanganyika. It suffered a decade of political
unrest because of ethnic tension between
the Hutu majority and the dominant Tutsi
minority. Most of Burundi's people are poor
and farm the land to feed themselves.

Tanzania

Area 364,900 sq miles
(945,087 sq km)
Population 46.2 million
Capital Dodoma
Currency Tanzanian shilling
Official languages English
and Kiswahili
Life expectancy 52 years

The United Republic of Tanzania was formed in 1964 after a merger between the mainland Tanganyika Republic and the island of Zanzibar. Tourism is an important source of revenue for Tanzania, and its biggest attraction is the wildlife-rich Serengeti National Park. Mount Kilimanjaro, Africa's highest mountain, is located here.

▲ MAASAI PEOPLE
The Maasai are seminomadic people who live mainly in Kenya and northern Tanzania. They still follow their age-old customs, and can be recognized by their distinctive bright clothing.

Malawi

Area 45,745 sq miles
(118,480 sq km)
Population 15.4 million
Capital Lilongwe
Currency Malawian kwacha
Official language English
Life expectancy 48 years

Landlocked in southeast Africa, Malawi lies on the Great Rift Valley and is dominated by Lake Malawi, Africa's third-largest lake. It gained independence from the UK in 1964 and was ruled by Hastings Banda for nearly three decades. It became a multiparty democracy in 1994. Malawi's major export earnings come from tobacco.

Mozambique

Area 300,496 sq miles
(801,590 sq km)
Population 23.9 million
Capital Maputo
Currency New metical
Official language Portuguese
Life expectancy 42 years

Located on the southeast African coast, Mozambique is divided by the Zambezi River. Following its independence from Portugal in 1975, Mozambique was affected by civil war for 17 years. A truce was declared in 1992, and Mozambique held its first multiparty elections in 1994.

Seychelles

Area 176 sq miles
(455 sq km)
Population 90,024
Capital Victoria
Currency Seychelles rupee
Official languages French
Creole, English, and French
Life expectancy 72 years

The Republic of Seychelles is made up of 115 islands in the Indian Ocean. Formerly a UK colony and then under one-party rule for 14 years, Seychelles became a multiparty democracy in 1993. The islands are home to unique flora and fauna, such as the Seychelles giant tortoise.

Comoros

Area 838 sq miles
(2,170 sq km)
Population 800,000
Capital Moroni
Currency Comoros franc
Official languages Arabic,
French, and Comoran
Life expectancy 63 years

The Union of the Comoros is an archipelago nation lying off the east African coast. It consists of three main islands and many islets. Since its independence from France in 1975, Comoros has faced many coups. The political instability has adversely affected the growth of its tourism sector.

Mauritius

Area 718 sq miles
(1,860 sq km)
Population 1.3 million
Capital Port Louis
Currency Mauritian rupee
Official language English
Life expectancy 73 years

The islands that make up Mauritius are in the Indian Ocean. The main island, from which the country takes its name, is of volcanic origin and surrounded by coral reefs. Mauritius has enjoyed considerable economic success following recent industrial developments and the expansion of tourism.

Madagascar

Area 226,657 sq miles
(587,040 sq km)
Population 21.3 million
Capital Antananarivo
Currency Ariary
Official languages French,
Malagasy, and English
Life expectancy 59 years

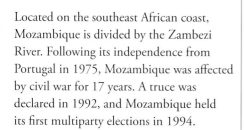

Lying in the Indian Ocean, Madagascar is the world's fourth-largest island. After being a socialist nation for 18 years, Madagascar became a multiparty democracy in 1993. It has a wealth of unique wildlife and plants—animals such as lemurs are not found anywhere else in the world.

▶ PANTHER CHAMELEON
Originally from Madagascar, the panther chameleon is a large chameleon species easily recognized by its vibrant color patterns.

Zimbabwe

Area 150,804 sq miles (390,580 sq km)
Population 12.8 million
Capital Harare
Currency Various foreign currencies in circulation
Official language English
Life expectancy 43 years

Zimbabwe is situated in southern Africa. The Zambezi River—on which lies the region's most spectacular natural feature, Victoria Falls—flows along its border with Zambia. Since its independence from Britain in 1980, Zimbabwe has been under the leadership of Robert Mugabe. The two main ethnic groups living here are the majority Shona in the north and the Ndebele in the south.

Botswana

Area 231,804 sq miles (600,370 sq km)
Population 2 million
Capital Gaborone
Currency Pula
Official language English
Life expectancy 50 years

Botswana is an arid, landlocked nation, with the Kalahari Desert occupying its western side. Nearly 80 percent of the people belong to the Tswana ethnicity. A multiparty democracy, Botswana is one of the most politically stable countries in Africa. Botswana is one of the world's top producers of diamonds. Its wildlife safaris are a major tourist attraction.

Lesotho

Area 11,720 sq miles (30,355 sq km)
Population 2.2 million
Capital Maseru
Currency Maloti
Official languages English and Sesotho
Life expectancy 43 years

The Kingdom of Lesotho is a mountainous country. It is entirely surrounded by South Africa; thousands of Lesotho people find employment in South Africa's gold mines. The majority of its people belong to the Sotho ethnicity, though there is a small community of European origin as well as an Asian minority. Textile export is an important revenue source for Lesotho.

Namibia

Area 318,696 sq miles (825,418 sq km)
Population 2.3 million
Capital Windhoek
Currency Namibian dollar
Official language English
Life expectancy 52 years

Namibia is a large country lying in southwest Africa. After many years of struggle, Namibia won independence from South Africa in 1990. The largest ethnic group, the Ovambo, mostly live in the far north. Namibia's original inhabitants, the San and Khoi (once called Bushmen), now make up a small minority. Namibia is one of Africa's leading mineral producers, with abundant uranium and lead reserves. The country is covered in the vast expanses of the unspoiled Namib and Kalahari deserts, where wildlife such as the African elephant and black rhinoceros can be found.

South Africa

Area 471,010 sq miles
(1,219,912 sq km)
Population 50.5 million
Capital Pretoria (Tshwane);
Cape Town; Bloemfontein
Currency Rand
Official languages Afrikaans,
English, and 9 African languages
Life expectancy 51 years

For nearly eight decades, South Africa was ruled by a white minority that practiced apartheid, or racial segregation. From 1990, South Africa underwent a political and social revolution, which led to its first multiracial elections in 1994. Antiapartheid crusader Nelson Mandela was South Africa's first elected president.

▲ CITY HALL, CAPE TOWN
This is the limestone façade of the City Hall in Cape Town. It was built in the early 20th century, using materials brought from Europe.

Swaziland

Area 6,704 sq miles
(17,363 sq km)
Population 1.2 million
Capital Mbabane
Currency Lilangeni
Official languages English
and Siswati
Life expectancy 41 years

The landlocked southern African kingdom of Swaziland is governed by a strong hereditary monarchy. Its current ruler, King Mswati III, is one of the world's last absolute monarchs. Swaziland is economically dependent on South Africa for employment, export revenue, and imported goods. Around 97 percent of the population belongs to the Swazi ethnic group.

▼ AFRICAN ELEPHANTS
This small herd of African elephants, including young ones, has assembled at a watering hole in the Etosha National Park, Namibia.

Asia

The world's largest and most populated continent, Asia is home to nearly four billion people. To its west are Europe and Africa and to its east is the Pacific Ocean. Asia is geographically, ethnically, culturally, and linguistically diverse. Many of the world's major religions, including Christianity, Islam, Hinduism, Buddhism, and Judaism, originated here.

▼ SAMPAN
A Vietnamese woman rows a sampan—a flat-bottomed wooden boat—on the Thu Bon River in the city of Hoi An, Vietnam.

Georgia

Area 26,911 sq miles (69,700 sq km)
Population 4.3 million
Capital Tbilisi
Currency Lari
Official languages Georgian, Abkhazian (in Abkhazia)
Life expectancy 71 years

A mountainous country, Georgia is sandwiched between the Greater and Lesser Caucasus mountains. It was one of the first countries to demand independence from the Soviet Union (USSR), in 1991. Georgia is famous for its traditional wine industry.

▲ KHACHAPURI
A traditional dish from Georgia, khachapuri is stuffed bread. The filling contains cheese, and sometimes eggs or meat.

Armenia

Area 11,506 sq miles (29,800 sq km)
Population 3.1 million
Capital Yerevan
Currency Dram
Official language Armenian
Life expectancy 72 years

Armenia is a landlocked nation in the Lesser Caucasus Mountains. It was the first country to adopt Christianity as its state religion, in the 4th century. Armenia has been a multiparty democracy since its independence from the USSR in 1991.

Azerbaijan

Area 33,436 sq miles (86,600 sq km)
Population 9.3 million
Capital Baku
Currency New manat
Official language Azeri
Life expectancy 72 years

Located on the west coast of the Caspian Sea, Azerbaijan was the first Soviet republic to declare independence. The Azeri people, who make up about 91 percent of the population, are Shi'a Muslims with close ethnic links to the Turks. Azerbaijan's economy is now growing, thanks to its vast oil wealth from the Caspian Sea oil fields.

Syria

Area 71,112 sq miles (184,180 sq km)
Population 20.8 million
Capital Damascus
Currency Syrian pound
Official language Arabic
Life expectancy 74 years

Located in Western Asia, the Syrian Arab Republic is bordered by Lebanon and the Mediterranean Sea in the west and Iraq in the east. Syria has been under a military-backed regime for almost four decades. In 2011, street protests broke out, demanding political and economic changes. Tensions have now escalated into civil war.

Lebanon

Area 4,015 sq miles (10,400 sq km)
Population 4.3 million
Capital Beirut
Currency Lebanese pound
Official language Arabic
Life expectancy 72 years

The Republic of Lebanon has a Mediterranean coast and shares borders with Syria and Israel. Once the commercial hub of the Middle East, Lebanon has been affected by regional conflicts, as well as a war with Israel in 2006. Lebanon has tried to regain its healthy economy with its growing tourism and strong financial services sector.

Israel

Area 8,019 sq miles (20,770 sq km)
Population 7.6 million
Capital Jerusalem
Currency Sheqalim
Official languages Hebrew and Arabic
Life expectancy 80 years

The world's only nation with a majority Jewish population, the State of Israel was created in 1948. Since then, it has been in conflict with Palestine and neighboring Arab countries over territory that is considered holy by the Jews, Christians, and Muslims. Israel has a modern infrastructure and a sophisticated, high-tech economy.

Jordan

Area 35,637 sq miles (92,300 sq km)
Population 6.3 million
Capital Amman
Currency Jordanian dinar
Official language Arabic
Life expectancy 72 years

The Hashemite Kingdom of Jordan is surrounded by the deserts of the Middle East. The vast majority of its population lives in the northwest, on the east bank of the River Jordan. Jordan is headed by a king, though multiparty elections were introduced in 1993. It is a predominantly Muslim country with Bedouin roots.

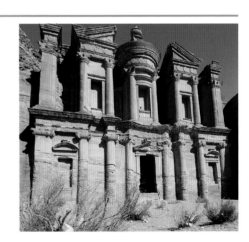

▲ PETRA
Jordan's most visited tourist attraction, Petra is an ancient Arabian city famous for its rock-cut architecture.

Saudi Arabia

Area 756,981 sq miles
(1,960,582 sq km)
Population 28.1 million
Capital Riyadh;
Jedda (administrative)
Currency Saudi riyal
Official language Arabic
Life expectancy 72 years

The world's largest oil reserves are found in the Kingdom of Saudi Arabia, where 95 percent of the land is covered in desert. Saudi Arabia contains Islam's holiest cities, Medina and Mecca. Each year, three million Muslims visit the cities for the *hajj* pilgrimage.

Oman

Area 82,031 sq miles
(212,460 sq km)
Population 2.8 million
Capital Muscat
Currency Omani rial
Official language Arabic
Life expectancy 76 years

The Sultanate of Oman is located at the entrance of the Persian Gulf. Most Omanis are Ibadi Muslims who follow an appointed leader known as the *imam*. Ibadism allows considerable freedom for women, who got the right to vote in 2002, and a few enjoy positions of authority. Oman's economy is dominated by the oil export industry.

United Arab Emirates

Area 32,000 sq miles
(82,880 sq km)
Population 7.9 million
Capital Abu Dhabi
Currency UAE dirham
Official language Arabic
Life expectancy 79 years

The United Arab Emirates (UAE) is a federation of seven states—Abu Dhabi, Dubai, Ajman, Fujairah, Ras al Khaimah, Sharjah, and Umm al Qaiwain—formed in 1971. Wealth from UAE's gas and oil exports have transformed it into a modern and well-developed country. Many foreign nationals come to UAE to work.

Yemen

Area 203,850 sq miles
(527,970 sq km)
Population 24.8 million
Capital Sana
Currency Yemeni rial
Official language Arabic
Life expectancy 62 years

Located in southern Arabia, the Republic of Yemen was formed in 1990 when two countries, the Yemen Arab Republic and the People's Democratic Republic of Yemen, came together. Yemenis are almost entirely of Arab and Bedouin descent.

Qatar

Area 4,416 sq miles
(11,437 sq km)
Population 1.9 million
Capital Doha
Currency Qatar riyal
Official language Arabic
Life expectancy 75 years

The State of Qatar is mostly flat, semiarid desert. Native Qataris were originally nomadic Bedouin. Today, the population includes a large number of workers from the Middle East, the Indian subcontinent, North Africa, and Southeast Asia. Qatar's large oil and gas reserves have made it one of the wealthiest nations in the region.

▲ BURJ AL ARAB, DUBAI
One of the most iconic buildings in the world is the Burj Al Arab. This luxury hotel, resembling a ship's sail, stands 1,053 ft (321 m) tall.

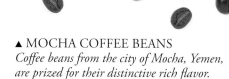

▲ MOCHA COFFEE BEANS
Coffee beans from the city of Mocha, Yemen, are prized for their distinctive rich flavor.

Bahrain

Area 239 sq miles
(620 sq km)
Population 1.3 million
Capital Manama
Currency Bahraini dinar
Official language Arabic
Life expectancy 76 years

Bahrain is an archipelago nation located between the Qatar peninsula and the Saudi Arabian mainland. It is the smallest and most densely populated Arab nation, as well as the most liberal. Since 2000, Bahrain has allowed women to participate in politics. It was the first Gulf state to export oil, though its reserves are now almost depleted.

Kuwait

Area 6,880 sq miles
(17,820 sq km)
Population 2.8 million
Capital Kuwait City
Currency Kuwaiti dinar
Official language Arabic
Life expectancy 78 years

With its huge oil and gas reserves, Kuwait is among the world's leading oil producers. It was invaded and occupied by Iraq in 1990, but was liberated by US-led forces in 1991. Kuwait's oil wealth has drawn in thousands of workers from other Arab countries and South Asia. There are more foreign nationals living here than native Kuwaitis.

Iraq

Area 168,754 sq miles
(437,072 sq km)
Population 32.7 million
Capital Baghdad
Currency New Iraqi dinar
Official languages Arabic
and Kurdish
Life expectancy 59 years

Iraq is an oil-rich nation located in Western Asia. In 2003, a US-led invasion ended the dictatorial rule of Saddam Hussein. In 2005, elections were held, which established democracy in Iraq. However, sectarian violence continues to affect Iraq's stability.

▲ PICKLING SPICES
Some of the spices used in Iran for pickling are dried aniseeds, coriander, ginger, golpar, powdered limes, cinnamon, and cumin.

Iran

Area 636,296 sq miles
(1,648,000 sq km)
Population 74.8 million
Capital Tehran
Currency Iranian rial
Official language Farsi
Life expectancy 71 years

Iran, formerly Persia, became an Islamic republic in 1979 when Ayatollah Khomeini overthrew the Shah's monarchy. Religious clerics, called *mullahs*, possess great political and moral authority. Iran has the world's second-largest oil and gas reserves.

Turkmenistan

Area 188,456 sq miles
(488,100 sq km)
Population 5.1 million
Capital Ashgabat
Currency Manat
Official language Turkmen
Life expectancy 63 years

A former Soviet republic, Turkmenistan became independent in 1991. The Turkmen were nomadic tribal people. Tribal units remain strong, and the largest groups are the Tekke in the center, the Ersary in the east, and the Yomud in the west. Turkmenistan is largely a Sunni Muslim country, with a small minority of Russian Orthodox Christians.

Uzbekistan

Area 172,742 sq miles
(447,400 sq km)
Population 27.8 million
Capital Tashkent
Currency Somi
Official language Uzbek
Life expectancy 67 years

Uzbekistan became a sovereign state in 1991, after splitting from the USSR. It is the most populous country in Central Asia and contains the ancient cities of Samarkand, Bukhara (Bukhoro), Khiva, and Tashkent, which once flourished as trade centers. Uzbekistan is one of the world's main cotton producers and is rich in natural resources.

Kazakhstan

Area 1,049,155 sq miles
(2,717,300 sq km)
Population 16.2 million
Capital Astana
Currency Tenge
Official language Kazakh
Life expectancy 66 years

Kazakhstan borders Russia to the north and China to the east. It was the last Soviet republic to declare its independence, in 1991. Kazakhstan is among the world's top 20 oil producers. It is ethnically diverse—Kazakhs make up more than half the population, and nearly a third is Russian, with a minority of Germans, Uzbeks, and Ukrainians.

Kyrgyzstan

Area 76,641 sq miles
(198,500 sq km)
Population 5.4 million
Capital Bishkek
Currency Som
Official languages Kyrgyz
and Russian
Life expectancy 68 years

Kyrgyzstan, officially the Kyrgyz Republic, is a small, mountainous nation in Central Asia. The Kyrgyz are a Turkic-speaking people, closely related to the neighboring Kazakhs. Their traditional nomadic lifestyle was forcibly changed when they were under Soviet rule, though many cultural practices linger, especially in rural areas.

Tajikistan

Area 55,251 sq miles
(143,100 sq km)
Population 7 million
Capital Dushanbe
Currency Somoni
Official language Tajik
Life expectancy 67 years

Tajikistan lies landlocked on the western slopes of the Pamir Mountains in Central Asia. Its language and traditions are similar to those of Iran. Ethnic Tajiks make up about 80 percent of the population. Uzbeks constitute the second-largest group, at around 15 percent. Tajikistan is one of Central Asia's poorest nations.

Afghanistan

Area 250,000 sq miles
(647,500 sq km)
Population 32.4 million
Capital Kabul
Currency Afghanis
Official languages Pashtu
and Dari
Life expectancy 44 years

Afghanistan is landlocked in Central Asia, and much of its terrain is inaccessible. Its political system, economy, and infrastructure have been devastated by decades of armed conflict. The Islamist Taliban militia came to power in 1996. In 2001, US-led attacks overthrew the regime, though the Taliban is trying to make a comeback.

Pakistan

Area 310,403 sq miles (803,940 sq km)
Population 177 million
Capital Islamabad
Currency Pakistani rupee
Official language Urdu
Life expectancy 65 years

Formerly a part of British India, the Islamic Republic of Pakistan was created in 1947. Initially, it included East Pakistan, present-day Bangladesh, which split from Pakistan in 1971. Punjabis account for more than 50 percent of the population, while Sindhis, Pathans (Pashtuns), and Baluchi make up most of the rest.

India

Area 1,269,345 sq miles (3,287,590 sq km)
Population 1.24 billion
Capital New Delhi
Currency Indian rupee
Official languages Hindi and English
Life expectancy 64 years

India is the world's largest democracy and the second most populous country after China. It is one of the fastest-growing economies in the world. However, wealth distribution is uneven and a huge gap exists between the affluent urban classes and the rural poor. The majority are Hindus, with a minority of Muslims, Christians, and Sikhs.

▲ THE TAJ MAHAL
A white marble mausoleum in Agra, the Taj Mahal is a World Heritage Site and one of India's most famous tourist attractions.

Nepal

▲ PRAYER FLAGS
Hanging prayer flags high up in the Himalayan mountains is an old Buddhist tradition to promote peace and compassion.

Area 54,363 sq miles (140,800 sq km)
Population 30.5 million
Capital Kathmandu
Currency Nepalese rupee
Official language Nepali
Life expectancy 63 years

Lying along the southern Himalayas, Nepal was an absolute monarchy until 1990. After years of revolt and much political chaos, Nepal was declared a republic in 2008. It has diverse ethnic groups, including the Sherpas, "Hill Hindu" Brahmans and Chhetris, Newars, and Tharus. Nepal's economy is mainly agricultural.

Bhutan

Area 18,147 sq miles (47,000 sq km)
Population 700,000
Capital Thimphu
Currency Ngultrum
Official language Dzongkha
Life expectancy 65 years

The Kingdom of Bhutan is formally a Buddhist state where power is shared by the king and the government. Perched in the Himalayas between India and China, it is 70 percent forested. Strict control over logging—thanks to traditional Buddhist values of respecting nature—has ensured that many of its forests remain untouched.

Bangladesh

Area 55,598 sq miles (144,000 sq km)
Population 150 million
Capital Dhaka
Currency Taka
Official languages Bengali
Life expectancy 64 years

Located around the fertile plains of the Ganges and Jamuna rivers, Bangladesh is one of the world's most densely populated countries. It was a part of Pakistan until 1971. Bangladesh's major economic sectors are jute, textiles, and agriculture.

▲ SAREE
The saree—a long cloth draped over the body in various styles—is a traditional garment of the women living in the Indian subcontinent.

Maldives

Area 116 sq miles (300 sq km)
Population 300,000
Capital Malé
Currency Rufiyaa
Official language Dhivehi
Life expectancy 68 years

The Maldives is an archipelago of 1,191 small coral islands in the Indian Ocean. Only 200 of these islands are inhabited. A popular tourist destination, the Maldives is known for its sandy beaches and abundant sea life.

Sri Lanka

Area 25,332 sq miles
(65,610 sq km)
Population 21 million
Capital Colombo
Currency Sri Lankan rupee
Official languages Sinhala
and Tamil
Life expectancy 75 years

The teardrop-shaped island of Sri Lanka, formerly known as Ceylon, is separated from India by the Palk Strait. Sri Lanka's domestic peace was marred by civil war between the majority Buddhist Sinhalese and the minority Hindu Tamils. The conflicts ended in 2009, when the army defeated the Tamil Tiger rebel group.

Mongolia

Area 604,249 sq miles
(1,565,000 sq km)
Population 2.8 million
Capital Ulan Bator
Currency Tugrik
Official language Khalka
Mongolian
Life expectancy 67 years

Mongolia lies landlocked between Siberia and China. Its various nomadic tribes were first unified by Genghis Khan in 1206. In 1990, Mongolia abandoned Communist rule and became a multiparty democracy. Mongolia has vast mineral resources, such as coal and oil. Its economy is being driven by the fast-growing mining industry.

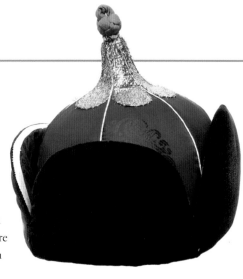

▲ MONGOLIAN HAT
The traditional silk-and-velvet hat with a topknot is worn by Mongolian men during celebrations, weddings, and other ceremonies.

China

Area 3,705,407 sq miles
(9,596,960 sq km)
Population 1.35 billion
Capital Beijing
Currency Yuan
Official language Mandarin
Life expectancy 72 years

▼ HONG KONG'S SKYLINE
With its skyscrapers and shopping malls, Hong Kong is one of the world's most modern cities. Controlled for a time by the UK, it came back under Chinese administration in 1997.

Covering a vast area of eastern Asia and bordered by 14 countries, the People's Republic of China is home to one-fifth of the world's population. The vast majority is Han Chinese, while the rest is made up of 55 minority ethnic groups. From the founding of the Communist People's Republic in 1949, China was dominated by Chairman Mao Zedong until his death in 1976. China's Communist Party is the world's largest political party, and holds absolute authority over its people.

Despite past domestic troubles, China has become an industrial and nuclear power. Today, China is a rapidly developing economy and has overtaken the US as the world's biggest manufacturer. China also plays an important role in the mineral trade—it is the biggest producer of steel and tungsten, and has the largest deposits of more than a dozen minerals. China also has ambitious space exploration programs and plans to launch a space station by 2020.

North Korea

Area 46,450 sq miles (120,540 sq km)
Population 24.5 million
Capital Pyongyang
Currency North Korean won
Official language Korean
Life expectancy 67 years

The Democratic People's Republic of Korea covers the mostly arid northern half of the Korean peninsula. North Korea is governed by a military regime that exerts total control over the lives of the population. A truce in 1953 ended the war with neighboring South Korea, though tensions continue to exist.

Japan

Area 145,883 sq miles (377,835 sq km)
Population 126 million
Capital Tokyo
Currency Yen
Official language Japanese
Life expectancy 82 years

Japan is a constitutional monarchy with an emperor as its ceremonial head of state. It is the world's third-largest economy. Made up of four principal islands in the north Pacific (Hokkaido, Honshu, Shikoku, and Kyushu) and many smaller islands, Japan is prone to frequent earthquakes and tsunamis.

Laos

Area 91,428 sq miles (236,800 sq km)
Population 6.3 million
Capital Vientiane
Currency New kip
Official language Lao
Life expectancy 64 years

The Lao People's Democratic Republic gained independence from France in 1953. This was followed by two decades of civil war. The Communist Lao People's Revolutionary Party (LPRP) has held power since 1975. There are more than 60 ethnic groups in Laos. Two-thirds of Laotians speak Lao, and many tribal dialects are also spoken.

South Korea

Area 38,032 sq miles (98,480 sq km)
Population 48.4 million
Capital Seoul
Currency South Korean won
Official language Korean
Life expectancy 78 years

The Republic of Korea covers the southern half of the Korean peninsula. South Korea is one of Asia's most affluent nations—it is the world's leading shipbuilder and has a well-developed high-tech industry. Its strained relationship with neighboring North Korea remains a major concern.

Burma (Myanmar)

Area 261,970 sq miles (678,500 sq km)
Population 48.3 million
Capital Nay Pyi Taw
Currency Kyat
Official language Burmese
Life expectancy 62 years

Burma, officially the Union of Myanmar, is a predominantly Buddhist country on the northeastern shores of the Indian Ocean. Ethnic conflicts rocked the nation following its independence from Britain in 1948. Burma was ruled by a repressive military regime from 1962 to 2010.

▲ SPIRIT HOUSE
Most buildings in Laos have a spirit house— a shrine where offerings to the spirits can be left to elicit good fortune.

▲ MARKET IN JEONGSEON
Many South Koreans frequent the five-day markets that are held every week in Jeongseon in Kangwon Province.

Vietnam

Area 127,244 sq miles (329,560 sq km)
Population 88.8 million
Capital Hanoi
Currency Dông
Official language Vietnamese
Life expectancy 71 years

The Socialist Republic of Vietnam lies on the eastern side of the Indochinese peninsula. The north and south of Vietnam, partitioned in 1954, were reunited only in 1976. It is now a single-party state ruled by the Communist Party. The most populated areas are along the Red and Mekong rivers.

Thailand

Area 198,456 sq miles (514,000 sq km)
Population 69.5 million
Capital Bangkok
Currency Baht
Official language Thai
Life expectancy 70 years

The Kingdom of Thailand, formerly Siam, lies in the heart of Southeast Asia. Since 1932, it has been a constitutional monarchy, though with frequent military governments. Its capital, Bangkok, is the main center for commerce and industry. Tourism is a major sector, drawing large numbers of visitors from across the world.

Cambodia

Area 69,900 sq miles (181,040 sq km)
Population 14.3 million
Capital Phnom Penh
Currency Riel
Official language Khmer
Life expectancy 59 years

Cambodia emerged from French colonial rule in 1953. From 1975 to 1979, the extremist Khmer Rouge regime headed by Pol Pot was responsible for killing almost a million Cambodians. Today, Cambodia is one of the world's poorest countries and relies heavily on foreign aid.

Singapore

Area 250 sq miles (648 sq km)
Population 5.2 million
Capital Singapore
Currency Singapore dollar
Official languages Malay, English, Mandarin, and Tamil
Life expectancy 80 years

An island nation, Singapore (meaning "lion city") was once a trading post of colonial Britain. Today, it is a wealthy nation known for its electronics and pharmaceutical industries, and its skilled workforce. The people of Singapore enjoy one of the world's highest standards of living.

East Timor

Area 5,742 sq miles (14,874 sq km)
Population 1.2 million
Capital Dili
Currency US dollar
Official languages Tetum and Portuguese
Life expectancy 57 years

East Timor achieved its independence in 2002 after a long and turbulent struggle against Indonesian occupation. Much of its infrastructure was destroyed during the violence, and the government heavily depends on foreign aid, especially from Australia and Portugal. Oil and gas from the Timor Sea forms its main source of income.

▲ MALAYSIAN TEXTILES
Textiles and clothing are one of Malaysia's main exports and the industry has contributed to the country's economic growth.

Brunei

Area 2,228 sq miles (5,770 sq km)
Population 400,000
Capital Bandar Seri Begawan
Currency Brunei dollar
Official language Malay
Life expectancy 77 years

Lying on the island of Borneo, the Sultanate of Brunei is divided in two by a strip of the Malaysian state of Sarawak. Independent from the UK since 1984, Brunei is ruled by decree of the sultan. Oil and gas revenue has made Brunei a wealthy nation with very high standards of living.

Indonesia

Area 740,100 sq miles (1,919,440 sq km)
Population 242 million
Capital Jakarta
Currency Rupiah
Official language Bahasa Indonesia
Life expectancy 68 years

Indonesia is the world's largest archipelago. Its 18,108 islands stretch 3,100 miles (5,000 km) from the Indian Ocean to New Guinea. Some islands, such as Java, Sumatra, Kalimantan, and Papua, are mountainous, volcanic, and densely forested. Indonesia is ethnically very diverse and has the world's largest Muslim population.

Malaysia

Area 127,317 sq miles (329,750 sq km)
Population 28.9 million
Capital Kuala Lumpur, Putrajaya (administrative)
Currency Ringgit
Official language Bahasa Malaysia
Life expectancy 74 years

Malaysia consists of the three territories of Peninsular Malaysia, Sarawak, and Sabah. Ethnic Malays make up about half the population, with a large Chinese minority. Malaysia's scenic beaches make it a key tourist destination in Southeast Asia.

Philippines

Area 115,830 sq miles (300,000 sq km)
Population 94.9 million
Capital Manila
Currency Philippine peso
Official languages English and Filipino
Life expectancy 71 years

Lying on the western rim of the Pacific Ocean, the Philippines is the world's second largest archipelago nation. Its three main island groupings are Luzon, Visayan, and the Mindanao and Sulu islands. Of the 7,107 islands, only 1,000 are inhabited. The islands are prone to frequent earthquakes.

▲ ORANGUTAN, SUMATRA
The endangered Sumatran orangutan is found only on the island of Sumatra, Indonesia, and lives mainly on a diet of fruit.

Oceania

More than 10,000 islands spread across the Pacific Ocean are collectively called Oceania. It includes the regions of Melanesia, Micronesia, Polynesia, and Australasia. The main continental landmass of Oceania is Australia. Many of the islands of Oceania have picturesque beaches, which draw tourists from across the world.

▼ MANA ISLAND, FIJI
This is a hilltop view of Mana Island, one of the most popular travel destinations in Fiji. The island is known for its beautiful coral reefs and marine life.

Australia

Area 2,967,909 sq miles
(7,686,850 km)
Population 22.6 million
Capital Canberra
Currency Australian dollar
Official language English
Life expectancy 81 years

An island continent located between the Indian and Pacific oceans, the Commonwealth of Australia is the world's sixth-largest country. It has a varied landscape that includes tropical rainforests, arid deserts, snowcapped mountains, agricultural land, and magnificent beaches.

Some of its most famous natural features are Uluru (also known as Ayers Rock) and the Great Barrier Reef. Most Australians are descendants of immigrants from Britain, Ireland, and other European countries. Native Aborigines today make up about two percent of the population.

▲ SYDNEY HARBOUR
Shown here is a panoramic view of the vibrant Sydney Harbour area—on the left is the famous Sydney Opera House, which hosts cultural performances.

Papua New Guinea

Area 178,703 sq miles
(462,840 sq km)
Population 7 million
Capital Port Moresby
Currency Kina
Official language English
Life expectancy 57 years

◀ CROWNED BIRD
Named after the British monarch Queen Victoria, the Victoria Crowned Pigeon is a large blue-gray pigeon with a unique white-tipped, lace-like crest. It is native to the New Guinea region.

Located on the eastern end of New Guinea Island, Papua New Guinea gained independence from Australia in 1975. It includes several other groups of islands in the North Pacific Ocean. With around 800 different languages and even more tribes, Papua New Guinea is the most linguistically diverse country in the world. The majority of the people are Christians, but local beliefs and traditions are still widely followed. Papua New Guinea is rich in minerals such as gold and copper, and its Porgera gold mine is one of the world's largest.

Micronesia

Area 271 sq miles
(702 sq km)
Population 106,487
Capital Palikir (Pohnpei Island)
Currency US dollar
Official languages English
Life expectancy 68 years

Situated in the Pacific Ocean, the Federated States of Micronesia is made up of four island-cluster states: Pohnpei, Kosrae, Chuuk, and Yap. Micronesia was formerly under US rule, but became independent in 1986. It still has a strong relationship with the US—receiving preferential trading rights and considerable aid. Micronesia's economic strengths are tourism, fishing, and the production of betel nuts and copra.

Marshall Islands

Area 70 sq miles
(181 sq km)
Population 68,480
Capital Majuro
Currency US dollar
Official languages English and Marshallese
Life expectancy 71 years

The Marshall Islands are made up of 34 widely scattered atolls in the central Pacific Ocean. Only 24 of these are inhabited. Most of the population live in Majuro, the capital and commercial center, and Ebeye Island. The Marshall Islands became independent from the US in 1986. However, the economy is almost entirely dependent on US aid, and rent from the US missile base on Kwajalein Atoll.

▲ ISLAND PARADISE
Many tourists travel to the Marshall Islands for the clear skies and unspoiled beaches, which are an ideal base for scuba diving and sport fishing.

Palau

Area 177 sq miles
(458 sq km)
Population 21,000
Capital Melekeok
Currency US dollar
Official languages Palauan
and English
Life expectancy 71 years

Palau lies in the western Pacific Ocean.
It is made up of more than 300 islands
in the Caroline Islands archipelago, only
nine of which are inhabited. Palau is
economically dependent on the US.

▲ GREEN SEA TURTLE
*The ocean surrounding Palau is home to
the green sea turtle. A threatened species,
the turtle's population is closely monitored.*

Nauru

Area 8.1 sq miles
(21 sq km)
Population 9,400
Capital Yaren
Currency Australian dollar
Official language Nauruan
Life expectancy 64 years

The world's smallest republic, Nauru lies
in the Pacific Ocean. Once a British colony,
it became independent in 1968. Its main
revenue has been from phosphate reserves,
which are now dwindling. Mining activities
have destroyed 80 percent of its ecosystem.

Kiribati

Area 277 sq miles
(717 sq km)
Population 102,000
Capital Bairiki
Currency Australian dollar
Official language English
Life expectancy 65 years

Kiribati, formerly known as the Gilbert
Islands, became independent from Britain
in 1979. Britain's sole interest in Kiribati
was its phosphate deposits, which ran out in
1980. The economy relies on the sale of
fishing rights, copra exports, and money
sent home by workers abroad. Kiribati is
also heavily dependent on foreign aid.

Samoa

Area 1,104 sq miles
(2,860 sq km)
Population 200,000
Capital Apia
Currency Tala
Official languages Samoan
and English
Life expectancy 71 years

Samoa, lying in the heart of the South
Pacific, is made up of nine volcanic islands.
Only four of these islands are inhabited—
Apolima, Manono, Savai'i, and Upolu.
Ethnically, 91 percent of the Samoan
population is Polynesian. An additional
8 percent is Euronesian (of mixed
European/Polynesian descent).

Tonga

Area 289 sq miles
(748 sq km)
Population 106,200
Capital Nuku'alofa
Currency Pa'anga
Official languages English
and Tongan
Life expectancy 73 years

Located in the South Pacific, the Kingdom
of Tonga is an archipelago of 170 islands.
These are divided into three main groups,
Vava'u, Ha'apai, and Tongatapu. Tonga's
eastern islands are low and fertile, while those
in the west are higher and volcanic in origin.
Tonga's economy is based on farming,
especially vanilla and squash production.

Tuvalu

Area 10 sq miles
(26 sq km)
Population 10,600
Capital Fongafale
Currency Australian dollar
Official language English
Life expectancy 69 years

Tuvalu is one of the world's smallest and
most isolated nations. It was a British
colony until it gained independence in
1978. Most Tuvaluans support themselves
by farming and fishing. In a move to
protect the environmentally fragile
islands, Tuvalu plans to switch entirely
to renewable sources of energy by 2020.

Solomon Islands

Area 10,985 sq miles
(28,450 sq km)
Population 600,000
Capital Honiara
Currency Solomon
Islands dollar
Official language English
Life expectancy 63 years

The Solomons archipelago has several
hundred islands, but most people live
on the six largest—Guadalcanal, Malaita,
New Georgia, Makira, Santa Isabel, and
Choiseul. The Solomon Islands, most of
which are coral reefs, draw many tourists,
especially for deep-sea diving. The islands
are rich in copra and minerals such as gold.

▲ LEAF FROG
*Varying in color from gold to brown to green,
this species lives in the tropical rainforests of the
Solomon Islands. It is also known as the eyelash
frog because of the projections over its eyes.*

Vanuatu

Area 4,710 sq miles
(12,200 sq km)
Population 200,000
Capital Port-Vila
Currency Vatu

Official languages Bislama,
English, and French
Life expectancy 70 years

In the South Pacific, Vanuatu is an archipelago of 82 mountainous islands of volcanic origin. It was formerly known as the New Hebrides. Ruled jointly by France and Britain from 1906, Vanuatu became independent in 1980.

Fiji

Area 7,054 sq miles
(18,270 sq km)
Population 900,000
Capital Suva
Currency Fiji dollar
Official language English
Life expectancy 69 years

Fiji is a volcanic archipelago in the southern Pacific Ocean, made up of two main islands and nearly 900 smaller islands and islets. Melanesians and ethnic Indians make up its population. Recent coups have affected Fiji's political stability.

▲ LEVUKA
Fiji's former capital, Levuka, is a picturesque town on Ovalau Island, with buildings that are unchanged since colonial times.

New Zealand

Area 103,737 sq miles
(268,680 sq km)
Population 4.4 million
Capital Wellington
Currency New Zealand dollar
Official languages English
and Maori
Life expectancy 80 years

Lying in the South Pacific, New Zealand is made up of the main North and South islands, separated by the Cook Strait, and a number of smaller islands. South Island is the more mountainous, while North Island contains hot springs and geysers.

The bulk of the population lives on North Island. Nearly three-quarters of the population are descendents of European migrants, while about 15 percent are Maori (migrants from Polynesia). Thanks to its small population and limited industry, New Zealand is one of the least polluted nations on Earth. It was also the first to give women the right to vote, in 1893.

▼ GLACIER WALKING
The Franz Josef Glacier (below) and the Fox Glacier on South Island's west coast are two of New Zealand's main tourist attractions. Thousands visit the glaciers every year.

Glossary

Algae Plantlike organisms that can make food using solar energy. Most are single-celled microbes.

Atmosphere The layer or layers of gas held around a planet or moon by gravity.

Atom The smallest particle of an element such as iron. Compounds have more than one kind of atom.

Axis An imaginary line that something spins around. Earth spins on such a line.

Bacteria Microscopic organisms that have a simple single-celled structure, and no cell nuclei or other distinct internal structures.

Batholith A very large mass of igneous rock such as granite, exposed in some places but mostly buried underground.

Biome A community of animals and plants on a large scale, defined mainly by vegetation—for example, rainforest.

Climate The typical or average weather in a particular area.

Cold front The leading edge of a moving mass of cold air, where it pushes beneath a mass of warm air.

Compound A substance containing two or more elements, formed by a chemical reaction that bonds their atoms together. Water is a compound of hydrogen and oxygen.

Condense To turn from a gas to a liquid.

Continental crust A thick slab of relatively light rock that "floats" on the heavier rock of Earth's mantle and forms a continent.

Continental shelf The submerged fringe of a continent, forming the relatively shallow floor of a coastal sea.

Convection Circulating currents in gases and liquids such as air and water, and even in hot, mobile rock, which are driven by differences in temperature.

Cyclone An area of low pressure, where warm air is sucked in and rises. It flows counterclockwise in the northern hemisphere and clockwise in the southern hemisphere. Also, a tropical storm in the Indian and southwest Pacific Oceans.

Delta A fan of sand and silt at the mouth of a river. The river usually flows through it in several channels.

Ecosystem The complex interactions of different organisms with one another and with their environment.

Element A substance that is made up of just one type of atom.

Equator A line of latitude around the middle of Earth at its widest point.

Erosion Wearing away, usually of rock, by natural forces such as flowing water or ocean waves breaking on the shore.

Evaporate To turn from a liquid to a gas or vapor.

Extinct Having died out completely. An extinct species has gone for good.

Fault A fracture in rock, along which rock masses move—this sometimes causes earthquakes.

Fissure A deep, narrow gap, such as between rocks.

Fjord A deep valley gouged by a glacier, which is now flooded by the sea.

Fossil The remains, imprint, or trace of a life form preserved in rock.

Fossil fuels Coal, oil, and gas made over millions of years from the remains of long-dead plants and microbes.

Genetic Relating to genes and inherited traits in living things.

Gravity The force of attraction exerted by a large object such as a planet, which holds things on the surface and in orbit.

Habitat A place where wildlife lives.

Hot spot A zone of volcanic activity caused by a plume of heat beneath Earth's crust. If the crust is moving, the hot spot creates chains of volcanoes.

Igneous rock Rock formed by the cooling of molten magma or volcanic lava. Most igneous rocks are made of interlocking crystals and are very hard.

Impermeable Rock that is waterproof and does not soak up water.

Infrastructure Services and structures such as power supply and road networks that allow society to function.

Latitude Distance from the equator. A low latitude is near the equator, and a high latitude is nearer the polar regions.

Lava Molten rock that erupts from a volcano and hardens into solid rock.

Lithosphere Earth's outer shell, consisting of the crust and the uppermost layer of the mantle.

Magma Molten rock lying beneath Earth's crust.

Mantle The deep layer of hot rock that lies between Earth's crust and the core.

Metamorphic rock Rock changed from its original state by intense heat, pressure, or both.

Microbe A microscopic living thing.

Mid-ocean ridge A ridge of mountains on the ocean floor, created by a spreading rift between two plates of Earth's crust.

Migrate To make a regular, often yearly journey in search of food or a mate.

Mineral A natural solid made of one or more elements in fixed proportions, usually with a distinctive crystal structure.

Molecule A particle formed from a fixed number of atoms. Two hydrogen atoms joined to one oxygen atom form a water molecule.

Monsoon A seasonal change of wind that affects the weather in the Indian subcontinent and Southeast Asia, causing wet and dry seasons.

Multicellular A living thing that is made up of many cells.

Nuclear Relating to the nucleus of an atom. If the nuclei of two atoms are fused together, or a single atomic nucleus is split, this nuclear reaction releases nuclear energy.

Nucleus The central mass of something, such as an atom or a living cell. The plural is nuclei.

Nutrients Substances that living things need to build tissue.

Oceanic crust The relatively thin crust of basalt that lies above Earth's mantle and forms the bedrock of the ocean floor. Oceanic crust is denser than continental crust, and always subducts beneath it.

Orbit To circle a planet or star. Earth orbits the Sun, and the Moon orbits Earth.

Ore A natural material from which valuable minerals can be extracted.

Organic A substance that is based on the element carbon, but usually meaning something that is—or was once—alive. Also, a type of farming and produce.

Organism A living thing.

Parasite An organism that lives in or on another. The relationship benefits the parasite but is detrimental to the host.

Peat The compacted remains of plants that have not fully decayed, because the oxygen vital to decay was excluded, usually because of saturation by water.

Permafrost Permanently frozen ground that covers large areas of the polar regions, especially in the Arctic.

Pesticide A chemical used to kill small animals, fungi, and weeds that attack or compete with farm crops.

Petrified Turned to stone.

Photosynthesis The process by which plants use the energy from sunlight to make sugar from carbon dioxide and water.

Phytoplankton Microscopic, single-celled organisms that drift in the sunlit surface waters of oceans and lakes and use photosynthesis to make food.

Plankton Living things that drift in lakes and oceans, usually near the surface.

Pluton A mass of igneous rock such as granite that formed below ground, but may now be exposed.

Porous A rock or similar substance that is not waterproof, and which may soak up water like a sponge.

Prevailing wind A wind that blows from a certain direction most of the time.

Protein A complex substance that a living thing makes out of simpler nutrients and uses to form its tissues.

Pyroclastic flow An avalanche of very hot rock and dust that cascades down the flank of an erupting volcano.

Radiation Light, heat, or other forms of energy such as X-rays that spread out through space from a source such as a star or a glowing object.

Reservoir A store of something, usually a liquid such as water.

Rift A widening crack in rocks or in Earth's crust, formed by tectonic plates drifting apart.

Rift valley A region where part of Earth's crust has dropped into the gap formed by the crust pulling apart.

Satellite Something that orbits (circles) a planet. The Moon is a natural satellite, but many of Earth's satellites are artificial, including the International Space Station, the Hubble Space Telescope, and dozens of communication, weather, and navigation satellites.

Scavenger An animal that eats the remains of dead animals and other scraps.

Sediment Solid particles such as sand, silt, or mud that have settled on the sea bed or elsewhere.

Sedimentary Describes a deposit or rock made of sediments.

Seismic Relating to earth movements caused by earthquakes.

Solar radiation Heat, light, and other forms of energy generated by the Sun.

Solar System The system of planets, moons, and asteroids orbiting the Sun.

Species The basic unit of classification of living organisms. For example, a tiger is a species of cat. Members of a species can reproduce by pairing with one another, but not with other species. A subspecies forms when there is a barrier—often geographical—between two populations of the same speciess.

Stalactite A cone-shaped structure created when groundwater deposits minerals on a cave roof.

Stalagmite A pedestal-shaped structure created when water drips from the tip of a stalactite and deposits minerals on a cave floor.

Star An object in space that is massive enough to generate energy by nuclear fusion reactions. The Sun is a star.

Strata Layers of sedimentary rock.

Stratosphere The layer of Earth's atmosphere that lies above the lowest layer (the troposphere).

Subduction The process of one plate of Earth's crust sliding beneath another, creating an ocean trench, causing earthquakes, and fueling volcanoes.

Subtropics The warm regions to the north and south of the equator that lie between the hot tropics and the cooler midlatitudes.

Tectonic plate Any one of about 17 pieces of Earth's rigid shell (made up of the crust and upper mantle) that drift slowly over the planet's surface.

Temperate A climate that is neither very hot nor very cold, or a region that has such a climate.

Trade wind A wind that blows steadily from east to west over a tropical ocean.

Tropics The hot regions to the north and south of the equator, between the Tropic of Cancer and the Tropic of Capricorn.

Troposphere The lowest layer of the atmosphere, where the weather happens.

Tsunami A fast-moving ocean wave generated by an earthquake on the ocean floor, by the collapse of an oceanic volcano, or by a coastal landslide.

Tundra The cold, almost treeless landscape that lies on the fringes of the polar ice sheets.

Ultraviolet Energy radiated by the Sun that is invisible, but attacks living tissues and destroys them.

Warm front The leading edge of a moving mass of warm air, where it slides up over a mass of cold air.

Water vapor The gas that forms when liquid water is warmed and evaporates.

Weathering The breaking down of rocks and minerals by rain, sunlight, ice, and other climatic effects.

Westerly wind A wind that blows from west to east.

Zooplankton Animals that mainly drift in the water, although some may also swim actively.

Index

INDEX

Acknowledgments

Smithsonian Enterprises:
Product Development Manager
Kealy Wilson; Licensing Manager
Ellen Nanney; Director of Licensing
Brigid Ferraro; Senior Vice President
Carol LeBlanc

The publisher would like to thank
the dedicated team of curators at the
Smithsonian Institution:
Bruce Smith, Senior Research Scientist,
Department of Anthropology, National
Museum of Natural History, Smithsonian
Institution; **Dr. Jeffrey E. Post,** Geologist
and Curator-in-Charge of the National
Gem Collection, National Museum of
Natural History, Smithsonian Institution;
Dr. M. G. (Jerry) Harasewych,
Research Zoologist and Curator of Marine
Mollusks, Department of Invertebrate
Zoology, National Museum of Natural
History, Smithsonian Institution;
Dr. Don E. Wilson, Curator Emeritus,
Department of Vertebrate Zoology,
National Museum of Natural History,
Smithsonian Institution;
Andrew K. Johnston, Geographer, Center
for Earth and Planetary Studies, National
Air and Space Museum, Smithsonian
Institution; **Julie A. Herrick**,
Volcanologist—Global Volcanism
Program, Department of Mineral Sciences,
National Museum of Natural History,
Smithsonian Institution; **Jennifer Zoon**,
Communications Assistant, National
Zoological Park, Smithsonian Institution;
Peter Liebhold, Chair and Curator,
Division of Work and Industry, National
Museum of American History, Kenneth E.
Behring Center, Smithsonian Institution;
Melinda Zeder, Curator of Old World
Archaeology and Archaeozoology,
Department of Anthropology, National
Museum of Natural History, Smithsonian
Institution; **Jim Harle**, Map curation
volunteer, National Museum of Natural
History, Smithsonian Institution;
Thomas F. Jorstad, Paleobiology
Information Officer, Department of
Paleobiology, National Museum of Natural
History, Smithsonian Institution; and
J. Daniel Rogers, Curator of North
American Archaeology, Department of
Anthropology, National Museum of
Natural History, Smithsonian Institution.

The publisher would also like to thank:
Clive Gifford for writing Chapter 7;
Archana Ramachandran for editing
Chapter 8; Debra Wolter for proofreading;
and Chris Bernstein for preparing
the index.

The publisher would like to thank the
following for their kind permission to
reproduce their photographs:

(**Key**: a-above; b-below/bottom; c-center;
f-far; l-left; r-right; t-top)

2-3 Dreamstime.com: Jiří Hruška (c). **4
Dreamstime.com**: Darko Plohl (b); Jay
Beiler (cra); Minyun Zhou (ca); Dink101
(cr); Daveallenphoto (crb); Goinyk
Volodymyr (br). **NASA**: (tr). **5 Corbis**: O.
Alamany & E. Vicens (bl). **Dreamstime.
com**: Basphoto (t); Colette6 (c); Mikdam
(ca); Steffen Foerster (cb); Stephen
Girimont (bc); Tiago Estima (tr);
Christopher Halloran (cra); Rainer Plendl
(cr); Janne Hämäläinen (r). **Fotolia**:
deviantART (c); Ojoimages4 (crb). **6-7
Dreamstime.com**: George Kroll (c). **6
Dreamstime.com**: Ruth Black (br); Steve
Estvanik (bl). **7 Dreamstime.com**: Steve
Allen (bl). **8 Dreamstime.com**: Wkruck
(tl). **9 Dreamstime.com**: Dmitry Pichugin
(cr); Vulkanette (c). **10-11 NASA**: (c). **10
NASA**: (crb). **11 NASA**: (br, bl). **12
NASA**: (bl, cl, crb). **13 NASA**: (cra, br, tr,
cla, cr, c, bl). **14 NASA**: (l). **15
Dreamstime.com**: David Gilder (cla, clb);
Satori13 (br). **16 Dreamstime.com**:
Oriontrail (c). **NASA**: (c). **17 NASA**: (br,
cl). **18-19 NASA**: (c). **20 Dreamstime.
com**: Njnightsky (cl). **21 Dreamstime.
com**: Showface (tr). **22 Dreamstime.com**:
Aaron Rutten (c); Intrepix (clb). **23
Dreamstime.com**: Colin & Linda McKie
(bc); Davinci (tr). **24-25 NASA**: (c). **26
Corbis**: Frans Lanting (tl). **Dreamstime.
com**: Robert Zehetmayer (bl). **27
Dreamstime.com**: Lpm (br); Steve
Estvanik (cl). **28 Dreamstime.com**: Walter
Arce (br). **NASA**: (cr). **29 Dreamstime.
com**: Arsty (br); Lnorah (bl). **NASA**: (cl,
tr). **30 Getty Images**: Pete Turner (bl).
NOAA: NOAA and NSF (ca). **31
Dreamstime.com**: Jiří Hruška (bc).
NASA: (cl). **32 NASA**: (bl). **33 Getty
Images**: James Balog (br). **NASA**: (cr).
NOAA: (cl). **34 Dreamstime.com**: Nigel
Spiers (bl). **35 Dreamstime.com**:
Oriontrail (tr); Yekaixp (br). **38 NASA**:
(bl). **39 Corbis**: AFLO / MAINICHI
NEWSPAPER / epa (tr). Dreamstime.
com: Yoshiyuki Kaneko (br). **NOAA**:
NGDC / NOAA (bl, bc). **40 Dreamstime.
com**: Petrakov (bc). **NASA**: (cla). **41
Dreamstime.com**: Jay Beiler (cr); Stephen
Finn (bc). **42-43 Dreamstime.com**:
Ebastard129 (c). **42 Dreamstime.com**:
Vulkanette (cl). **NASA**: (bc). **43 Corbis**:
Alberto Garcia (br). **44-45 Dreamstime.
com**: Juliengrondin (c). **46 Dreamstime.
com**: Rudolf Tepfenhart (l). **47
Dreamstime.com**: Victorpr (bl);
Warrengoldswain (tc). **NASA**: (br). **48-49**

Dreamstime.com: Dmitry Pichugin (c).
48 Dreamstime.com: Huub Keulers (bl);
Minyun Zhou (br). **49 Dreamstime.com**:
Paul Whitton (cr). **NOAA**: (tc). **51
Dreamstime.com**: Richard Semik (cl);
Underwatermaui (c). **52 Dreamstime.
com**: Vasilyev (bl). **Fotolia**: Tatesh (tl, tl);
Tatesh (tl, tl). **Fotolia**: Tatesh (tl, tl);
Tatesh (tl, tl). **52-53 NASA**: (c). **53
Dreamstime.com**: Dink101 (br). **54
Dreamstime.com**: Underwatermaui (c).
54-55 Science Photo Library: JAMES
STEINBERG (c). **55 Dreamstime.com**:
Simarts (cl). **56 Dreamstime.com**: Gozzoli
(cr). **57 Dreamstime.com**: Jan Hofmann
(tr). **58-59 Getty Images**: Carsten Peter /
Speleoresearch & Films (c). **60-61
Dreamstime.com**: Richard Semik (bc). **60
Corbis**: Bernardo Cesare (bl). **62
Dreamstime.com**: Jeremy Richards (crb).
Fotolia: Celso Diniz (br). **NASA**: (cl). **63
Dreamstime.com**: Jeffreyho (bl); Sdbower
(tr). **64 Dreamstime.com**:
Firebrandphotography (bc); Pavle
Marjanovic (cl). **65 Dreamstime.com**:
Andrew Millard (br); Daleinus (tl). **66
Dreamstime.com**: Riekefoto (bl). **66-67
Dreamstime.com**: Dean Pennala (c). **67
Dreamstime.com**: Leah Mcdaniel (clb);
Oleg Znamenskiy (tr). **68-69
Dreamstime.com**: Tirthac (c). **70
Dreamstime.com**: Paskee (cla). **Fotolia**:
Mark Eastment (bl). **71 Dreamstime.com**:
Donsimon (bl); Linda Bair (crb); (tl). **73
Corbis**: Louie Psihoyos (clb). **74
Dreamstime.com**: Gunold Brunbauer
(bl). **76 Dreamstime.com**: Jing-chen Lin
(cl). **77 Corbis** (tr). **Dreamstime.com**:
Charles Bolin (tl). **80 Dreamstime.com**:
Gail Johnson (cl). **81 Dreamstime.com**:
Siimsepp (br). **82 NASA**: (br). **82-83
Dreamstime.com**: Vulkanette (c). **83
Dreamstime.com**: Daveallenphoto (br);
fstockfoto (tr); Peter Mautsch / Maranso
Gmbh (cra); Islandsofaloha (clb). **84
Dreamstime.com**: Ivica Milevski (bl); Svat
(tr). **85 Dreamstime.com**: Darko Plohl
(cla); Ruud Glasbergen (crb). **86-87
Dreamstime.com**: Mikdam (c). **87
Dreamstime.com**: Alan Ward (cr); Erectus
(cl); Alfonso D'agostino (c). **88
Dreamstime.com**: Adeliepenguin (tc);
Sanyam Sharma; Steve Allen (t); Svetlin
Ivanov (tl). **NASA**: NASA Goddard Space
Flight Center (tr). **89 Fotolia**: Olivier
Tuffé (bl). **90 Dreamstime.com**: Porojnicu
(bl). **91 Dreamstime.com**: David
Mcshane (tl); Sunflower799 (tr). **Getty
Images**: Wigwam press / Joanna Vestey
(clb). **NASA**: NASA Earth Observatory /
Jesse Allen / Robert Simmon (bl). **92
Dreamstime.com**: Goinyk Volodymyr (t);
Mariusz Jurgielewicz (br). **93 NASA**:
NASA / Jesse Allen (bl, bc, br). **94-95
Dreamstime.com**: Andrey Pavlov (c). **96**

Dreamstime.com: Alexey Stiop (cr).
96-97 Dreamstime.com: Leonid Spektor
(bc). **97 Dreamstime.com**: Hugoht (tl);
Stephen Bures (cr). **98 Corbis**: Bettmann
(bl). **99 Corbis**: Patrick Bennett (cl).
Dreamstime.com: Eti Swinford (tr);
Pseudolongino (br). **100-101
Dreamstime.com**: Brian Hendricks (bc).
100 Dreamstime.com: Sergio Boccardo
(cl). **101 Dreamstime.com**: Basphoto (tr);
George Burba (br); Pancaketom (clb). **102
Dreamstime.com**: Veronica Wools (bl).
103 Dreamstime.com: Alfonso
D'agostino (bl); Conchasdiver (br);
Erinpackardphotography (tr); Cazuma (cl).
104-105 Dreamstime.com: Nico Smit
(c). **106 Dreamstime.com**: Nicku (cl);
Whiskybottle (bl). **NASA**: NASA / Jesse
Allen (crb). **107 Dreamstime.com**:
Kotourist (tl); Vit Kovalcik (b); Maigi (tr).
108 Dreamstime.com: Alexandr Malyshev
(b); Elena Elisseeva (cr). **109 Dreamstime.
com**: Alain Lacroix (cl); Alan Ward (tr);
Kacmerka (br). **110 Dreamstime.com**:
Most66 (c). **NASA**: (bl). **112
Dreamstime.com**: Erectus (b). **113
Dreamstime.com**: Annworthy (br);
Cosmopol (tr); Peter Leahy (cla);
Supachart (clb). **114 Getty Images**: Arnulf
Husmo (b). **115 NASA**: (cr). **116-117
Dreamstime.com**: Paul Topp (cl). **118
Dreamstime.com**: Rcpphoto (br). **119
Dreamstime.com**: Colette6 (c); Paul
Lemke (br); Darrensharvey (tl). **120
Dreamstime.com**: Marylooo (bc);
Youssouf Cader (tr). **120-121
Dreamstime.com**: Oliver Purser (c). **121
Dreamstime.com**: Justmedude (cr);
Robyn mackenzie (crb); Xxlphoto (cra).
NASA: (tr). **122-123 NASA**: (c). **122
Fotolia**: Valdezrl (tl). **123 Dreamstime.
com**: Ferguswang (cr); Paul Maguire (cl);
Thor Jorgen Udvang (c). **124-125
Dreamstime.com**: Snaprender (bl). **125
Corbis**: Redbull / Handout / redbull
content pool (cl). **Dreamstime.com**:
Dink101 (tr); Pajche (br). **Fotolia**: Paul
Fleet (cr). **126 Dreamstime.com**: Dannay
(crb); Fleyeing (cr). **127 Dreamstime.
com**: Kyolshin (br). **128 Dreamstime.
com**: Ferguswang (b); Mikdam (cb). **129
Dreamstime.com**: Jessamine (tr). **Getty
Images**: Michael S. Nolan (cla). **NASA**:
(b). **130 Corbis**: Rosemary Calvert (bl).
131 Corbis: Frans Lanting (br).
Dreamstime.com: Mettesd (cr);
Scubabartek (tr); Npoizot (bl). **132
Dreamstime.com**: Dmitry Berkut (b).
NASA: AIRS Science Team, NASA / JPL
(cl). **133 Corbis**: Dean Conger (cl).
Dreamstime.com: Kjersti Joergensen (cr);
Thor Jorgen Udvang (br); Victor Pelaez
Torres (tr). **134-135 Getty Images**: David
Santiago Garcia (c). **136 Dreamstime.
com**: Darryn Schneider (br). Fotolia:

ACKNOWLDGMENTS

Lance (cr). **137 Dreamstime.com:** Christian Kohler (cr); Jorg Hackemann (b). **Getty Images:** PATRICK BAZ (tl). **138 Corbis:** Craig Connor (cr). **Dreamstime.com:** Connect1 (cl). **139 Dreamstime.com:** Sinake (b). **NASA:** (cl). **140 Dreamstime.com:** Shailesh Nanal (c). **140-141 Dreamstime.com:** Lars Christensen (c). **141 Dreamstime.com:** Hasan Can Balcioglu (cl). **143 Dreamstime.com:** Leaf (cl); Rcaucino (t); scol22 (crb); Vladius (cr); Portokalis (tr); Pcphotohk (bl). **144 Dreamstime.com:** The44mantis (b). **Fotolia:** deviantART (cla). **145 Dreamstime.com:** Jixue Yang (cl); Paul Maguire (t); Svlumagraphica (br). **146 Dreamstime.com:** Andrei Calangiu (t). **Fotolia:** Daniel Loretto (cr). **147 Dreamstime.com:** James Horn (r). **148-149 Getty Images:** Carsten Peter (c). **150 NASA:** NASA GSFC (t). **151 Corbis:** Marcos Delgado (bl). **Getty Images:** Ian Cumming (tr). **NASA:** Rob Simmon / USGS / NOAA. (cr). **152 Fotolia:** pomkajamik (tl). **153 Dreamstime.com:** Jubalharshaw19 (c); Richard Kittenberger (cl); Vito Werner (cr). **154 Dreamstime.com:** Katrina Brown (c); Leonidtit (bl). **Getty Images:** M I Walker (br). **155 Dreamstime.com:** Cathy Figuli (cr); Orionmystery (clb); Robert Bayer (tl). **156 Dreamstime.com:** Christophe D (bc); Ivan Cholakov (cl); Robyn mackenzie (br); Jubalharshaw19 (cr). **157 Corbis:** Frank Krahmer (b). **158 Dreamstime.com:** Gumenuk Vitalij (b). **Fotolia:** James Thew (cr). **159 Dreamstime.com:** Rachwal (cla); Steffen Foerster (c). **160 Corbis:** Solvin Zankl (cl); Wim van Egmond (br). **Dreamstime.com:** Koi88 (t). **Fotolia:** Convit (bc). **161 Dreamstime.com:** Eric Gevaert (tl); Steffen Foerster (r); Valeko (clb). **162 Corbis:** Gavriel Jecan (b). **Dreamstime.com:** Karen Wunderman (tr). **163 Dreamstime.com:** Alleks (cr); Richard Kittenberger (br); Hugoht (tl); Brandon Alms (cl). **164 Dreamstime.com:** Pavla Zakova (l); Timhesterphotography (ca). **165 Dreamstime.com:** Kav777 (b); Yury Maryunin (cla); Menno67 (cr). **166-167 Dreamstime.com:** George Kroll (c). **168 Dreamstime.com:** Elena Elisseeva (clb); Savenkov (c); Valery Shanin (br). **169 Dreamstime.com:** Arvidas Saladauskas (cl); Panady (bl); Erik Mandre (r). **170 Corbis:** Ashley Cooper (bl); Wilfried Krecichwost (c). **171 Dreamstime.com:** Bevanward (br); Tom Curtis (t); Neal Cooper (l); Vito Werner (cr). **172 Dreamstime.com:** Andreyshot (cr); Evgeniya Moroz (cl). **Fotolia:** Thomas Barrat (b). **173 Dreamstime.com:** Krapels (br); Stephen Girimont (tl); Nan Li (bl).

174 Dreamstime.com: Darko Komorski (cl). **Fotolia:** Eric Isselée (t). **Getty Images:** Nigel Pavitt (br). **175 Dreamstime.com:** Brian Sedgbeer (tc); Markbeckwith (b). **176 Dreamstime.com:** Braendan Yong (l); Vallefrias (crb). **177 Dreamstime.com:** Bevanward (cr); Nico Smit (tr); Marcel Klimko (cl). **178 Dreamstime.com:** Attila Tatár (cl); Gorshkov13 (b). **179 Corbis:** Martin Harvey (br). **Dreamstime.com:** Bevanward (tr); Sdbower (clb). **Fotolia:** forcdan (cla). **180-181 Dreamstime.com:** Anton Foltin (c). **182 Corbis:** O. Alamany & E. Vicens (bl). **Dreamstime.com:** Seread (c). **183 Corbis:** Thomas Marent / Minden Pictures (tr). **Dreamstime.com:** Angela Sharp (cl); Olimpiu Alexa-pop (tl). **Fotolia:** Wusuowei (bc). **184 Dreamstime.com:** Checco (c). **Fotolia:** Leonid Ikan (bl). **185 Dreamstime.com:** Mirceax (cr); Yaroslava Polosina (br); Pictureguy66 (cl). **Fotolia:** Delmas Lehman (t). **186 Corbis:** Flip Nicklin / Minden Pictures (clb). **NASA:** Jeff Schmaltz / MODIS Rapid Response Team / NASA (cl). **186-187 Dreamstime.com:** Brett Atkins (b). **187 Corbis:** Norbert Wu / Minden Pictures (cra). **Dreamstime.com:** Outdoorsman (cr). **188-189 Getty Images:** Fritz Poelking (c). **190 Corbis:** Flip Nicklin / Minden Pictures (cl). **NOAA:** Public domain (cr). **190-191 Dreamstime.com:** Harald Bolten (b). **191 Dreamstime.com:** Ruth Black (tr); Stacy Barnett (ca). **Fotolia:** vilainecrevette (tl). **192 Fotolia:** Steven Brown (bl). **Getty Images:** Reinhard Dirscherl (cr). **NOAA:** Public domain (cl). **193 Corbis:** David Wrobel / Visuals Unlimited (cl). **Getty Images:** DEA PICTURE LIBRARY (tr). **NOAA:** Public domain (br). **194 Dreamstime.com:** Bin Zhou (b); Daexto (cl). **195 Corbis:** Gary Bell (br). **Dreamstime.com:** Boris Pamikov (tr); Nataliya Taratunina (bl). **196-197 Dreamstime.com:** Irochka (c). **198 Dreamstime.com:** Brian Maudsley (bl); Tiago Estima (tr). **Fotolia:** Svenni (br). **199 Dreamstime.com:** Aji Jayachandran (cr); Nico Smit (b); Zzvet (tl). **200 Dreamstime.com:** Inna Yurkevych (tl). **200-201 Dorling Kindersley:** Jamie Marshall (c). **201 Dreamstime.com:** Aksakalko (c); Heisenberg85 (cl); Alexander Mitrofanov (cr). **202 Corbis:** Gianni Dagli Orti (bl). **Dreamstime.com:** Alexander Mitrofanov (cr). **203 Dreamstime.com:** Heisenberg85 (br); Natalia Bratslavsky (tl). **Getty Images:** Roger Sutcliffe (cr). **204 Corbis:** David Stoecklein (br). **Dreamstime.com:** Thor Jorgen Udvang (cr). **205 Dreamstime.com:** Aksakalko (c); Inavanhateren (bl); Davidmartyn (tr).

Getty Images: Jean-Luc PETIT (br). **206-207 Dreamstime.com:** Gnomeandi (c). **208 Dreamstime.com:** View7 (cr). **Fotolia:** Greg Pickens (b). **209 Dreamstime.com:** Christopher Halloran (tr); Labdog (bc). **210 Dreamstime.com:** Damian Chung (cr); Rainer Plendl (br); Steve Estvanik (cl). **211 Corbis:** TWPhoto (tr). **Dreamstime.com:** Americanspirit (br). **212 Dreamstime.com:** Ella Batalon (t); Leon Viti (br); Wan Rosli Wan Othman (c). **213 Corbis:** Proehl Studios (cl). **Dreamstime.com:** Speculator27 (br); Xiaofeng123 (cr). **214 Dreamstime.com:** Sova004 (cl). **Fotolia:** Cardaf (cr). **214-215 Dreamstime.com:** Fabio Cardano (b). **215 Dreamstime.com:** Dan Breckwoldt (clb). **NASA:** METI / ERSDAC / JAROS, and U.S. / Japan ASTER Science Team (tr). **216 Dreamstime.com:** Ken Cole (b); Steve Allen (cr). **217 Dreamstime.com:** Mikael Damkier (tl); Zhudifeng (cl). **Fotolia:** QQ7 (br). **218-219 NASA:** (c). **220 Dreamstime.com:** Andrey Shchekalev (crb). **Fotolia:** Vladimir Melnik (c). **221 Dreamstime.com:** Arne9001 (r); Naluphoto (clb); Jinlide (cla); Danny Hooks (cra). **222 Dreamstime.com:** Achim Baqué (cr). **223 Dreamstime.com:** Aleksandr Klimashin (tr); Sophie Vigneault (b). **Fotolia:** Jean-Paul Bounine (tl); Philipus (cr). **224 Digital Vision:** (bl). **Dreamstime.com:** Seread (cr). **225 Fotolia:** Luisapuccini (c); wusuowei (cla); Ojoimages4 (bl). **226-227 Fotolia:** Sergey Nivens (c). **227 Dreamstime.com:** Atanasbozhikov (c); Yuri Yavnik (cl); Robert Gubiani (cr). **228 Dreamstime.com:** Belopez (cl). **Fotolia:** Inna Felker (bl). **229 Corbis:** Peter Essick / Aurora Photos (tr). **230 Dreamstime.com:** Gabriella S.bognár (c); Svetlana485 (bl). **231 Dreamstime.com:** Biserko (cla). **232 Dreamstime.com:** Jeremy Richards (bl); Tomas Sereda (cla). **233 Dreamstime.com:** Jan Dufek (tr). **234 Dreamstime.com:** Pictureguy66 (cr). **235 Dreamstime.com:** Jf123 (bl); Phillip Gray (bc). **236 Dreamstime.com:** Jborzicchi (cr). **237 Dreamstime.com:** Janne Hämäläinen (cl, cl); Janne Hämäläinen (cl, cl); Johnny Lye (br). **Dreamstime.com:** Janne Hämäläinen (cl, cl); Janne Hämäläinen (cl, cl); Johnny Lye (br). **237 Dreamstime.com:** Janne Hämäläinen (cl, cl); Janne Hämäläinen (cl, cl); Johnny Lye (br). **Dreamstime.com:** Janne Hämäläinen (cl, cl); Janne Hämäläinen (cl, cl); Johnny Lye (br). **238 Dreamstime.com:** Honourableandbold (cl). **239 Dreamstime.com:** Jenifoto406 (bl); Serban Enache (cra). **240 Dreamstime.com:** Edwardje (cr). **241 Dreamstime.com:** Sergey Uryadnikov (l).

Fotolia: Erichon (cb). **242 Dreamstime.com:** Bevanward (cl); Yuri Yavnik (bl). **243 Dreamstime.com:** Robert Gubiani (tr). **244 Dreamstime.com:** Johncarnemolla (bl). **245 Corbis:** Kim JongBeom / TongRo Images (br). **Dreamstime.com:** Atanasbozhikov (tr). **246 Dreamstime.com:** Andrey Pavlov (cl); Bernard Breton (bc). **247 Corbis:** Paul A. Souders (tr). **248 Fotolia:** Semisatch (tl). **248-249 Dorling Kindersley:** Jamie Marshall (c). **256 Dorling Kindersley:** Jamie Marshall (c). **272 Dorling Kindersley:** Jamie Marshall / Jamie Marshall (c). **272 Dorling Kindersley:** Diego Barucco / Jamie Marshall (c). **274 Dorling Kindersley:** © Angus Beare (tl). **278 Dorling Kindersley:** Powell-Cotton Museum, Kent (tr). **279 Dorling Kindersley:** Thomas Marent (cr). **281 Dorling Kindersley:** Thomas Marent (br). **284 Dorling Kindersley:** Jamie Marshall (c). **291 Dorling Kindersley:** Thomas Marent (br). **293 Dorling Kindersley:** Thomas Marent (cl).

Jacket images: *Front:* **Corbis:** Angelo Cavalli / Robert Harding World Imagery bl; George Hammerstein fbr; Frans Lanting br. **Getty Images:** Photolibrary / David Davis fbl; Stone / Demetrio Carrasco t. *Back:* **Corbis:** Arctic-Images t; Image Source fbl; George Lepp bl; Stocktrek fbr; Torleif Svensson br. *Spine:* **Corbis:** Frans Lanting.

All other images © Dorling Kindersley
For further information see:
www.dkimages.com

Finally, the publisher wishes to note that the area and population figures for the cities in this book follow UN data for 1992–2011. How cities are defined can vary considerably: some estimates apply to the city proper; others also include the urban agglomeration around the city. This book gives the latter where available.